"William M. Akers defies the old adage that those who can't, teach. He's both a great writer *and* a great teacher — in my experience a combination as rare as rocking-horse doo doo. *Your Screenplay Sucks!* lays out in crystal-clear language all the things that most screenwriters have learned the hard way but don't want you to know, because why should you have it easy? This book is a lifetime of lessons in the screen trade recounted by someone with the intelligence to see, the talent to understand, and the generosity to share — laid out with the engaging and deceptive ease of a natural-born storyteller. If Mark Twain wrote screenplays, this is the advice book he'd write."

— Jon Amiel, director, *The Singing Detective, Entrapment*

"If you want a pat-you-on-the-back, feel-good book on writing, read *Chicken Soup for the Writer's Soul*. If you want the sucker-punch-you-in-the-throat, down-and-dirty truth about screenwriting for Hollywood, read *Your Screenplay Sucks!*".

— Linda McCullough, Columbia College, Chicago

"A book about screenwriting that reads like a good screenplay. It is so full of great stories, examples, and advice that I couldn't put it down."

— Tom Schulman, Academy Award–winning screenwriter for *Dead Poets Society, Honey I Shrunk the Kids, What About Bob?*

"A thoughtful guide to finding your way out of the many creative cul-de-sacs that bedevil the form."

— John Requa, co-writer, *Bad Santa, Bad News Bears*

"A well-written recipe for avoiding the mistakes which young or inexperienced screenwriters often make... It is a luminous guide and light is, after all, what we are after."

— Benedict Fitzgerald, writer, *Wise Blood, The Passion of the Christ*

"Don't take it personal; your screenplay *does* suck. Almost all screenplays suck until you beat them into shape. William M. Akers's book is an excellent guide through the pitfalls and easy mistakes that first-time screenwriters face. His advice is honest and simple. He will make your screenplay suck less — as long as you're willing to do the work."

— Larry Karaszewski, writer, *Ed Wood, The People vs. Larry Flynt, Man on the Moon*

"Will Akers takes a straightforward, no-nonsense approach to the process of writing and fixing your screenplay. He cuts through the crap and gets right to the heart of what is wrong and simply tells you how to fix it. Fantastic book."

— Matthew Terry, screenwriter, teacher, columnist for *www.hollywoodlitsales.com*

"Among the many books on screenwriting, William M. Akers' *Your Screenplay Sucks! 100 Ways to Make It Great* is a clear standout. His hundred ways range from the inspirational to the procedural to the minutely practical, but they are all inordinately useful. Whatever other books you own on the craft of screenwriting, this one needs to be among them."

> — Robert Olen Butler, Pulitzer Prize–winning author of *From Where You Dream*

"I repeatedly found you saying things that I've been saying to writers I know. It also provided me with many useful reminders for my own work, that I knew, but sometimes forget to practice. Your manner is direct and clear and your examples are strong and logical. Kudos."

> — Greg Beeman, Executive Producer, *Heroes, Smallville*

"Will's book is a must for the novice screenwriter. Not only will it help them write a better script, they will write a better, more commercial script, increasing the odds that it will interest the people who make movies (and the people who read their scripts for them). Even experienced screenwriters can pick up helpful tips from this entertaining and edifying book."

> — Peter Heller, Loyola Marymount University

"It's a terrific travel guide for the writer's journey with a sharp eye on 'which neighborhoods to avoid.'"

> — Kevin Wade, writer, *Working Girl* and *Meet Joe Black*

"Great screenwriting books begin and end with William M. Akers' *Your Screenplay Sucks!* Not only is it jammed full of terrific information on screenwriting, but it's a damn good read as well. I was alternating between learning and laughing all the way through. A must have for the serious screenwriter."

> — Kelley Baker, author of *The Angry Filmmaker Survival Guide*

"William M. Akers is a renaissance man of film who is at once a big studio screenwriter, independent writer/director, and caring, insightful teacher. He also knows every trick in the book when it comes to fixing a script. And this is that book! A must for any writer facing the 'dark night of the script.'"

> — Blake Snyder, author, *Save the Cat!, Save the Cat! Goes to the Movies*

Your Screenplay Sucks!

100 ways to make it great

by

William M. Akers

MICHAEL WIESE PRODUCTIONS

Published by Michael Wiese Productions
12400 Ventura Blvd. #1111
Studio City, CA 91604
(818) 379-8799, (818) 986-3408 (FAX).
mw@mwp.com
www.mwp.com

Cover design by MWP
Interior design by William Morosi
Copyedited by Paul Norlen
Drawing on page 32 by Alex Echols
Printed by McNaughton & Gunn

Manufactured in the United States of America

Library of Congress Cataloging-in-Publication Data
Akers, William M., 1956-
 Your screenplay sucks! : 100 ways to make it great / by William M. Akers.
     p. cm.
 Includes bibliographical references.
 ISBN 978-1-932907-45-2
 1. Motion picture authorship. 2. Motion picture plays--Editing. I. Title.
 PN1996.A47 2008
 808.2'3--dc22

                         2008009848

Dedicated

to my teachers

Bob Baldwin, Jim Boyle, Ken Robinson, John Truby

and

my students,

from whom I learned even more.

Without you, this book would not exist.

Table of Contents

Act II: Physical Writing

Welcome to Writing

Format

Characters

Scene Description

Rewriting

Picky, Picky, Picky

Act III: What Now?

Don't Be a Jackass, Be Professional

The Industry

Acknowledgments

Thank you, first and foremost, to Blake Snyder. From the beginning, he thought this foolishness was a swell idea.

Second, Fransisco Menendez, who invited me to speak to his class at UNLV. The resulting 100-page handout eventually became this book.

My understanding family, Kate McCormick, Scott Pierce, Cathie Pelletier, Tom Schulman, Linda McCullough, Melissa Scrivner, Nick Morton, Alex Beattie, Jessica Stamen, Mark Kurasz, Richard Hull, Kelley Baker, Randy Feldman, Willard Carroll, Margaret Matheson, Coke Sams, Mark Cabus, Beth O'Neil, Jason Blum, John Cherry, Carol Caldwell, Dave Brown, Kerith Harding, Steve Bloom, Ryan Saul, Jenny Wood, Pam Casey, Chris Ruppenthal, Jon Amiel, Shian Brisbois, Rob Muraskin, Suzanne Kingsbury, Tony Cane, Max Wong, and Miles Davis.

Introduction

"Honest criticism is hard to take, particularly from a relative, a friend, an acquaintance, or a stranger."
Franklin P. Jones

Your Screenplay Sucks! grew from an idea born while critiquing screenplays.

I've had three scripts made into feature films. I'm a Lifetime member of the Writers Guild. I've written screenplays for twenty years. I've critiqued scripts for friends the whole time, and have been paid to critique the past seven years or so. Not to mention the hundreds of scripts I have shepherded through my screenwriting classes.

Through my reading and critiquing, I discovered that beginning writers consistently make the same mistakes. Mistakes which, in Hollywood, can cause the reader to… (gasp!) *stop reading…*

They can do that, you know.

I found myself telling writers the same things over and over: "Don't have character names that rhyme." "Every character's voice sounds just like every other character." "Your hero doesn't have a clear goal." Repeat *ad nauseam*. I decided to create a simple checklist so, before sending me their screenplay, writers could do a rewrite, cleaning up this nuts and bolts stuff, and then we could discuss plot and character and structure, instead of wasting time on generic stuff like, "run your damn spellcheck." That short checklist turned into this book.

"I read to the first typo."
Hollywood agent

Welcome to Hollywood.

"If it were easy, everyone would do it."
Every producer in Los Angeles

In theory, readers have to read the whole thing. Some do. Some don't. Producers are not bound by such niceties. While they do hope to find the next *Raiders of the Lost Ark*, they're also looking for any excuse to put it down by page ten. So don't give them one, okay! That's the point of this book, removing land mines from your screenplay that will cause the reader to pitch it into the trash.

And believe me, that is what they do.

Ninety-nine percent of people who will read your script do not have the ability to say "Yes," but every single one can say "No." They are just itching to use that power.

"Fight the power!"
Rosie Perez in *Do the Right Thing*

One fine sunny Los Angeles afternoon, I was sitting in an assistant's office, waiting for the producer, and her door was closed. Probably inside her kitsch-packed office playing paddle ball. I'll never know. Anyway, killing time, I looked above the assistant's desk, and there were two shelves overflowing with screenplays. They ran around three walls of the room. For mental gymnastics, I estimated how many scripts there were. 1,400. One thousand four hundred screenplays, and they all had agents.

It is nearly inconceivable to an outsider, to someone at a typewriter or a computer in a city other than Los Angeles, far from the agent's desk, or the producer's office... it is impossible to conceive of the staggering volume of material the system has to contend with. The number of scripts that gushes over the transom of every producer, or agent, or executive, every week, boggles the mind. You're one writer sitting in your room, or at a park, or coffee shop, writing your screenplay. There are thousands of people sitting in parks all across this great land of ours, writing screenplays too. So, what you're writing has to be really good.

While the competition you face is gigantic, it is not monolithic. There are chinks and cracks in the armor, and a well-written script can wriggle through. But it has to be extremely well written. If your script isn't perfect, or as close to perfect as you can get it, then it doesn't stand a chance. It is supremely arrogant to think that something you dash off in a couple of weeks, and don't rewrite, is anything more than a waste of your time.

When you're in a producer's office, take a gander at the Matterhorn of scripts. Each was written by somebody just like you. Obviously, screenwriting is not for the faint of heart.

Writing a spec screenplay [writing on "speculation," hoping to sell it] is all about the *reader*, not your mom, or a friend who critiques your material, but someone who is paid to read your stuff. You know, a reader with fifteen scripts to plow through each weekend. If you're not actually *in* the business, you have no idea how monumentally difficult it is to find someone "real" to read your material. If you ever get that chance, you don't want to mess it up.

While it's true a reader really, really wants to unearth a fantastic screenplay, and opens each one with that uncrushable hope in mind, he is also dying to *quit reading* so he can flop by the pool with a delightfully refreshing umbrella drink. Therefore, if you give him any excuse to toss your script, he'll take it. And *poof!*, all your effort will be for naught. A big fat waste of six months of your life. Or a year. Or seven years, like one guy I know.

For some of you, this may come as heartbreaking news: the only people who *want* to read your work are your parents, maybe, and your boyfriend or girlfriend, depending on how new the relationship is. Remember the umbrella drinks? Readers want something that reads like lightning. Something with plenty of white space. Something where they don't have to fight to figure out what you're trying to say.

You are asking upwards of $100,000 for said work. You're asking someone to spend from $100,000 to $100,000,000 to produce something you just made up. You need to get this stuff *right*. You need scene description that sings. You need to have lively minor characters. You need to run your spellcheck. Like that.

What I'm telling you is simple to execute. It has nothing to do with talent or mythic story structure or round characters. I'm not telling you "how to write a great script." There are plenty of good books for that. What I am giving you are guidelines to make sure the reader *keeps reading*.

I once sat next to a producer on a plane and watched her read six pages and put a script down. That writer spent months and months on his script but, for some reason, blew his chance by page six. Probably for a long list of reasons.

I'm going to help you check a hundred reasons off that depression-inducing list!

> *"If the story confuses, it's the writer who loses."*
> Johnny Cochran (not really)

For the reader, reading a screenplay is like sprinting through a dark swamp across a hundred yards of floating lily pads while getting shot at by savages. The last page is the shoreline the reader is desperately trying to reach. If something breaks her concentration, even slightly, she may stumble, lose her balance and fall into the piranhas. Do everything you can to keep her on the lily pads!

As the Joe Gideon character says in *All That Jazz* (written by Robert Alan Aurthur and Bob Fosse):

```
"Listen. I can't make you a great dancer.
I don't even know if I can make you a
good dancer. But, if you keep trying
and don't quit, I know I can make you a
better dancer."
```

If you follow the *Your Screenplay Sucks!* checklist, by the time you finish this book, you'll be a better writer. No problem.

I hope you find the book incredibly useful.

William M. Akers
on the beach in Zihuatanejo*
August 2008

* Not really, but doesn't it just sound great! Maybe if I sell a few books....

ACT I:

Storytelling

**This is where you earn the money.
The rest is mechanics.**

"If a person can tell me the idea [of a film] in twenty-five
words or less, it's going to make a pretty good movie.
I like ideas, especially movie ideas, that you can
hold in your hand."
Steven Spielberg

"A writer is someone for whom writing is more difficult
than it is for other people."
Thomas Mann

"The task of the writer is to make you hear, to make you feel
— it is, before all, to make you see. That — and no more,
and it is everything."
Joseph Conrad

"Write about what you're afraid of."
Donald Barthelme

FADE IN:

"All serious daring starts within."
Eudora Welty

Here follows the most important lesson in this book, and maybe the most important single lesson in all of screenwriting. Actually overheard by me:

Two guys in line to buy tickets for *Finding Forrester*.
First guy says, "What's this movie about?"
And his buddy says, "Sean Connery."

Don't you *ever* forget it.

Contrary to what you may believe, you're not trying to write a great story. You're not writing a blueprint so a studio can make your movie. You're not writing something that's going to cure cancer or win a Nobel Prize. What you're writing is *actor bait*.

When the movie business first started, actors' names weren't on screen. Even then, producers weren't stupid. Very quickly, the public found actors who caught their fancy. They started writing fan letters to "The Biograph Girl." The actress getting the fan mail told Biograph Pictures that in her next contract, she wanted her *name* on screen. The producers were forced to relent. That actress was named Mary Pickford. The rest is history.

What those producers knew is that the public is only interested in movie stars, not story, not directors, not, for God's sake, writers. Just actors. When someone says, "We're sending this script out to talent," the "talent" is actors.

If your idea doesn't excite an actor, if they don't think that character and dialogue is going to win them an Oscar, make them look cool, make people cry, or get them laid, then your movie won't get made. In order to excite an actor, you have to excite a producer, and in order to excite a producer, you first have to excite the development executive, and, to excite a development exec, you must excite a reader.

And, for a reader to recommend your script to his boss, she has to *read the damn thing*. All of it.

Therefore, you need to make sure you do everything to get everyone to read to the last page of your screenplay. If your screenplay sucks, they'll stop reading.

So, let's roll up our sleeves and find out *why* your screenplay sucks. The good news is that most screenplays can be rewritten and repaired. Something that sucks today doesn't have to *always* suck.

Unless you've got a bad idea. Then you're dead.

Once you've chosen your idea, you're committed. Like a pig at breakfast.

> *"What's the difference between 'involved' and 'committed'? At breakfast, the chicken is involved. The pig is committed."*
> Anonymous

With that firmly in mind, here are 100 reasons your screenplay sucks. And a bunch of ways to fix it!

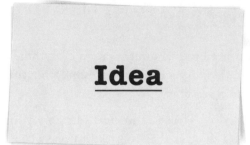

Idea

☑ 1. You have not written something you care about!

Write about something that fascinates you, that boils your blood, that gets you out of bed in the middle of the night, that you argue about at cocktail parties, that might cost you an old friend.

> *"Write a screenplay that will change your life. If you don't sell it, at least you will have changed your life."*
> John Truby

Take a cue from Mr. Truby, one of Hollywood's legendary screenwriting teachers. Are you writing about something that is of deep interest to you and therefore might be of deep interest to other people? Though it may be buried seventeen layers below the surface, are you writing a story that is "*about* something"?

If you have something to "say," then your script will be worth reading. Even if you're writing an all-nude bank heist musical, it helps to be invested in it.

Writing is not for wimps. It takes colossal mental and spiritual energy. It's hard work. Do it long enough, you'll have hemorrhoids and a bad back. If you're only trying to make money, you'll never survive the bone-grinding difficulty of the process. So, for God's sake, have something to say.

Why do you want to write? Why are you passionate? What matters to *you*!? What can you write, that you care about, that people will be interested in reading, that you *know* about? What story do you have the right to tell, more than any other writer out there?

If you're just writing a surfer horror movie because the last seven surfer horror movies made a mint, you're in it for the wrong reasons and the reader will smell it like gangrene. You can write the goofiest movie in the world — and if there is something in there that's got its hooks in your guts — you've got a chance at writing something wonderful.

Consider *Wedding Crashers*. At first blush, it seems pretty silly. Two guys sneak into weddings to get laid. Wish I'd thought that up when I was single. Really wish I'd thought of it last time I sat down to brainstorm a screenplay! But, when you look at the story, it's *about* something. Something profound: the relationship between two friends. It's a bromance, a love story between two guys, like *Tombstone* or *Superbad*. And, at its core, *Wedding Crashers* is real and touching. It's not a stupid comedy. It's a lovely, heartwarming story.

> *"Ain't no son of a bitch alive knows what's gonna hit."*
> Ray Charles

You can't know what's going to sell. No way. No one does. Another reason to write what *you* care about, because you can't even know the kind of script someone wants to read. A producer can tell you what he *thinks* he wants, but he doesn't actually know. He will *act* like he knows, and his reasoning may be convincing, but remember, he also believes his kids aren't stealing his liquor, so why listen to him? The same is true for agents, actors, or anybody alive on the planet.

You must write what matters to you, because:

> *"No matter what they say, that ain't what they want."*
> Barefield's Law

Going back to 1976: if you asked someone on the street what kind of movie they wanted to see, they'd say, "Whoa, dude. What a question. I wanna see something like *Jaws*. That shark was cool, man."

But, he only *thinks* he wants to see something like *Jaws*, because he liked it. What he really wants to see is something amazing and wonderful and new and nothing like *Jaws*, but he can't articulate that because — *he doesn't know what he wants to see because he hasn't seen it yet*. What audiences actually wanted to see hit theaters in 1977, and it was called *Star Wars*.

Same is true for producers. They will know what they want when you give it to them. So give it to them!

They will put their efforts into what they believe is going to have the best shot at selling — so write something you think someone is going to be able to sell. But, since it probably *won't* sell, at least write something you really, really want to write!

A book that may help you find *your* story is *Telling Your Own Stories* by Donald Davis. Highly recommended.

One way to choose what to write is if an idea keeps bobbing to the surface, saying "Listen up, Bud. I'm the story you have to tell!" Have you been interested in a particular subject for a long, long time? Maybe there's a way to turn that fascination into a movie. If it's been digging at your innards for eons, scratch that itch! It's so much easier if you write something you are dying to write. The reader will sense your enthusiasm.

There are lots of ways to approach subject matter. You can write something you think up. An original idea. You have total freedom here. You can create the world, the characters, the events, even the history of your world. You're in charge. Go wild. Have fun! Or, you can plunder history and write *Troy* or *300*. You can take a public domain novel, like *Emma* by Jane Austen, turn it on its head and, presto! you've got *Clueless*. You can spend money and option a short story, someone's life rights, a book, or a magazine article. Doesn't matter.

Whatever you choose to write, make sure you create characters who get our attention. Good writing is about the human condition. The more movies get bogged down in plot, action, special effects and things that are not revelatory of character, the more they go astray. Look at *Die Hard*. You worry about McClane and his wife and the cop outside and even the kid in the limo in the garage. If we don't care about your people, it's over. If we connect with the characters, you're home free.

You're the first audience for your idea, and it must interest you.

Can you sustain that interest over the years it may take you to write it? You don't want to lose sight of the spark and go down into the garden of forking paths. How is your idea so great, exciting, and compelling? How can you pull the reader through to the end? Do you think you can sell it? What is new about your approach?

Will a producer want to walk barefoot across broken glass to make your movie?

☐ 2. Your idea isn't vibrating with originality!

Go to the movies! See what gets made. Look at movies that are interesting and original like *Eternal Sunshine of the Spotless Mind* or *Three Kings*, which starts as a simple little war story but turns into something way more fascinating!

> "The oldest and strongest emotion of mankind is fear, and the oldest and strongest kind of fear is fear of the unknown."
> H. P. Lovecraft

Take us to a world we've never been to, and give us a ride we never expected. *Stranger than Fiction* is a uniquely delightful movie. When it came out, *2001: A Space Odyssey* was wholly fresh. Heck, it still is! *Ferris Bueller's Day Off. City of God. Being John Malkovich. My Life as a Dog.*

Each was wonderfully original. If you're not taking your reader to a place he's never been, why ask him to read past page one?

Here. My gift to you. A world you've never seen in a movie, not once! It's a world that exists a few miles from where you live.

Yet no one has ever set a movie in this arena. Ask yourself the hard question: "How can you take us on a journey that, on some level, is *this* new and fascinating?" *Rising Tide* by John Barry is a stunning piece of non-fiction. In the mid-19th century, an engineer in a makeshift diving bell is walking *on the bottom of the Mississippi River*:

> Without light, Eads could not see the river. He felt it. The bottom sucked at him while the current embraced him in darkness and silence. The current also buffeted, whipped, bullied, pulled. A diver had to lean against it, push against it. Unlike the wind, it never let up. He later wrote: "I had occasion to descend to the bottom in a current so swift as to require extraordinary means to sink the bell. ...The sand was drifting like a dense snowstorm at the bottom... At sixty-five feet below the surface I found the bed of the river, for at least three feet in depth, a moving mass and so unstable that, in endeavoring to find a footing on it beneath my bell, my feet penetrated through it until I could feel, although standing erect, the sand rushing past my hands, driven by a current apparently as rapid as that on the surface. I could discover the sand in motion at least two feet below the surface of the bottom, and moving with a velocity diminishing in proportion to its depth."

Whoa. What an amazing world. And were you to set a movie there, it would be a place none of us had ever been. But, then again, Westerberg High School in *Heathers* is not a world we'd ever been to either.

Just because you *think* an idea is wildly clever doesn't mean it's something you should write. Not everything you come up with is genius.

Spend time bouncing it on its head, turning it inside out, twisting it around to make it more interesting. Ask questions. What can I do to make this better? Is this like another movie I saw? Is there something here we've never seen? Why will anyone care about this story? Is this something people will be busting to tell their friends? Will it force a strong emotional reaction? Have we seen it before? How have I turned the genre on its head? What can I do to make it cooler, niftier, groovier? Am I just rehashing somebody else's movie, or is there a piece of my soul here? How can I take this idea and explode into something amazing?

> *"The competition is grotesque."*
> Richard Sylbert, production designer
> on *Chinatown* and *Dick Tracy*

You better believe it. If you're out there raising money for your fabulous feature film, you better have a very sharp script. Amazingly enough, people can raise money for a bad screenplay. They can make a movie based on a bad screenplay. However, this does not mean they *should* make a movie based on a bad screenplay. The amount of time and money wasted on boring, mediocre material is staggering. Experience shows that dentists will invest in damn near anything, but why should you want to waste their money, their time, the grip's time, the gaffer's, the actor's, the editor's, and *your own precious time*, of which you don't actually have that much, on something that wasn't GREAT? Do another ten drafts; make sure your script is original as hell, absolute, titanium-clad and bulletproof. If people read it and don't ask you what they can do to help you get it made, then you haven't written a fresh piece of work. It is as simple as that.

Just because you make a movie and show it to your buddies, your uncle, or a room full of giddy investors, does not mean you made a successful film. If someone buys your film and it goes to iPods, cell phones, or, dare I say, movie theaters, *then* it is successful. Remember the old advertising adage: "It's not creative unless it sells."

Right now, you're only worried about writing it. You also need to be worried about how someone is going to sell it, because, after all, this is the movie *business*.

Consider, when you're sitting down to think of your idea for a movie, "What parts are going to make it *sell*?" What have you got in there someone can take to a distributor and get them revved up about? Are there explosions or steamy romance they can show in the trailer? Drama, to me the most interesting storytelling form, is also the hardest to sell, because there are no "exploitable elements." You only have people talking to, or sometimes yelling at, each other. Unless they're throwing furniture, you don't have much action for a trailer. A horror film has "exploitable elements," in that there is goo and gore. But what about your movie? Is your script going to have WOW moments that will get your film sold?

Ask yourself which ground-breaking scenes *you* remember from movies — and then create some that work that strongly for your story. Here are some that work for me.

In *Say Anything* when John Cusack holds the boom box above his head and plays the song for the girl he loves: it's romantic and unforgettable. The food fight in *Animal House*. In *Cinema Paradiso*, when Alfredo moves the glass on the movie projector and the image slides across the walls of the projection booth. When Bambi's mother dies. In *Pulp Fiction*, when Samuel L. Jackson recites the Bible verse and kills the drug dealers. In *To Kill a Mockingbird* when Boo Radley comes out from behind Jem's bedroom door. In *Lawrence of Arabia*, when Lawrence has to kill Gasim, the man he saved in the desert. In *Miracle on 34th Street*, when Kris Kringle speaks to the little girl in Dutch.

At the climax of *The Full Monty*, Gaz, who's been promoting the strip show for the entire movie, admits he's too afraid to go onstage, and then is encouraged by his son. Watching that scene in a theater, I laughed and cried at the same time.

With the idea you're considering, can you deliver to that level?

☐ 3. You picked the wrong genre!

Genre is a huge topic. Books are written about genre. It's worth some major study.

You need to know what your story's genre is and you need to communicate it to the audience clearly, quickly, and early. If you're writing a genre you don't know backwards and forwards, it's going to be much more difficult.

Is it one clear, established, simple to understand genre? Is it a western, caper film, love story, drama, gross out movie, sci fi, horror, coming of age story... what is it? If you're not sure, and we aren't clear by page ten that you *are* sure, then you're toast. The reader has to know, right quick, what kind of story she's in.

Are you writing a genre you like? Are you writing a genre you're good at? If all you ever watch are cop movies, but you're writing a romantic love story set on the heaths of England in the 1700s, perhaps you are doing your talent a disservice. If you find you rent more westerns on Netflix than any other genre, give a long thought to writing a western.

Did you seize on a genre because that's what's popular in theaters this month? Death on a cracker.

It will take you six months to a year to write the script, another year to get somebody to want to buy it, if you're lucky. By then, that flavor *du jour* genre will have petered out and died, so you will have wasted your time. There are only so many screenplays you'll be able to write, so pick carefully what you choose to spend irreplaceable time on.

Sometimes you can just be a victim of bad luck. Once upon a time my school chum, Bob Rodat, decided to write a gangster movie. He wrote it. He had the massive misfortune to send it to his agent the same week three gangster movies opened and bombed. His agent threw his script away. He didn't give up. Soon thereafter, he wrote *Saving Private Ryan*.

Try not to pick a genre just because it's popular right now. Try not to pick a genre just because it's something you could make money with. Pick a genre you are comfortable with, pick a genre you love. But know that someone out there may be doing something a lot like yours…

☐ 4. Your story is only interesting to you!

Don't bore the reader.
Don't bore the reader.
Don't bore the reader.

> *"When you go to a cinema, you should come out like having a rocket up your ass."*
> Gary Oldman

A lot of this book, you're welcome to take with a grain of salt. Disagree with me if you like. Cast aspersions on my character if I say something you think is moronic. But, whatever you do, don't be boring. That's the only inviolable rule. If a scene, or your idea, or the main character is ever boring, stop writing until you figure out a way to un-boring it.

This is tough, especially if your tale is autobiographical.

Telling people, "Yo, when it happened to me, it was so intense" is, sadly, not enough. Just because it was exciting when you lived through it, doesn't mean it's going to work for the reader. Just 'cause you cried when your doggie died doesn't mean the reader will. Especially if Fido croaked when a safe fell on him.

Your life is probably not a good subject for a movie, so beware adapting it into drama; however, do dig deep into your life for *emotion*. You can make a fantastic movie about how you *felt*, as a strong emotion will be universal and will suck the reader in like quicksand.

We probably don't care what you did when you were nine, but we sure do care how you felt. My script about the fall of Saigon came from my watching *The Sound of Music* as a child and being terrified for the family trying to get out of the country before the Nazis captured them. I tapped into my own deep fear to write the screenplay. Turns out, other people related to it too, and the script sold.

Once upon a time, Billy Bob Thornton, working as an actor, was mistreated and miserable. In a wretched spiritual place, he hid out in his trailer, made faces in the mirror and started talking to himself about how he felt. From his shattered soul and searing mirror-diatribes, he squeezed the amazing character, Carl, in *Sling Blade*. Carl is not Billy Bob, but they share the same emotional connective tissue. Landed himself a nice, shiny Academy Award for tapping into his sadness.

What do you care about competitive ballroom dance? Nothing, right? Watch the first ten minutes of *Strictly Ballroom* and the filmmakers will convince you that competitive ballroom dance is the most important thing in the world!

> *"The fact that no one understands you does not make you an artist."*
> bumper sticker

Just because you dig it, doesn't mean anyone else is going to care. Just because *you* think it's a great idea doesn't mean it is a great idea. If your idea isn't great, you're wasting your time. And I mean a GREAT idea. On *X-Files*, a writer would sometimes work ten hours a day for six months to come up with *one* idea that would become an episode. It's *that* difficult to do.

The good news, at this stage: it's only your time you're wasting. Well, that and money you could have made had you been out getting paid to lay bricks instead of sitting in a coffee shop writing a screenplay based on an idea only you will care about.

Just because you take the time to write it, is anyone going to want to read it? Or see the movie? Really and truly? Don't waste your time. Or anyone else's.

"Write what you know."
every creative writing teacher

"He wrote what he knew. It didn't take long."
Howard Nemerov

Nemerov was poet laureate of the United States. He knew a thing or two about writing! In some respects, if you're a real writer, you *can't* write just what you know. You have to be out there on the end of the diving board, blindfolded… reaching, reaching…. You can use what you know in your writing, sure, but you are allowed to move outside your comfort zone. Do you think the guy who created the series *Prison Break* served time? *The Sopranos* creator is neither a therapist nor a mafia don. Mario Puzo was Italian, so he knew about pasta and family and honor and what it meant to be Italian-American. He made up the rest and it became *The Godfather*.

"Write what you know" at its most useful means: take something churning inside you and use it in your writing. It doesn't mean that, if you're a second grade teacher, you can only write about second grade teachers. But if you are a second grade teacher, and you're writing about a second grade teacher, make certain she is in the middle of an emotional story that is going to hook everybody, deep.

☐ 5. Your story is about miserable people who are miserable the whole time and end miserably! Or worse!!

It is not my job to tell you what to write. You have to write something that will get you up in the morning, or get you to stay up late at night, or get you to dictate in your car, or sit in a park and write instead of being at home getting yelled at by your spouse because you're not looking after *your* children.

Write what you wanna write. However, for a topic, I don't suggest misery, especially relentless, unending misery. It may be your life, but we want a *story*.

It's very, very, very hard to get a movie made. Quadruple or quintuple that degree of difficulty when your movie is about endless grim horribleness. If there is no spiritual uplift at the end, the reader is going to heave the script into their fireplace and cackle as it burns. Why should the audience suffer along with the character only for it to have been in vain?

Patrick Marber adapted the Zoe Heller novel *What Was She Thinking* into the screenplay *Notes on a Scandal*. After all the characters' trials and tribulations, the book ends with them in a low, dark, awful place, with zero hope for redemption. The suicide zone. NOT how you want to end a movie. Marber, clever lad, reworked the finale to give us hope for the main character. Not a lot, but enough for the audience to think, "Oh, she's gone through this whole wretched experience and at least she's learned something, and maybe can save her marriage!" Whew.

Let the reader end on a note of hope or redemption. *Million Dollar Baby*, by Paul Haggis, has a grim ending which is then followed by the lead character's at last doing what he'd always wanted to do. We leave the theater with a smidgen of an uplift. Though we're sad, we feel good for the hero, as he's managed to find something happy in the midst of his sadness. Good plan, Mr. Writer!

Either have a happy ending or figure out a way to give the reader some hope!

☐ 6. You haven't spent enough time thinking up a fantastic title!

Is your title a good title or a stupid title? Does it give no hint about your story? Is it a title no one will understand and no one will care about? Is it so weird that it's going to be off-putting? Is it the main character's name? Is it hard to pronounce or spell?

If you have a less-than-stellar title, change it.

If the title makes you smile or laugh or get a warm and fuzzy feeling, keep it. If it tells the reader what the movie's about, keep it. The title is the first thing people learn about your script. If you have a dumb title, they'll think it's going to be a stupid screenplay. I cannot emphasize this enough.

I was on the phone with one of my former students, an agent's assistant in Los Angeles, and he had a choice of two screenplays to read. He picked the one with the cool title. He figured that if someone could think up a good title, maybe the script would be good too. From time to time, I wonder if that other screenplay ever got read.

My favorite title is *Blade Runner*. It's cool and compelling and makes me want to read the script or see the movie. I'd be happy naming every movie I write: *Blade Runner*. Yeah!

These are good: *Alien, Rich and Famous, Gone with the Wind, Trouble in Paradise, Gladiator, A Beautiful Mind, Tremors, Used Cars, Herbie: Fully Loaded, The Madness of King George, Speed, Oldest Living Confederate Widow Tells All, Robocop, His Girl Friday, Ernest Saves Christmas, Dog Day Afternoon.*

These are, um, less good because you have no idea what the movie is about: *The Island, K-Pax, SwimFan, She's the Man, The Man, Monster, Signs, Tomorrow Never Dies, Go, The Grudge, Fur, The Neverending Story, Music and Lyrics, Freddy Got Fingered, Gigli, Manos: The Hands of Fate, Jeeper's Creepers, August Rush.*

How about *Wedding Crashers, The 40-Year-Old Virgin*, and *Knocked Up*? What GREAT titles — delightfully intriguing, and they tell you what the movie's about! Unfortunately, they're taken.

Is yours the best you can come up with? Try to think of at least 50 titles for your film. Email your friends and ask them to suggest titles. Ask them to choose between your top ten. Visit a music store and look at song titles. Go to imdb.com and steal a title from a film made in 1934. Make the effort to find the best title you possibly can.

It will make a difference.

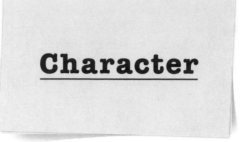

Character

☐ 7. You picked the wrong main character!

You'd be surprised how often people write an entire screenplay only to find they've written it with the wrong person as their hero. This is a tough one to get right, and is demoralizing to discover you've goofed. But, it's better at this stage to throw the script out and rewrite it around the right person than give it to someone real and squander the only read they'll ever give you.

What tells you you've got the right main character?

Hero Litmus Test

1) Your hero must be active.
He must seize control of the action, his problem, or his destiny and struggle without quitting until he has triumphed over the bad guy. A hero who is not active will never engage the audience or the reader. Dr. Richard Kimball, the Fugitive, never gives up. No matter what problems are thrown at him, he fights and fights to find a solution and continues the struggle.

Does she initiate action or allow other people to think up the stuff that happens? Yes, you can write a screenplay about a character who sits still and takes no action and makes no decisions and is quiet and passive the entire time, but Natalie Portman won't play her.

A passive main character is a one-way ticket to Palookaville.

2) Your hero must have a well-defined problem.
One problem. It must be simple. It must be clear to the reader, and that reader needs to know about that problem in the first

ten pages. There can't be several problems. There can only be one main problem, which is what the movie is about. A movie is closer to a short story than a novel. Keep it simple.

One problem.

3) The hero's problem must be interesting to an audience.
Just because you think it's fascinating, I may not. You have to engage us. The problem must be strong enough to drag us all the way through 110 pages. Don't think tiny, think huge.

The bigger the hero's problem, the more engaging it will be for the reader. This does not mean every movie has to be about a guy blowing up a rogue asteroid to stop it from crashing into earth and wiping out life as we know it. The problem has to be the most difficult problem *your* character would ever have to deal with. In *Breaking Away*, the hero struggles to find out if he's a bike rider or a stone cutter. In *Superbad*, he wants to get some liquor so he can go out with the beautiful girl.

It may not be a big problem to the Universe At Large, but it had better be HUGE for the people in the movie.

4) Hero must solve his/her own problem.
No one can save him in the big moment. He must gut it through on his own. He can have allies, but in the final battle, your hero has to down the forces of evil (if you're British: eeevil) on his own.

Does she come up with a great idea and save herself at the end, or does someone else do the saving? That someone else might be a good candidate for Main Character!

In *Prince of Egypt*, the Israelites are running away from the Egyptians and come smack up against the Red Sea. There's no way they aren't going to get caught — guaranteed 100% cannon fodder. Suddenly, out of the blue, comes a pillar of fire that stops the bad guys juuuust long enough for Moses to figure out how to part the Red Sea and hustle everybody to safety. Moses doesn't solve his own problem. It's such an egregious example of *deus ex machina* that I looked in the Bible to see if had actually happened, because that would have been the only way the fine folks at Disney would have allowed such crummy writing. Okay, so the pillar of fire happened in the Bible, but it's incredibly poor screenwriting.

In *Pinocchio*, every time Pinocchio gets in a jam, the Blue Fairy swoops down and gives him a clue he's been unable to find on his own. *Deus ex machina* is a low level way to move a story forward. Avoid it.

If you have trouble with the above four guidelines, give your main character a serious re-think.

Ask yourself: Is your heroine in the crusher all the time? Is she the one having larger and larger problems thrown at her, faster and faster?

Are her emotions big enough to hang a whole story on?

Is her problem one you're fascinated by, or is it really her aunt, who's building a fighter plane in her kitchen, who blows your dress up? Is the story really and truly "about" her? Perhaps the story is really "about" someone else, say the lead character's little brother. This is why you give your rough draft to a friend to read and ask, "Do you think Betty is the lead, or is it Veronica?"

Is she on screen most of the time?

Is she the one who fights her way through a fiery furnace to be transformed at the end? The actress who does the changing is often the one with the Oscar.

If you've chosen the wrong main character, rejoice! You've done heaps of good work which will serve your *new* story. You can sail forward knowing that at last, you're on the right path. Best of all, you didn't send your script out. Then your heaps of good work would have been a waste of time.

Be glad you found out now, instead of when you got hold of CAA's coverage.

☐ 8. You haven't constructed your main character correctly!

Don't forget the all-important *Finding Forrester* lesson. You're writing actor bait.

Actors will attach to your script because they want to play the characters you construct. Construct them well!

Plot comes from character. Things happen because of who they are. Early in *Raiders of the Lost Ark*, we learn Harrison Ford is terrified of snakes. It's part of his character. So, at the climax, it has to be snakes! In *Lawrence of Arabia*, he has a passion to avoid bloodshed; later, he changes and enjoys killing. In *Casablanca*, Rick steadfastly won't stick his neck out for anyone, and finally, that's exactly what he does.

Let's talk about character change. The character's "arc." Who they are at the beginning versus who they are at the end. Actors sometimes look at the first ten pages and the last ten pages to see if there is a big change. If the character doesn't change, they put down the script. As Sergeant Rock would say, "ARGGGGGHHHH!"

Character transformation is important. It happens so seldom in life: we want goodness and justice to triumph, but we also want the characters to figure something out about themselves, becoming something that they weren't at the beginning.

Remember *How the Grinch Stole Christmas*? When the story starts, the terribly unpleasant Grinch's heart is too small. By the end, it grows two sizes and he smiles and is nice to folks in Whoville. Massive change. In *Regarding Henry*, Harrison Ford is a jerk. He gets shot, rediscovers his life, and ends a better person. In *The Wizard of Oz*, Dorothy hates Kansas and ends up thrilled to come home. In *My Fair Lady*, Liza Doolittle starts as gutter trash and finishes a lady. In *The Mask*, Stanley Ipkiss is a sniveling obsequious loser, and the Mask releases his inner self. Boy, is he different at fade out!

The main character doesn't always have to change. Does the Man With No Name in *A Fistful of Dollars* have a character arc? Naaaaaaaaaah.

In Billy Wilder and I.A.L. Diamond's *The Apartment*, Jack Lemmon is a *nebbish* (and his neighbor calls him one!) who learns to be a *mensch* (which he calls himself).

At the start:

> Jack is desperate to work his way up in the insurance company, and to that end, buys snacks and liquor for the VPs using his apartment to um, entertain their mistresses. He's lonely and eats frozen food. He washes dishes after someone else's party. He's a doormat with ambition.

> When he allows himself to be convinced to leave his apartment in the rain so one of his bosses can screw some ditzy babe, he's angry, but keeps his yap shut. It's clear his job is on the line if he doesn't let them use the apartment.

Later on:

> He gives the apartment key to Fred MacMurray, who goes there to have sex with the elevator girl, the girl Jack Lemmon has fallen in love with! But, he does get that big promotion he'd wanted.

Then, way further down the road:

> Jack no longer can tolerate this arrangement and tells Fred he can't use the apartment any more. Jack gives up his job, after deciding to become a *mensch*, a human being. Everything about him is different. Even his tone of voice has changed. And, once he's transformed, he finally gets adorable Shirley MacLaine to play cards with him. Voilà.

Jack changes. A lot. Your main character should too.

When you're figuring out why your characters are the way they are, build the layer cake in this order:

> Who are they, basically? Is he an art thief or a priest? She's from Chicago and is an underwater welder. He's a gladiator in Ancient Rome. He's a weird kid with scissors for hands. She's a nun who can fly. He's a businessman with a gambling problem.

Are they in conflict inside themselves? Is Sally weak and strong at the same time? Is there good and evil inside her, a demon on one shoulder, an angel on the other? Sally wants to be the good girl homecoming queen, but she also wants to murder her competition.

Specific characteristics of their character? Personality traits. Cultural influence. Financial background. Historical period. Occupation. All this influences how they talk, move and act. What are their beliefs? Morals? How do they feel about their parents or their children or their coworkers? Is she excitable? Does he hate liars? Is he a liar? Was he frozen in a lump of ice ten thousand years ago, so a pencil is a miracle? Is she a gardening fanatic? and on and on.

Readers love details. So do actors. Does your guy love to speak French when he kisses his wife on her neck? Does he carry a St. Christopher medal in his pocket? How does being left-handed affect her? Does she line up her plucked eyebrow hair on the edge of the sink? Does she stutter when she has to say, "Father."

Finally, are they consistent throughout the story? No wild card surprises just because you need one. Once you've defined his core personality, everything he does must fit that character. He can't be a vegan and suddenly start eating bacon.

Each character must want something, very badly. But, what they *need* is different from what they want, and they must get *that* by the end. (More about this when I pontificate about structure.)

That desire must be strong enough to drive the whole movie. It also has to be simple. In *The Trip to Bountiful*, the old woman wants to go home. The old woman in *Driving Miss Daisy* wants independence but her son wants her not to drive, and forces her to hire a chauffeur.

Characters must not be faced with an easy decision, like "Do I marry the homecoming queen or do I go to jail?" Give them a bone-crushing moral decision: 1) I love my husband but I want to move in with my student. 2) A good man kills a bad one. Do you hang him? 3) If I tell my clients the truth, they'll settle out of court. If I lie to them, I might be able to win big in court.

The ghost (like in *Hamlet!*) is the spear point at your hero's back, driving him forward. In *Chinatown*, in the past, Gittes wanted to protect a woman, but she ended up getting hurt. He desperately doesn't want that to happen again. In *Ironweed*, the hero dropped his baby and it died. The ghost of that child is eating him alive. In *The Wild Bunch*, Robert Ryan betrayed his best friend, William Holden, to the law. In *Casablanca*, Rick's ghost is what happened in Paris; he had love and lost it. That drives him to want to hold onto love the next time he gets a chance. In *Ordinary People*, before the movie opened, one son died and the other tried to kill himself. The ghost of the dead, better-loved son pushes all the characters toward the brink.

Backstory is different from ghost. Backstory explains why they are the way they are because of specific events from the past. It can be ten things or six or two. It's not the ghost (the stone in the hero's shoe) but it's that he grew up in New Jersey, raised pigeons, came from a family of longshoremen, was a boxer, took falls for short end money, and could have been a contender.

Ghost is part of a larger backstory. Don't spend a lot of time talking about ghost and backstory. *We* see the tip of the iceberg, but *you* know everything that's below the surface.

In *Rain Man*, Tom Cruise was a great kid. One time he got all As and asked his father for the keys to the treasured Buick. The Old Man said no. Tom took it out with his friends anyway, and his father called the car in as stolen. They all went to jail. The other boys' fathers came and got them. Not Tom's. He left him for two days. A guy tried to rape him and knifed him. When he got out of jail, Tom left home and never went back.

How Tom *feels* about what happened in the past affects his every move in the present.

Last thoughts on character:

Is your hero 100% good? No one should be. Make sure they've got a flaw or two.

Are there any characters you don't need, or two or three you could combine into one character?

Make sure none of your main characters disappear for too long.

Do we learn about your characters by what they *do* — not through dialogue? A man beats his wife, cries and says he's sorry, but keeps on beating her. Character must be visible with the sound turned off. Watching a guy wash his cans of vegetables before putting them in the pantry trumps his saying, "I'm a neat freak."

If you have two people in a scene, make them WILDLY different from one another. It becomes much easier to write if they have contrasting personalities. One worships Clinton. The other has Bush stickers all over her cubicle. Imagine them at lunch! Imagine them at lunch, drinking!

Have you given your character as many moments as possible to *take action*? In the novel, *The Enchanted April,* Mrs. Wilkins knows Mrs. Arbothnot from church and asks her to rent a villa in Italy with her. In the screenplay, Mrs. Wilkins places an ad in the paper searching for people to share rent the villa, a much greater risk, and that is how she meets Mrs. Arbothnot. It's a more interesting character choice from the writer.

Again, and not for the last time: does your character change? The bigger the change, the easier it will be to write. In a 114-page script, if Toby changes from A all the way to Z, imagine how many steps along the way you can write about. But, if he only goes from A to F, that's not much of a change. Tough to write.

Tough to turn into actor bait!

☐ 9. You are not specific about EVERYTHING when you create a character!

Here's a conversation I had with a student. Her character, Linda, is a patient in a hospital. Robin is her nurse.

> "So, tell me about Linda."
> "She's sick."
> "How is she sick?"
> "From an infection."
> "What kind of infection?"
> "She has a tube in her side and it got infected."
> "Why has she got a tube?"
> "She's got cancer."
> "What kind of cancer?"
> "Does it matter?"
> "Well, yes. What kind of cancer affects how she appears, how she feels, and how we feel about her. If she's got breast cancer, you've got pink ribbons and a lot of political agenda that doesn't come with, say, pancreatic cancer."
> "Really?"
> "And if she's got pancreatic cancer, she's for sure going to die, and it will be fast but it won't be too painful."

Long pause.

> I said, "So you see how it really matters that, if she's sick, that you know exactly why she's sick, because it will affect everything."
> "Yeah, sure. Now I do."
> "Now, tell me about Robin, the nurse."
> "She's very upset with where she is in her life."
> "How do we see this?"
> "She steals pills."
> "What kind of pills?"
> "I don't know. Just pills."
> "Uppers?"
> "Maybe. That might work."
> "What about downers? A person who steals uppers is going to have very different personal problems and a different character makeup than someone who steals barbiturates. Does she take pain killers? Why? What part of her personality directs her to

steal Oxycontin, or morphine? Her story will be very different, depending on what kind of pills she steals."
"Oh, yeah, cool."

And it went on from there. At the end of the conversation, she had a much better idea of what she needed to do, and she understood what I meant when I said, "You're not being specific."

You need to ask yourself these same questions. If you say something about a character, like "He's sad," that's not enough. Is he "sad" or "suicidal," and then, of course, you have to know why.

If you find yourself saying *anything* in a story, figure out a way to make it specific. Don't say, "He graduated from a well-known university." Tell us what school!

The actor will want to know these things. So will the reader. Be specific. Be very specific.

☐ 10. You haven't made "place" a character in your story!

Here's some lousy writing:

```
FADE IN:

EXT. NONDESCRIPT TRACT HOME      DAY

A nice home in an average city.
```

Give yourself all the help you can. This isn't helping.

There is no such thing as an "average small town." No such thing as "a medium-size city." Probably not in real life and certainly not in a movie. If you are not incredibly specific with your choice of location, be it country, city, or particular room in a house, you will not write as well as you should.

A sense of place should be treated as a separate character. Does your story happen in the correct time and location for what you're trying to get across? Where you put people is crucial.

When you pick a place for your story, don't say "suburbs" when you should say Hamtramck, Michigan. Pick a city or a town and make it a character. People who live outside Detroit are going to be affected by their locale in a different way than, say, people who live outside Key West. Read the novels of Tim Gautreaux if you want to see how place really matters to a story.

> *"People behave differently depending on where they are. Imagine an argument that takes place between a husband and wife in their front yard. Now, move it to the back yard. How does that change the nature of the argument? People behave differently when they know their neighbors are not watching."*
> Joan Tewkesbury, writer of *Nashville*

I wrote a script for the producer of *Risky Business*. It was based on his first year of college and a girl he had been in love with. His girlfriend had gone to school in Philadelphia and her parents lived in New York, and he'd been a life guard on Long Island. For some reason, the story didn't work. We worked on it and worked on it, and I finally realized (after months!) that we were stuck on what had happened in real life. I changed it so the girl and her parents were in New York. They lived there and she was in school there. It changed everything and made the story work. Just because I decided to have her live in New York.

Does your story happen in the best possible year? The right season? Imagine how different your story will be if it takes place in Nome, Alaska in the dead of winter with three feet of snow, or perhaps on the beach in California. How will people react to an event if they are from Nebraska or from Selma, Alabama?

A sense of place will affect not only your entire story, but individual scenes.

While this example from *Rocky* doesn't actually spring from the writing, let's pretend it does. Stallone's script called for Rocky and Adrian to finally go on a date. He's asked her out and she's refused, but he's at last worn her down. They go to a restaurant. They have a lovely conversation. It's a wonderful first date, right?

Well, when it got around to shooting the scene, they couldn't afford to rent a restaurant and pay for all those extras. They had to find a cover set that was cheap to rent, requiring no extras. What did they use? An empty ice rink that was closing for the night.

The rest is movie history. Putting Adrian on wobbly skates and Rocky walking beside her while they had their sweet, halting conversation — same dialogue they'd have used in a restaurant — was a sublime choice. A little conflict thrown in from the Zamboni guy saying they have to leave in a few minutes, and you have one of my favorite scenes in any movie. All by changing where the scene takes place.

Go through your script, scene by scene, and see if you can turn a few boring locations into something magical.

☐ 11. We have no rooting interest in your hero!

This does not mean we want her to dig for truffles.

> *"The easiest way to attract a crowd is to let it be known that at a given time and a given place someone is going to attempt something that in the event of failure will result in sudden death."*
> Harry Houdini

We need to desperately want your hero to win. This does not mean "have a sympathetic lead character." *Your hero does not have to be sympathetic.* He doesn't have to be nice. Just because development people or writing teachers say your main character has to be likeable, doesn't mean you have to listen. If all your friends jumped off a cliff, would you?

Look at Jack Nicholson in *As Good As It Gets*. Is he sympathetic? First thing we see him do is drop an adorable little dog down a garbage chute! That's not likeable. When he gets thrown out of a restaurant, all the patrons applaud because everybody hates him.

And this is the story's hero?

He's not sympathetic. Not at all. But. We do feel *empathy* for his situation. We identify with his feelings. We understand his problem. And we very much want him to overcome it.

We're rooting for him.

While the Jack Nicholson character is not sympathetic in the slightest, he sure is *fascinating*. We want him to get Helen Hunt at the end. We want him to win!

If your lead character is not mesmerizingly compelling to the reader, it's all over but the crying. She can be the biggest jerk in the universe, but if she's *interesting*, we're hooked. Look at Shakespeare's Richard III. Now, there's a world-class, 24 karat evil bastard. Not remotely likeable, but we can't take our eyes off the guy. Think about Mr. Pink. He doesn't tip. Or Mr. Blonde. He cuts off Mr. Nice Policeman's ear. Those guys aren't "sympathetic." They're horrible! You'd never invite them over for lasagna, but, you sure want to watch them in a movie.

Take Alan Arkin, the incredibly grumpy old man in *Little Miss Sunshine*. Now there's an unpleasant old geezer. But, he loves his granddaughter and spends a ton of time helping her with her dance routine, so we want him to win.

We want the boy to win the race in *Breaking Away*. We want Sandra Bullock to catch the bad guy in *Miss Congeniality*. We want Humbert Humbert to nail Lolita. We want Tom Cruise and Dustin Hoffman to work out their problems in *Rain Man*. We want Bruce Willis to defeat the Hans Gruber Gang in *Die Hard*. We want Tom Robinson to be found innocent and we want Scout to be safe from Mr. Ewell.

You must set up the character so we want him to get what he wants. *But, we don't have to "like" him.* Here's my pick for "guy we loathe the most, but who we still want to win!"

In Todd Solondz' *Happiness*, Dylan Baker plays a deeply closeted pedophile. At a child's slumber party, he laces the kids' ice cream with sleeping pills. Not so sympathetic. What he wants to do is illegal and immoral and nothing we would ever applaud, but as obstacles get in the way of his desire and the more he has to struggle to get what he wants, the more we want him to get it — even though down in our guts we know what he wants is wrong! wrong! wrong! wrong! Yet, we still want him to win. It's amazing.

We have to be pulling for your guy to win, or you've got no story anyone will care about.

☐ 12. Your opponent is not a human being!

"Evil New York City" is not a good bad guy for a movie. "Man's inhumanity to man" is not an opponent for John Denman, tough and crusty Oklahoma City private investigator. "A dark and oppressive presence" was not what threatened Sigourney Weaver in *Alien*. It was a monster. A big, drippy-fanged creature — just like Mr. Hand in *Fast Times at Ridgemont High*. Spicoli had to do battle with a *person*.

And so should your hero.

Your bad guy shouldn't be a disease or "the system" or guilt or the weather. These can be part of the hero's problem, but he must face off with a human being. People can make plans, have complex wants and needs, have a set of beliefs in direct opposition to the hero's, and can be in a room to yell at him!

You can argue that *Shaun of the Dead* had zombies as an opponent, but I will counter that there was plenty of human conflict ripping that little group of people to pieces well before the undead attacked the pub.

If you want the evil being to be "the medical profession," create a doctor or nurse to embody the loathsome corporate transgressions of Big Medicine. Look at Nurse Ratched in *One Flew Over the Cuckoo's Nest*. Louise Fletcher is in near-mortal conflict with

Jack Nicholson. It's horrible for the audience when she does mean things to him and his hospital buddies, and it's terribly satisfying when he, at long last, defeats her. Because she's a person.

You have to have a person for the hero to fight against. If you don't have one, find one.

Plus, you can't write nifty dialogue for a "dark, oppressive presence." Actors want to say cool stuff. And producers won't make your movie if actors don't want to be in it.

☐ 13. Your Bad Guy isn't great!

Your hero is only as interesting as the dude he's in the ring with.

> *"In science-fiction films the monster should always be bigger than the leading lady."*
> Roger Corman

This is my memory of the *Space Jam* poster: Michael Jordan with a big, scary, fanged monster looming over him.

Lookee here. The hero is a nice, clean-cut basketball player. He's smart, strong, and good looking. The perfect movie hero. Who is he in conflict with? Not little Timmy from down the street, a squirt he could mop the floor with, no, but a huge, ghoulish, fanged space alien who has super strength and devious ways. Plus, a savage jump shot. A worthy opponent!

The opponent, or bad guy, or antagonist has to be stronger than the good guy or you've got no movie. If, at the start of your story, we're not quaking in our boots when faced with the opponent, you have some rewriting to do. This does not mean she has to have a ray gun. It can be Mary Tyler Moore in *Ordinary People*. That mom is one strong, implacable, relentless opponent.

Your bad guy must always be taking action. He's always plotting. Planning, stealing, killing, wounding, belittling, or scraping cheese off your pizza. If the bad guy isn't constantly making (more and more clever) moves, he's not much of a bad guy.

Are your bad guy and good guy in the room together as much as possible? Figure out ways for them to be face to face. Get them off the phone and into a car together. If there is a way for the bad guy and the good guy to be business partners instead of crosstown rivals, do it.

Don't make him 100% bad. Just like your hero isn't 100% good, your opponent shouldn't be a total jerk. If he's a terrorist, let him like fine wine. In *Casablanca*, Major Strasser is not a drooling villain; he has good reasons for doing what he does. The Godfather is motivated by love for his family. Gordon Gekko is driven by success and ambition. Captain Jas. A. Hook suffers because "no little children love me."

What about your bad guy is set up precisely to punch the good guy's buttons? If the good guy feels horrible because he doesn't make much money at his prestigious university teaching job, the bad guy lives across the street and makes twice that money, teaching.

Without a good opponent, your hero can't be heroic. If Muhammad Ali had faced off with Grandma Moses, who'd have paid to see that? Joe Frazier made Ali the champion he is today. Without Frazier, there'd be no Ali.

☐ 14. The opponent is not the hero's agent of change!

Without the opponent, your hero will never evolve to who he/ she needs to be.

Most main characters are transformed. Actors know they won't win an Oscar if the guy doesn't show some growth. So, how does your hero reach that dazzling Grail known as "character change?"

At the beginning of your tale, your hero is in a bad place in his life, treats other people shabbily, and has a hole in his soul you could drop a Mack truck through. At the end of the movie, he'll be happier, better adjusted, and the rest of his life will be a snap.

All because of the opponent.

In *Die Hard*, John McClane is in a bad marriage. He's not been treating his wife very well. He's separated and on the slippery slope to divorce. Enter Hans Gruber.

Gruber kidnaps everybody in sight, including McClane's wife, and plans to kill them all. McClane is forced to step up to the plate. By having to save his wife from this clever robber, McClane realizes how much he loves her, and, at the end of the story, they are back together and their marriage has been saved. McClane becomes the man he needed to be at the start of the story. Hans Gruber, marriage counselor.

Pick any movie.

At the start of *Casablanca*, Rick Blaine is a selfish jerk. At the end, he's a totally different guy, having given up the one woman who will make him happy in order to help the war effort. That's a gigantic character arc. Because it's a love story, the opponent is Ilsa Lund. Were it not for her turning his life inside out, he would remain a jerk and die in Casablanca.

In *Crash*, Terrance Howard has trouble dealing with racism and his place in the white world, not to mention a lot of "issues" with his wife. He has his buttons pushed by Matt Dillon and, after nearly becoming hamburger, comes out of the meat grinder a better, stronger person. No Matt Dillon: no happiness.

In *Shopgirl*, Claire Danes isn't interested in Jason Schwartzman (the guy she should be with) until she is put through the wringer by Steve Martin — and she only changes because of her relationship with him. Then, and only then, does she have the self confidence she needs to end up with Jason.

So, look at your script and see what causes the main character to change.

It had better be the opponent.

☐ 15. The Bad Guy doesn't feel he's the hero of his own movie!

The bad guy has good reasons for what he's doing.

In *Extreme Measures*, Gene Hackman is Hugh Grant's unscrupulous opponent. But he's far from a serial killer. He's a renowned surgeon, getting on in years, searching for a cure for paralysis. He knows that, since FDA approval for his protocol will take longer than he has to live, he must resort to untraditional methods to bring about the cure he believes in so strongly. Now there's a noble goal!

Except — whoops! — he does it by experimenting on homeless people and some of them, um, die. He thinks it's justifiable because a cure would be wonderful and the homeless guys are forgotten and have no reason to live anyway. He's doing bad things but for an understandable (and sympathetic) reason.

There should be an emotional component to what the bad guy wants.

In *The Shawshank Redemption*, the Bible-believing Warden wants order in the prison. Totally laudable. But there's just one problem. He's a sadist.

In *Ferris Bueller's Day Off*, the bad guy wants order in the school — a totally sympathetic, understandable desire. "I have to catch him this time. To show these kids that the example he sets is a first class ticket to nowhere." Rooney's doing the right thing. Unfortunately, if he succeeds, he's going to ruin Ferris's life.

Even the Wicked Witch of the West has a reason to be upset. How would you feel if someone dropped a house on your sister and stole the magic shoes that you had been counting on from your mother's inheritance? So, she too is the heroine of *her* movie.

☐ 16. You don't give your bad guy a Bad Guy Speech!

This is how we learn he's the hero of his own movie. It's amazing how often you see the bad guy talk about how he feels and why he's doing what he's doing.

In *The Last of the Mohicans*, written by Michael Mann and Christopher Crowe (and based on the novel by James Fenimore Cooper), Magua is a delicious bad guy! He's smart, ugly, mean, and hates Munro and his daughters with an unquenchable purple passion. We're scared to death of Magua. All he wants to do is hack these sweet little girls to bits… But, were that his sole characteristic, like the shark in *Jaws*, he would just be a killing machine.

Magua remains one-dimensional until he gets a chance to tell his side of the story. First, he scares us. (It's Chapter 12 — Magua's Hate — of the DVD, btw.) When Montcalm asks why Magua hates the Grey Hair, he says he wants to kill the Grey Hair and eat his heart, but before he dies, Magua has a special treat for him. "Magua will put his children under the knife so the Grey Hair will see his seed is wiped out forever."

That's a showstopper. Interestingly, he doesn't answer Montcalm's question, "Why?" We only know he wants to kill those two little girls and eat their father's heart. Step back, Jason and Freddy, a master has entered the room.

What's great about this Bad Guy Speech is that Michael Mann and Christopher Crowe break it into two parts. After the first half, we get some more excitement, some kissing, a *soupçon* of death and intrigue — and we see what a tough mother Magua really is — but we still don't view him as anything other than a bloodthirsty animal.

Then, in Chapter 21 — Magua's Pain — Montcalm and the reader hear what's boiling Magua's guts. What's cool, he's in the right, 1,000%.

Montcalm sees huge scars on Magua's back and asks who did it. Magua slowly tells him that his villages had been destroyed and that his children had been killed by the English. Magua was enslaved by Indians who fought for the Grey Hair, and finally, worst of all, Magua's wife thought he was dead and married another man. All this, because of Magua's enemy, the Grey Hair.

Whoa! No wonder he wants to kill him and his sweet little girls. We totally sympathize with the guy. Suddenly, he becomes a fascinating character, and his conflict with the hero is all the more rich and rewarding.

Bad guy speeches rock!

☐ 17. Your characters do stupid things to move the story forward, a.k.a. they do stuff because you make them!

If your character does something that they'd *never actually do it in real life*, reconsider.

If Lily is your heroine, and she's a smart, with-it, on-her-game woman, and Sean gets her pregnant, and he's a complete jerk about it — why would she want him?

```
                    SEAN
                (deliberately)
        Lily, I am standing here willing to take
        you back.

                    LILY
        Sean, I'm sorry I didn't tell you about
        my pregnancy, but I--

                    SEAN
        --I left a God-damned dinner with
        Senators for you--

                    LILY
        --I promise you can share my child. And--

                    SEAN
        --I don't want shared custody! I'm giving
        you another chance. You can't do this
        alone!
```

If he treats her like garbage — and she takes it — the reader will think she's a moron and won't invest any more time reading about her.

If you've got a super-intelligent serial killer who is diabolically clever in how he approaches, tracks, and kills his victims, but leaves a nice, juicy clue in each one's dresser drawer for the detectives to conveniently find so they can solve the crime, that's not something a smart guy would do. You can make it work, however. If he is, for instance, totally vain and thinks police detectives are stupid.

Have you sealed off every avenue for your character to take except the one they take?

If Little Miss Muffet shivers alone on her tuffet in a dark room afraid the killer is coming to poison her curds and whey — *with a telephone next to her* — you have a problem. If she'd call 911 in real life, she'd call 911 in the movie. Have the killer cut the phone line or make the local constable be thirty miles away knocking back a beer. You're a writer. Be creative.

In *Crimes and Misdemeanors*, Woody Allen needed Martin Landau to kill his mistress. The story hinged on it. So, knowing he had to march his hero down a very tight path, Allen closed every door along the way. Landau couldn't tell his wife the truth. He couldn't go to the police. He couldn't reason with his girlfriend 'cause she was crazier than a shithouse rat. Finally, the only option was murder. So he kills her and the movie can proceed, happy in the knowledge that the viewer totally buys that the nice man would murder that awful woman.

At the beginning of Jean-Pierre Melville's *Le Samourai*, Alan Delon, a hit man, walks out of his apartment building and steals a car. Why would a guy who's that smart steal a car that could belong to someone in his own neighborhood? When he comes home and parks the car, even though he's changed the license plate, the real owner might see it. It's just such a boneheaded thing to do; why not steal the car in a different neighborhood?

In *The Client*, the kid climbs up in a rowboat hanging from a boathouse ceiling. Bad guys come into the boathouse and he can overhear their nefarious conversation. Up there, he's totally unseen. Scared silly, all he has to do is lie still and no one will find him. So *what does he do*? He tries to crawl out across some ceiling beams! I wanted to run screaming from the theater. I also wanted them to shoot him because he was so dumb.

In *Pirates of the Caribbean 3*, the dumbest thing a character does is during one of the many climaxes, when Lord Beckett's ship is attacked from both sides. He is an excellent bad guy, not a dim bulb, but when the two good guy ships start blasting away, he freezes and doesn't give the order to open fire! Why would he do that?! His ship is turned into flying toothpicks while he mumbles something about this being "good for business." He stares into space like he's stoned — and does NOTHING. He's always been Mr. Evil Quick-Decision Maker. Suddenly, he's Caspar Milquetoast on Nembutal. That character would never, ever do something like that. Never.

It should have been infuriating to, at least, *somebody*.

Make a pilgrimage to this site: *www.moviecliches.com*. Learn the clichés and avoid them. For example: Any apartment in Paris will have a view of the Eiffel Tower, and, if a main character dies in a war, his sweetheart back home will have nightmare at that exact same moment.

Another super website: If I Ever Become An Evil Overlord (*www. eviloverlord.com*). My particular fave: "My ventilation ducts will be too small to crawl through." Duhh.

The world champ granddaddy of characters doing stupid things is in *Alien*. A hideous monster (world champ granddaddy bad guy, btw!) is gobbling up the crew of a spaceship in grim, icky ways. The crew makes a pact to "stick together" and then what happens? Yaphet Kotto goes off in a giant dark room looking for a cat. By himself! And doesn't turn on the light. And gee, what happens? He gets eaten. Which he richly deserves.

The cat, of course, is fine.

☐ 18. Your minor characters don't have *character!*

Make all characters, even in small roles, have specific, fascinating, memorable *character.* It will raise the overall level of your script an amazing amount.

Consider Ted Danson, assistant D.A. in *Body Heat.* Lawrence Kasdan gave him a great little bit: he pretends he's Fred Astaire, always doing little dance steps here and there, throwing out his arms and gliding across the room. It's weird, but cool. It makes his character more interesting than 99% of the assistant district attorneys we see in the movies.

Watch the most excellent *Down Periscope.* Get an understanding of how quickly, and how well David Ward establishes the secondary characters, giving Lt. Dodge, the captain, all these wonderful goofballs to react to. What fun for the writer! Here are a few:

> Executive Officer "Marty" Pascoe — By-the-book military, officious, with anger-management issues. Shortest man on the crew, he uses intimidation to compensate. When Lt. Dodge gives him an order, Marty repeats it to the crew by yelling at the top of his lungs. He asks for a transfer to another ship because the crew is "a bunch of idiots."

> Seaman 2nd Class E.T. "Sonar" Lovacelli — Loyal, and uncouth with an amazing sense of hearing. He has a collection of whale noises on tape. When confronted by an enemy ship in the war game, he makes the sounds of whales having sex to divert the attention of the enemy.

> Engineman 1st Class Stepanak — Belligerent, rude, lazy, tattooed tough-guy. He hates the Navy, but stays because his father is the Admiral. When asked by Lt. Dodge why he didn't give away their position when they were being hunted by the enemy, he says "that would be unethical. I just want to fuck myself so I can get out of here. Not fuck everybody else."

> Nitro, the electrician — Incredibly dumb, somewhat erratic, but efficient at his duties. He seems to have lost his intelligence because of all the shocks over the years. For Lt. Dodge to

communicate with his superiors, Nitro makes the connection by shocking himself.

Lt. Emily Lake, diving officer — Top of her class, diligent, and determined. Overconfident despite lack of real-life experience. She's so attractive that the crew drools over her. She flaunts her success in simulations by telling Lt. Dodge that she scored better than he did. Yet when asked to do real-life tasks on the ship, she's overwhelmed with anxiety and fear of failure.

Chief Engineer Howard Elder — Sailor with tons of experience. Seems slightly wacky because of it. He wears a dirty Hawaiian shirt and is poorly shaved. It is as if he was traumatized during Pearl Harbor and never changed clothes since.

All supporting characters are distinctive and easy to separate one from the other.

When you finish your first draft, pull out just the secondary character's dialogue. Work on it. Make them real, living, breathing people, don't let them just have a "function." Make them compelling. Give them attitude and interesting business.

If a Waitress' one line is "Here's your coffee," at least have her bring it over and grumble "Here's your damn coffee, freak." If you have a Water Meter Reader, give him a zany personality and awesome dialogue. Remember, even if the role is tiny, the producers have to find someone who wants to play it. This is especially true if you are in Low-Budget Land and can't pay the actor. Give him world-class dialogue, he'll pay you!

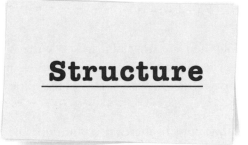

Structure

☐ 19. You worried about structure when you came up with your story!

If you did, I'm sorry. You missed some of the most joyous moments in writing. Character and story come first. Before anything. Certainly before all that Act One, Two, and Three crapola.

When you're teasing out your story, make lots of notes. Think out loud. Talk to a tape recorder. Make more notes. Fill up oceans of 3x5 cards. Write on yellow legal pads. Write on white legal pads. Scribble on napkins or beer coasters. Write down cool stuff for characters to do that may never find its way into the movie. Make notes and more notes and more notes, but do not trouble yourself with structure.

Screw structure. Have fun.

Structure is for later. For now, just let your incredibly creative mind run free. Make notes about character and plot and story and funny moments and locations you'd like to visit. Tape record dialogue for your characters. Use different voices for each one. You'll be astounded what you come up with! Think about old boyfriends and how this stunt pilot character reminds you of the sole charming one. Free associate. Remember your grandmother and how she used to serve you Fritos and 7-Up when your mother wouldn't. Think about the time you saw your father cry at his best friend's grave. Make stuff up. Make more stuff up. Steal from real life and make it your own. Steal from other people's lives. Listen to music up loud and use what it suggests. Write it down. Make notes. Go for a long walk with a tape recorder and say whatever comes into you head. Make more notes. Enjoy this part of the process!

It's easier to think up cool material if you don't have to worry if it fits.

One of my most creative moments, ever, came in the middle of an afternoon when I lay on my bed with a pocket tape recorder on my chest. I was working on a story, and had music playing as I slowly drifted toward sleep. There's an amazing space just before actual sleep where I could still think and talk, and my mind connected with the music, cut loose, and got *incredibly* free. With ideas tripping on themselves to get out, I dictated idea after idea triggered by the music. I'd force myself awake, holding onto that zone unfettered by normal thought, talking into the tape recorder as I drifted in semi-consciousness — and finally I fell asleep.

After I woke up from my nap, I transcribed the notes. Some were garbage, but some were amazingly inventive. It was an extraordinary way to come up with story ideas.

Whatever works, works!

If you get all constipated agonizing about proper structure, you won't be creative. Creativity sells. Worrying about rules and page numbers will only cloud your mind.

For now, have fun.

Structure is important, but it's not fun. That said, shall we ease into structure?

☐ 20. You don't have enough tension!

If there is no constantly building tension, you've lost the reader.

Readers love to worry. You jam them in a corner, make 'em nervous, and then turn up the heat. This does not mean car chases and explosions. That's action, not tension. Tension is: a father deciding if he should lower a drawbridge and keep a passenger train from crashing into the river — or leave it up and not crush his son who's fallen into the machinery. That was the tension in the short film *Most* and the woman beside me in the theater was sobbing uncontrollably.

What you want as a writer is tension.

It doesn't have to be Cold War finger-on-the-button level tension, either. It can be small — as long as it's not small to the characters. In *Remains of the Day*, Anthony Hopkins (butler) is in his little room reading. Emma Thompson (maidservant), who has a wee crush on him, comes to his room with a question. The instant she opens the door, he covers his book's title. SLAMMO! Tension City. She desperately wants to know what he's reading, but he desperately doesn't want her to know. He tells her it's just a book. They're all very polite and no one speaks above a hush, but the tension is killing!

Tension will keep a reader turning pages. Can you find a way to maintain and then heighten tension all the way through your story?

Another form of tension is stakes. Not like the ones you overcook on the Weber, which can be quite tense if the whole neighborhood is standing there, waiting, but stakes like "what's at risk for my lead character?"

I wrote one of the Ernest movies. "Best of the series," said the *Boston Globe*! I learned a lot from John Cherry, who directed it. He told me, "If it's not about world domination, it's not about anything at all." What do you think that means? And why should something that applies to a goofy comedy created for little kids to watch with babysitters apply to your *magnum opus*?

In a James Bond movie, world domination means just that. In *Ordinary People*, they're fighting for control of a home. It's still world domination.

If your characters aren't playing for all the marbles, the reader is going to pack up and go home. If the stakes in your story are small, ratchet them up. Later, find a way for them to increase even more — because your story has to get more intense as it goes along.

At the beginning of *A Few Good Men*, Tom Cruise's attorney character is trying a big case. The stakes are high — if he loses, his clients go to jail for a long, long time. Then, partway through, the stakes go up. If he takes on Jack Nicholson, and loses, his Navy legal career is over. For a guy whose dad was U.S. Attorney General, those are all the marbles in the world.

Is that true for the main character in your story?

Do not make the mistake a lot of my students make, which is no tension at the beginning. Stakes do not start low and get high. Stakes are high from the start and get way higher and then higher still. Start with your guy *already* on a high wire, and then have the wind start blowing and when he's halfway across, his wife yells from the far end of the wire that she's leaving him. When he's three-fourths of the way across, his doctor throws him a paper airplane. It's a note saying he's got cancer.

Whatever you do, don't start with your guy still on the ground. The story must be tense from the beginning.

In *Casablanca*, Victor Lazlo, who is essential to the Allied war effort, must escape Casablanca or he will be sent to a concentration camp, or back to German occupied France, or, worse, be killed in Casablanca. Rick knows this. He's a patriot, but is in love with Lazlo's wife. Rick faces personal happiness by keeping the only woman he's ever loved — or personal damnation by helping lose the war — some stakes!

In *Night of the Iguana*, Richard Burton lost his church congregation and has ended up in Mexico at the end of his rope. He works for Blake's Tours and there's "nothing lower than Blake's Tours." Last month, he was on probation because he had a bad tour. If he loses this month's tour, he'll get sacked. When he's doing battle with the prim woman who wants him fired, we understand what's at risk. Everything.

If your hero is not in the crusher, all the time, with the pressure getting worse and worse, you're writing a story no one will care about.

To see how good Hollywood writers are, read *Clear and Present Danger*, then see the DVD. In the book, Jack Ryan doesn't even go to South America. He's never in danger! First thing the screenwriter did was put the hero in harm's way, which makes the reader worry.

Another way to think about tension is "jeopardy." Is your hero in constant, escalating peril? This applies to being attacked by aliens, of course, but also visiting grandmother. If your bitch-on-wheels granny wants you to eat your grilled cheese sandwich, but you won't because she burned it, and she asks you what your mother does when *she* burns the grilled cheese sandwich, and you say, "She doesn't burn my grilled cheese sandwich," you're in jeopardy, big time.

Make your reader feel the tension, every step of the way. Take a tip from Bob Falfa in *American Graffiti*: "You're gonna be hangin' on for mercy once I get this sucker rollin'."

☐ 21. You have no time pressure!

Always helps to have a ticking clock.

In *Millions*, the two boys have only a limited amount of time before the fortune in cash they found is worthless, as all currency is about to be converted to Euros. They are forced to solve their problem before the suitcase of money is useless.

In *16 Blocks*, Bruce Willis has to get Mos Def to the courthouse in the next two hours. Anything you can do to put time pressure on the characters, makes a huge difference. How many movies can you think about where they have to get the diphtheria serum to Nome in the next *48 hours*? How about a movie *titled 48 HRS*?

Die Hard takes place in one night!

It's all about making the events happen in as compressed a space as you can. If you've given the character six months to accomplish his task, see what happens if you give him a month. How does that change your story? What about a week?

The tighter you can squeeze down your time period, the more satisfying it is to write because you make it more difficult for your character.

If not an actual ticking clock, is the time over which your story happens screwed down as tightly as possible? The film version of *To Kill a Mockingbird*, written by Horton Foote, took a year and a half. The book took place over three years. The result is a more powerful experience for the audience.

Is there *anything* you can do to make your story happen in less time?

☐ 22. You don't give the reader enough emotion!

Give the reader an emotional experience or you're wasting your time. It doesn't matter what that emotion is, but make damn sure he or she *feels* something. The stronger, the better.

Are you spending enough page length on the moments that are supposed to be the most emotionally affecting for the reader and audience? Don't gloss over something. Don't miss an emotional moment. Make sure you are milking them enough and, at each step of the way, think how each character reacts and ask if that is the correct and appropriate response.

Think about this, too: If your hero has an emotional moment, has he or she *earned* it?

Emotion can be anything. Laughter. Fear. Compassion. Heartache. Lust. Give your story emotion like in these scenes:

In *Rear Window*, Grace Kelly comes to Jimmy Stewart's house with her Mark Cross overnight case. She opens it and we see her nightie. We shiver with anticipation, realizing she had packed that case knowing she was going to sleep with him.

In *Hoosiers*, the coach tells the team to measure the size of the gym they have to play in for the championship. It's the *same size* as their old gym back home.

The old man remembers the "girl in the white dress" in *Citizen Kane*. Once you've seen it, you'll never forget it. It's the most emotional moment in the film. I think about that old guy often.

I sent out a call via email for my friends' favorite emotional scenes. I got back an amazing list.

> My favorite scene is in *The Night Porter*, when Charlotte Rampling locks herself in the bathroom and shatters a glass, forcing Dirk Bogarde to walk barefoot across the glass to get to her, thereby reversing the role he once played of torturer/sadist and turning ideas of romantic or correct love on its ear. The masochist becomes the sadist, and the sadist likes it.

> Near the end of *Heaven Can Wait* when Julie Christie is lost in the locker room tunnel and asks Warren Beatty for help. (Warren, her fiancé, has died and come back in someone else's body. Knowing he was going to die, he told her that she might meet someone and see something in his eyes, and he might even be the quarterback.) In the tunnel, they talk, he invites her for coffee, because he feels something, but she declines. Then she looks at him and says something like "You're the quarterback." It is so simple, but it says it all. She knows kind of, but she doesn't know how, that he is the guy. They go off together.

> *On the Waterfront*. The scene in the backseat where Marlon Brando confronts Rod Steiger about the thrown fight, when he realizes his brother ruined his life. "I could have been a contender. I could have been somebody." It is so powerful and poignant, and it breaks my heart.

I still get goosebumps every time I see Elliott and E.T. take off and fly for the first time, silhouetted against the moon. It is unexpected and magical.

In *The 400 Blows*, when Jean Pierre Léaud says he missed school because his mother died, but he was just playing with a friend, and then the parents appear.

In *The Miracle Worker*, when the little girl succeeds in associating the word "water" and the water. It is the beginning of the real life for this girl. The actress is great. One really believes she is actually handicapped, her face during this scene is so expressive.

There is a funeral scene in *Waking Ned Divine* that is very clever and emotional. Ned Divine, the lottery winner, is dead, and the town has conspired to put Michael in his place in order to split the money. Jackie is giving Ned's eulogy when the Lottery representative happens into the chapel, looking for Ned. The rep, who suffers hay fever in the country, sneezes — everyone now knows he is in the room. This is a tense scene. The plot converges marvelously, and, for the townsfolk, all is either won or lost in this moment; they will either be rich or jailed. Jackie, at the lectern, all eyes on him, thinks fast, and instead eulogizes his longtime friend Michael, who is sitting in the front row (whom the Lotto rep thinks is Ned). Some very sweet and poetic things are said about friendship and life, and the scene is a wonderful example of how a comedy can suddenly switch gears and give a light story a beating heart.

The scene that makes me cry, *every* time I tell it to my students, is in *Throw Momma From the Train*, written by Stu Silver. Billy Crystal's a writing teacher and his most annoying student is Danny DeVito. Danny invites him over for dinner. Not only does Billy not want to go, *we* don't want him to go, 'cause Danny's so damn aggravating. Danny's beloved father is dead and his mother is *horrible*. The actress, Anne Ramsey, had had cancer and part of her tongue had been removed, so, on top of being fantastically ugly, she had a sluggishly painful voice. "Owen, you don't have any friends!"

The dinner is awful. The mom is awful and all Billy Crystal wants to do is leave. He despises Danny DeVito and so do we. Just after mom has retired to her lair, and Billy thinks he's out the door, Danny asks if he wants to see his coin collection.

Billy has no choice but to say yes. He and Danny get on the floor. Danny pulls up the carpet. He removes a floorboard. Pulls out a rusty tobacco tin.

You have to understand how much the viewer loathes Danny at this point. Up to now, he hasn't done anything that's not irritating, and we never want to see him again.

Danny dumps about ten coins on the floor. A couple of ratty quarters, dimes, and a nickel or two. Billy is mortified. "That's it?" he's thinking. We're thinking it too. And then, in a mind-blowingly amazing turnabout, the writer makes you LOVE Danny DeVito.

Danny picks up a coin, shows it to Billy — I'm tearing up as I type this — and he says, "This one here, I got in change, when my dad took me to see Peter, Paul, and Mary. And this one, I got in change when I bought a hot dog at the circus. My daddy let me keep the change. He always let me keep the change." It's wonderful.

For the *rest* of the movie, Danny DeVito can do no wrong! We adore him. He's still annoying, but we love him. I'm sitting here, working on this book, and I have tears in my eyes because of a scene in a movie I saw twenty years ago.

That's emotion. Do that.

☐ 23. You bungled your story structure!

Bad structure = hell for eternity.

Plot construction is fairly simple. Well, not that simple, because if everyone could do it, every writer would live in a big house that's paid for.

Your story needs to be "about" something. This is your theme. Tape it to your monitor and keep looking at it. Whatever your theme is, the hero needs to deal with it at the end. His character growth has to be tied into that theme. That's the foundation of story structure.

Here's my favorite description of story, from *Writing to Sell* by Scott Meredith:

> "A sympathetic [*or fascinating!*] lead character finds himself in trouble of some kind and makes active efforts to get himself out of it. Each effort, however, merely gets him deeper into his trouble, and each new obstacle in his path is larger than the last. Finally, when things look blackest and it seems certain the lead character is finished, he manages to get out of his trouble through his own efforts, intelligence, or ingenuity."

This is *so* useful. Let's break it down.

> *"A sympathetic lead character…"*

I talk about this elsewhere to a degree, but it's important for the reader to be interested in the main character. My suggestion of "fascinating" works too, because it's not crucial that we find him sympathetic. We do have to understand his problem, and we somehow have to empathize with him. Your reader must make an emotional connection with your main character. She doesn't have to like him. She doesn't have to think he's cute and may not want to take him home for supper, but she has to want him to *win*.

This is what Blake Snyder calls the "Save the Cat" moment. Make them do something nice, or interesting, or funny, so we can hitch our emotional wagon to them.

Because the reader is desperate to attach to somebody from the moment she opens your screenplay, as a general rule of thumb you want us to meet the main character first. We can meet the villain first if you want, but you better find us somebody important to latch onto in the first five pages.

I just took a book-on-tape back to the library. I listened to side A of the first tape and gave up. Characters were wandering around some men's club in London having all sorts of silly conflict-free dialogue, and the story never quite got started. My little antennae were out waving around trying to find *somebody* I could lock onto, and I failed. Just as I was shoving the box into the library slot, I read the synopsis. To my surprise, with black-hearted delight, I noticed the book was about a woman named Elizabeth, a character I had not even met yet!

> "...*finds himself in trouble of some kind...*"

The trouble needs to be like the main character, interesting. *And not just interesting to you!* It must be a large and difficult problem, so intense that, if she doesn't solve it, the rest of her life will be wreckage.

The trouble must be poised to destroy her entire world. Period. If it's not a BIG problem, to her, then why are we reading about it? It doesn't have to be a problem that can be seen from space, mind you, but it has to threaten to rip the hero to bits. You can make a short film about a kid in wintertime who licks a metal flagpole. That's a BIG problem to him, and therefore, to your reader.

> "...*and makes active efforts to get himself out of it.*"

What's the key word here? Active! The Dalai Lama would not make a very good movie hero because he sits on a golden throne and waves his hand, and other people go out to solve his problems for him. When you think of things for your character to *do* to get out from under the rock you've dropped on him, he must never stop squirming and trying to fix it himself. The minute you have another character step in and try to solve his problem for him, the reader will stop turning the pages.

> "*Each effort...*"

This is important because it gives you the idea of repetition. Your girl tries Plan A, which fails. Then she revs up Plan B, which is bigger than Plan A. It fails, worse. Then Plan C, etc. This has been the structure of motion picture storytelling since the dawn of celluloid. Hal Roach knew about it when he first started making movies, as it is the structure for most one-reel comedies.

Never say die! That's your hero's mantra.

> "*Each effort, however, merely gets him deeper into his trouble...*"

Do you ever watch *Entourage*? Look at that band of interesting idiots! When they come up with a plan, does it work? Not only no, but hell no! It *can't* work, or the story stops right there. When something goes wrong, and they try to solve *that* problem, they just sink deeper into quicksand.

This part of your tale is where things get worse, a whole lot worse, and a whole lot faster. Your hero's falling down a mountain, tumbling along, gathering snow, sticks, mud, and squished alpine skiers, and the slope gets steeper and steeper, and soon he is in free fall, accelerating at 32 feet per second per second.

> "*...and each new obstacle in his path is larger than the last.*"

The obstacles have to get bigger, otherwise, as the character struggles along, getting smarter and stronger, he will be able to defeat the villain. Also, and a more pertinent reason, if the obstacles don't get bigger, the reader will get bored.

Who does the hero face at the end of *To Kill a Mockingbird*? Since the obstacles get bigger, she faces, not the rabid dog, or Mr. Ewell (who tried to kill her and failed), but *Boo Radley*. Her entire life, Scout has been afraid of Boo.

```
              DILL
    I wonder what he does in there? I wonder
    what he looks like?

              JEM
    Well, judgin' from his tracks, he's about
    six and a half feet tall. He eats raw
    squirrels and all the cats he can catch.
    There's a long, jagged scar that runs all
    the way across his face. His teeth are
    yella and rotten. His eyes are popped.
    And he drools most of the time.
```

We are terrified of him too.

At the end of the film, in an incredibly emotional reveal, Jem is in bed with the broken arm he got from Mr. Ewell. His father, Atticus, is there with Scout, his sister.

Scout doesn't know who stopped Mr. Ewell. Her father tells her he's right there, behind the door. The door is swung open and reveals Boo Radley. The object of her fear. The biggest obstacle of them all.

> *"Finally, when things look blackest and it seems certain the lead character is finished…"*

This part is easy when you're writing a sword and sorcery movie because the main character goes underneath the Pit of Eternal Darkness, into the Cave of Doom, and loses his Sword of Glory and Light — just as Mordred the Wicked steps up with the Nunchucks of All Power….

This step is harder if you're doing a courtroom drama, but not that hard. It's a really difficult step when you're writing a romantic comedy. There's got to be a moment, the Low Point, where we think the hero has lost it all. Everything he's wanted the entire movie is destroyed. What's worse (but better for the reader!) is that it gets destroyed because of a mistake he made. For instance, she catches him in bed with his old girlfriend, and dumps him flat. Now, you, as the writer (ha ha ha!), have to figure out a sympathetic reason he was bopping his old girlfriend, but that's not my problem.

In any event, however you get him there, he's got to be near death and in pieces on the ground.

> *"He manages to get out of his trouble through his own effort, intelligence, or ingenuity."*

I can tell you this: If he doesn't manage to get out of trouble, you've written a French movie, and you may as well give up trying to sell it to Hollywood. If he doesn't get out of trouble by saving himself, you should probably give up trying to sell your script to dentists, because you won't get a distributor.

Okay, now, a bit more on structure.

Read Blake Snyder's *Save the Cat*, Christopher Vogler's *The Writer's Journey*, and John Truby's *The Anatomy of Story*. Take what you need from those books and press on.

When you're reading a screenwriting book, it helps to have a story in mind already. As you read, little light bulbs will go off! You'll make all kinds of notes about your story. I have one student who will not write a screenplay without *Save the Cat* open beside her. I have other students who swear by the Vogler book. Hopefully you will feel the same way about mine!

Because everyone who reads your script has bought into Three Act Story Structure like a drowning man clutching whatever gets heaved at him, it's crucial to understand it. You must comprehend their eeevil plan before you can use it against them.

You have to know where you're starting with this character. You have to know where she's going to be at the end. That's her arc. Her transformation. Her change. Sometimes you can think about the end first: "Who is she going to be when all this is over — strong, kind, alive?" and work backwards — "Who will she be at the start: weak, irritating, in danger?"

You open, Once Upon a Time, with your hero stuck in his difficult spot, which is not going well. He's in the middle of a serious problem, which you establish right away. If he hasn't got a problem, why are you telling his story? Give him a weighty, difficult, interesting problem.

How is he off-kilter with society? How is she adrift in the world? How is he being mean to other people? What is the hole in her soul? Once you establish this problem, well and swiftly, it will be your goal, for the rest of the screenplay to find the answer to this one single burning question. For you to spend 110 pages dealing with one problem, it had better be a helluva problem. It's this problem he *wants* to solve.

"Want" established, it's time to look at "Need" — what the character desperately needs to become at the *end* of the story, which, at the beginning, he had better not be aware of. Mick and Keith put it best — "You can't always get what you want" but if you try (real hard!), "you get what you need."

Michael Corleone wants to marry Kay and stay out of the family business, but he *needs* to become the new Godfather.

Development people gotta have an "Inciting Incident." It will happen someplace between pages 5 and 15, and it's what gets the story going. Once we meet the hero and have a decent handle on the world he's struggling in, something happens that jars that world. Dostoyevsky supposedly said there are only two stories in all of literature, "A man goes on a journey and a stranger comes to town." The Inciting Incident is when the man starts his journey or the stranger comes to town.

> The hero discovers his boss is stealing!
> The private detective has a mysterious client knock at her door!
> A little girl gets a phone call telling her she has a slot in the beauty contest!
> Atticus Finch is hired to defend Tom Robinson.

And we're off to the races.

We need to know the hero's problem and how she is going to try to solve it and how the opponent is going to try to clobber her. Ask yourself these two questions: How quickly do you tell us what the good guy wants? How quickly do we know what the bad guy wants?

You gotta have something big happen at the end of Act One. You gotta have something enormous happen at the end of Act Two. Plus, these events have to be really, really obvious. Clear, not just to you, but to a blind man. I can't tell you how many times I've talked to writers about their act breaks and got told about some dinky scene where a little tiny thing happened — that I hadn't even noticed. Just because you think it's an act break doesn't mean the reader is going to catch on. The character's world must be turned upside down at the end of Act One and twisted inside out at the end of Act Two! Make it obvious! Allow the reader to go, "Aha! Here's the first act break! This writer sure knows his structure! Maybe I can get my boss to write him a check!"

Another way to chart the big steps in your story is by looking at decisions the character makes. The First Act is her moving under increasing pressure to a moment where she has to make a big decision. This decision will be the wrong decision. If it were the correct decision, heck, the movie'd be over! The second act is a long string of your hero's decisions: bigger and bigger ones in the midst of struggle, trouble, struggle, trouble, struggle, trouble. End of Act Two is a huge decision she makes that pushes her into the finale.

In the opening scene of *The Verdict*, attorney Paul Newman decides to give business cards out at funeral homes. An ambulance chaser! A drunk! A loser! His first BIG decision, which is dishonest, comes when he decides to turn down the diocese's settlement offer without consulting his client. He could be disbarred! And the rest of the movie proceeds from that horrible choice.

In *Body Heat*, Ned Racine's first big decision is to heave a chair through Matty Walker's window and, um, engage in sexual congress with her on her front hall floor. Bad call, Ned! It gets him in a world of trouble.

So, you've got the first part of your screenplay under a good head of steam. Wasn't that easy? Things are happening. We're finding out new information. Time for the end of Act One.

In *Chinatown*, the end of Act One comes when Jake Gittes finds out that the adultery case he has been pursuing is a set-up, and the woman who hired him was only pretending to be Mrs. Mulwray. He learns this the hard way on page 23 when the real Mrs. Mulwray shows up with her attorney and coolly announces that he is going to get tough with Gittes.

The end of Act One in *Die Hard* is when McClane throws a body out the window and it lands on a cop car. Until then, *Die Hard* has been a battle inside the building between McClane and Gruber. As we enter the uncharted waters of Act Two, McClane opens the world up, enlarges the problem, brings in more players, and makes things worse for himself.

In *Thelma and Louise*, the end of Act One is when Louise shoots the rapist and their little vacation trip suddenly becomes two women on the lam.

Twenty-five minutes into *Casablanca*, Ilsa walks into Rick's bar. Pow!

In my screenplay *105 Degrees and Rising*, the end of Act One is when the hero discovers that the Americans might not take out their key Vietnamese workers, who they have promised for twenty years not to leave behind. The hero's world is bowled over, and he enters into the murky void known as Act Two.

The best description of Act Two is "things get worse." In a well-structured second act, YOUR second act, things get much, much worse, and faster and faster. By the end of Act Two, the whole thing needs to be going so wrong for the hero, so fast, that he's on his way to hell in a handbasket. Check out the middle of *Before the Devil Knows You're Dead*. Staggering example of "Things Get Worse."

Every so often, something interesting has to happen. It must be surprising to the character and the reader. You can call them plot points, reversals, plot twists, revelations, I don't care what, but *you better have a new one every fifteen pages or less*, at least.

It's like *The Simpsons*. If you don't like a joke, wait five seconds because here comes another one. Not enough reveals, your script is burnt toast. Try to have a *lot* of them. How about more than twelve!

Act Two is where the hero gets deeply involved. No way to get out. Obsessed.

```
                    GITTES
               (now inches from her)
         -- I goddamn near lost my nose! And I
         like it. I like breathing through it. And
         I still think you're hiding something.
```

Can't you hear Jack Nicholson saying that? In *Chinatown*, by Robert Towne, once the opponent's attacks get personal, there's no way Gittes is going to turn this one loose. Even when Mrs. Mulwray tries to get him to drop the case.

Act One, as I'm sure you know, needs to end somewhere between pages 25 and 35. Act Two needs to end somewhere around 80 or 90. Again, it doesn't matter where these things happen, exactly, as long as there's enough going on so a Page 80 Freak can latch onto one of your revelations and say, "What a clever lad he is! Act Two ends right at the right spot! I'll keep reading!"

The end of Act Two in *105 Degrees and Rising* is when the North Vietnamese shell the Saigon airport and everyone's evacuation plans go up in smoke. For the past 80 pages, everyone has been counting on the airport and now it's gone. Suddenly, the characters are thrown into a mad scramble to get the hell out of Dodge.

In *Chinatown*, the end of Act Two is when Gittes learns that Mrs. Mulwray's sister is *also* her daughter — a moment that comes out only via the most explosive conflict. Everything Gittes has believed about this case is suddenly wrong.

In *Thelma and Louise*, the end of Act Two is when they decide they're not going to go home: they're going to stay on the road, no matter what.

Act Two break in *Casablanca*: Rick and Ilsa kiss. Love is back, and *nothing will ever be the same again*. She tells him, "I ran away from you once, I can't do it again."

Now you've got your Inciting Incident and the end of Act One and the end of Act Two. Are you home free? Nope.

If two big fabulous act breaks are *all* you come up with, you're dead in the water, torpedo bait. You'll have a big weak spot in the middle of your story where the reader is looking around wondering why is nothing interesting happening! Plan a lot of surprises along the way. The reader will be happier and you'll be happier because it will be much more interesting to *write*.

Have a big event in the middle too. The character wins big. The character loses big. We think everything is great or we think everything is garbage. Something happens where the story turns in a new direction. Watch some movies; check out the Midpoint. It's there!

Another way to look at structure is: "Who's got the power?" Who's taking action and who's taking action against them?

Power should shift from the opponent to the hero to the opponent to the hero throughout the story. One makes a move and gets the upper hand for a while before being overtaken by a *stronger* countermove from the other party. A beautiful example is *The Luzhin Defense*. Luzhin is a head-in-the-clouds chess genius. His despised and feared former teacher, Valentinov, hates him and wants him to lose the championship. Luzhin's new girlfriend, Natalia does "battle" with Valentinov.

At a match, Valentinov notices Luzhin smiling at Natalia. Later, as Natalia is about to tell Luzhin that she'll marry him, Valentinov interrupts — terrifying Luzhin. Later, Valentinov says that Luzhin should be proud to have gotten this far: Natalia says he's going to win. Later, Valentinov plants an article in the paper which destroys Luzhin's confidence — and he has a draw. So, Natalia makes love to him for the first time. His game improves and he starts winning with verve. On the defensive, Valentinov arranges for Luzhin to be whisked away after a match and left in a field. This time, he suffers a complete nervous collapse.

With each battle, the power shifts from Natalia to Valentinov and then back. Each move/countermove is stronger than the one that came before.

Don't forget these steps:

Low Point. The hero thinks all is lost. His secret weapon has failed and he's about to be destroyed by the opponent. He must reach into his soul and find the strength to continue. In a courtroom drama, this is where the bad guys get to his most important witness.

Battle and climax. Put hero and bad guy in a ring with barbed wire around the top. They face off and try to kill each other. Figuratively or literally. You've been preparing the reader for this, now deliver!

Final resolution. The hero resolves his need and becomes a better person. The story is over and he has (probably) won.

Whole New World. The hero and his world have been permanently transformed. Now that everyone has survived the fiery furnace that is your story, nothing will ever be the same.

Whew.

What a lot of bother!

Now, after you've thought about it for awhile, you actually have to *write* the damn thing.

How you take these structure beats and transform them into screenplay is up to you.

You can work out your outline in enormous detail, with 3x5 cards color-coded, all over your dining room table, sitting in your lap, or on a cork board. You can buy computer software that will manage your 3x5 cards for you at *www.writersblocks .com*. Heck, you can work out your story on a napkin.

You can outline tightly, you can outline loosely. You can outline only the main story beats, finding out the rest as you discover what you characters want to do. You can write character biographies and start writing and let your characters dictate the story.

You can proceed with no bios and no outline at all, which is like a beginning tight-rope walker working without a net, but, hey, it's your time you're 'a wastin'.

One of the best screenplays I ever wrote, I wrote without an outline. One of the worst screenplays I ever wrote, I wrote without an outline. It's a hell of a lot more fun to write with no outline, but it's a lot more dangerous.

At the minimum, you will need to know your theme, how your character changes, what some of the main story surprises are, and you certainly need to know the end. It's crucial to know where you're going. It's death, or a giant waste of time, which is the same thing, blindly to start out in the dark with your cane tapping your way across the Bonneville Salt Flats.

A book that attacks your (and my) particular brand of insanity is *From Where You Dream* by Robert Olen Butler. It's about how to write a novel, but he's gifted at explaining how to outline a story. Another excellent book about fiction writing is called, funnily enough, *Writing Fiction: A Guide to Narrative Craft*, by Janet Burroway. It's out of print. Look for it at *www.abebooks.com*.

So, that's a smidgen about structure. Here's more!

☐ 24. You have not done, and then redone, and REDONE, a one-line outline!

A one-line outline is such an important writing tool! Without it, it's impossible to see your story. If you have a 115-page script, you can't see the storytelling machinery. A Zen description of what happens in every scene is the only way to approach story.

You can use the one-line outline to create your story. A "just the facts, ma'am" way to create narrative building blocks.

You can also do a one-line outline when you have a complete draft of your script and you're ready to rewrite. Write down what each scene is supposed to accomplish. Or better, what each scene *does* accomplish. Try to get your head into the mind of the reader, so you're reading the script from their point of view. What *you* think is happening in a scene may not be what the reader is getting.

Here's part of a one-line outline. For each scene, only crucial information is included. The entire screenplay can be seen on five pages, which you can then spread out on a table and ponder, and ponder, and ponder....

105 DEGREES AND RISING

second draft, A

Tuesday, April 22

Xuan Loc. Small child grabbed by parent. ELLEN and TU give news report. Woman shoves baby in Huey. Vietnamese swarm chopper. Ellen in agony as baby is left behind.

Saigon. Embassy with black guard in dress uniform. MARTIN looks at tamarind tree. MCKILLOP, HUMMEL, OSCAR, et al., watch Ellen's report. McKillop worries Da Nang could happen again. Hummel thinks they'll negotiate.

NBC control. Ellen & cronies watch the report. She's displeased with her performance.

Sydney. PETERSON watches report. South Vietnamese bomb presidential palace. He sees KHANH on TV. Thieu makes speech.

Saigon. Roof of building. Deserters, LEVERETT & LOOSE WRAP watch Thieu's speech. Estab. Girlfriend & her brother. Thieu wants the B52s to come back. Loose Wrap doesn't want to go back to jail. Smugglers.

La Coupole. VAN CAO and TRANG watch TV. Van Cao is headed to U.S.

Apartment. LAN watches speech. UNCLE says not to trust American to take her out. She feeds GRANDMOTHER.

Caravelle Hotel. CARTER smokes opium while speech finishes. Estab. tape recorders.

Embassy. Thieu resigns. McKillop thinks it's hitting the fan.

Night. Tan Son Nhut. Peterson lands. Saigon is a mess.

Night. McKillop's balcony. He watches the war.

Wednesday, April 23

Morning. **PAGE 10** Martin's office. McKillop asks Martin about the Evac plans. Martin says solution will be diplomatic.

Consulate. McKillop worries Vietnamese will die if we leave, asks Hummel about the tree. Ambassador doesn't want to cut it down. McKillop gives Oscar a list of questions, including chain saws. He thinks settlement is likely.

La Coupole. Van Cao serves Policeman. Peterson talks to Van Cao. Carter sits down, gives Peterson tape recorder.

NBC office. Ellen complains about her assignments to Tu. Wonders if they are going to negotiate or not. Scarce: gold, sleeping pills.

VNAF ready room. Peterson, a bit shy, hires a pilot.

Above Xuan Loc. Pilot will get Peterson in eight hours. Leaves him in Xuan Loc.

La Coupole. Van Cao leafs through scrapbook. Trang watches, leaves him alone.

409 Club. Tough Whore hates Americans. Lan argues.

A one-line outline is an amazing useful tool. Now you've seen one. Do your own.

You can mark it up by acts, scenes, action scenes, or track emotional levels.

You can tell if these three scenes need to move up earlier. It's a great way to decide to combine scenes — take this scene from there, move it down, and combine it with that one. You can tell by looking at five scenes in a row how they flow and if they're out of order. I find this MUCH easier to do with a one-line outline instead of a whole script.

I update the one-line outline for every single draft, and most of my structural rewriting is done on the one-line outline. Once I get it cut and pasted the way I want, I go into the screenplay and start shuffling scenes around.

When you do your one-line outline, mark revelations and reversals, so you know if there are any looooooong periods with no surprises.

Color coordinate each character — see how often they appear, or for how long they disappear. You don't want an important character to drop out for twenty pages.

The one-line outline is the Swiss Army knife of screenwriting. Use it in good health.

☐ 25. You have not done a "random thoughts" outline!

Of course you haven't. I haven't told you what it is.

Once I get an outline, I'm always hell for leather ready to start writing screenplay pages. Writing script is WAY more fun than outlining. I loathe outlining and once I start writing script, I never want to work on the outline again. I just want to write! Even if the outline isn't ready. Ooops. To combat this cunning, baffling, powerful weakness in my soul, I do a "random thoughts" version of my outline.

It's a ton of fun, actually. It's a last chance to be really creative with story before I get locked into screenplay pages, which I find are tougher to change than an outline.

I take my outline and copy it in a new file: Random Thoughts Version A. Put hard page breaks in so each scene starts on its own page.

#1. Big City. ROBERT gets daughter GRACE up for school. Is a loving,
if inattentive father. Preoccupied with business. Wife, MARLENE sleeps.
Robert sings "Twinkle, Twinkle Little Star" to Grace while making her
breakfast. Estab. NANNY, full-time help.

Now, turn the music up loud. Get your kids out in the yard with some water balloons and the dog. Whatever it takes to be alone for a while. It's time to just MAKE STUFF UP.

With the tiny guide to your scene in front of you, start generating whatever random ideas you can, from every direction, about any aspect of the scene. Wardrobe, dialogue, character, stuff that might tie in later, motivation, production design, plot — ANYTHING you want to throw in.

It's kitchen sink time.

#1. Big City. ROBERT gets daughter GRACE up for school. Is a loving, if inattentive father. Preoccupied with business. Wife, MARLENE sleeps. Robert sings "Twinkle, Twinkle Little Star" to Grace while making her breakfast. Estab. NANNY, full-time help.

Big city or not? Time of year? What is his work?

Real estate deal going south? Is he a caterer. He loves to cook.

Estab. her photos on the wall. Her dark room. NICE dark room.

Ink Spots song over titles. Creepy.

Maybe lose the Nanny.

He reads while she has her breakfast. Does she play a musical instrument?

Title sequence? Drifting through the house.

Watches TV news. Reads novel. Reads self-help book about marriage. Has a pile of self-help books, all unread. Still in bookstore bags.

Marlene calls, asks for coffee, which he has already ready. He hides the marriage book.

Robert ties his tie perfectly. Mr. Precise. Doesn't listen to Grace when she tries to tell him something. How else is he a lousy father?

Marlene sleeps in nightgown. Later, she'll be naked. After she leaves him.

Home movies at start?

He's a good dad, only distracted. Newspaper carries word of his big deal.

Does his brother call, warning him about article in paper?

Wakes Grace up. Loves doing that. Estab. that Grace really adores him. They have their routine.

Louis Armstrong's "What a Wonderful World." Her CD. Plays it at night before bed. Grace plays trumpet. Lessons today?

Is she sick at the beginning, give him something to do?

She reads her book. He ignores her. Is he a bad father here, so he can get good later, or will we hate him from the get-go if he's a cruddy dad?

Marlene comes in, looks at mess in kitchen. Disapproves. Sleepy with great hair. Hot.

Secretary calls with bad news.

Talk to Axson about real estate nightmares. Specific dialogue and woes. How can we make a real estate developer sympa?

Grace cuts her finger. Robert puts on band-aid. Good father!

This kind of idea generating can go on for pages and pages. When you've finally exhausted every drop of creativity in your body about THIS scene, start on the next scene. Same way.

And, as you go through the outline, you'll continually bounce back to Scene #1 with ideas triggered by something you think about for Scene #121. It will take eons to work your way through your entire story. That's okay, because you're coming up with superb material for your scenes.

When you're completely done with Version A of the Random Thoughts outline, save it as Version B, whip out your highlighter and mark the genius bits you want to keep. Cut the chaff, and lo and behold, a creative, detailed outline you will use to write your screenplay!

Congratulations. Now that you have an outline, it's time to fix it.

☐ 26. You have not used the Kerith Harding Rule of Drama!

I didn't know this one until one of my former students taught it to me. Now I see it everywhere.

> *"Just when everything seems hunky dory, everything is so not."*
> Kerith Harding, creative executive

In *Strictly Ballroom*, the hero finally gets to kiss the girl. It's delovely!

                                                              CUT TO:

In the next scene, he is told horrible news about his father's disastrous past. His world collapses.

In *Risky Business*, Joel's parents are out of town, he has his big party, the college admissions guy happily comes and goes. It's a triumphant moment. He and Lana, his hooker girlfriend, are having a wonderful time. In the morning, he comes back from spending the night with her. He picks up his father's now-repaired Porsche, and drives home at five careful miles an hour. Nothing could be better! Everything is hunky dory.

CUT TO:

Joel walks in his house, smiling — and, Oh My Holy God!, *everything* has been stolen! All the furniture, everything, is gone. Including his mother's uber-precious crystal doodad. Guido, the killer pimp, has struck back!

Right when everything seems totally perfect and blissful, everything is ruined. Once you know it's in the atmosphere, you can see the Kerith Harding Rule coming a mile away.

Lawrence brings his army safely through the blistering Nefud desert. Akaba lies ahead, a succulent grape for the taking — all is right with the world — for a glorious instant.

CUT TO:

A gunshot splits the night. A man killed a man from a different tribe, and the tenuous alliance will disintegrate unless Lawrence, who has no tribe, kills him. To his horror, it turns out to be Gasim, the man he had risked his life to save. Everything was hunky dory, and now, Lawrence not only kills a man, he *likes* doing it. Now everything is so incredibly *not* hunky dory.

Here's a perfect example of the Kerith Harding Rule of Drama from Garrison Keillor's *The Writer's Almanac*.

> Lincoln spent [a] little more than four years serving as President, and for most of those four years, there weren't many people who thought he was doing a good job. The Civil War went on for longer than most people thought it would, and it was far more brutal than anyone expected. Lincoln had a hard time getting his generals to aggressively pursue the enemy, and the Confederates came close to capturing Washington, D.C. In the second week of April 1865, he received word that Robert E. Lee had surrendered his army.
>
> On the afternoon of April 14, 1865, Lincoln took a ride in an open carriage with his wife, and he was the happiest she'd ever

seen him. He told her, "I consider *this* day, the war has come to a close." That same night, he and his wife went to the theater, and Lincoln was murdered by John Wilkes Booth.

Just when everything seems hunky dory….

☐ 27. Your B story does not affect your A story!

In other words, "Why have a subplot if you don't use it?"

Generally, and you have to remember I don't know *everything*, but generally, a B story should only exist if it affects the A story. Once the movie gets going, the A and B stories can wander along, in parallel sometimes, and then, right toward the end of the movie, the two railroad tracks must cross, the trains will smash into one another, and kablooey, nothing will ever be the same.

In *To Kill a Mockingbird*, the A story leads to Tom Robinson's trial and the subsequent hatred of Atticus Finch by Bob Ewell. The B story is Jem and Scout's developing "relationship" with Boo Radley. At the end, the A and B stories tie together when Mr. Ewell tries to kill the children and Boo stabs him and saves their lives.

In *Rocky*, at the end of Act II, Rocky realizes that he's never going to beat Apollo Creed. He's done all this training and all this dreaming and it's all for naught. He is going to lose the fight. It's a soul crushing revelation. But, lucky guy, he's got his girlfriend, Adrian, with him. Because of her, he figures out that if he just manages to go the distance with the Champ, he'll be okay. It's a transfiguring moment and Adrian exists to make it happen. She's the B story and she has a huge effect on the A story. Without Adrian, Rocky would lose the fight and be a loser. With her, he loses the fight but becomes a man.

In *Jerry Maguire*, the A story is Tom Cruise's relationship with his wife. The B story is his relationship with his "show me the money" client and *his* wife. Tom isn't sure if he loves Renée Zellweger, his wife. But, at the end of the B story, the client is on the field hurt and his wife is worried out of her skin. Tom sees their love and it forces him to realize how much he loves his own wife. He would never solve the problem in the A story without the B story there to help him along.

If you have a B story that does not strongly affect the A story, rewrite it or cut it.

☐ 28. You don't use Set Up and Pay Off to your advantage!

You introduce a pistol in Act I. It goes off in Act II. That's set up and pay off. But, like Joe Louis, you don't want to telegraph your punch — you want the reader to be surprised when you knock 'em out.

Set up and pay off is a standard storytelling device. Hitchcock said, "If you want the audience to feel the suspense, show them the bomb underneath the table." After hanging out with me quite a bit, while watching a movie, my seven-year-old would shout, "Here's a set up!" Once you know it's there, you see it everywhere.

In *Thelma and Louise*, the pay off is that Thelma is being raped in a parking lot and Louise pulls a pistol out of her purse and blows the dirtbag away. How did the writer "hide" the set up, so we're not spending all our time thinking about that pistol in her purse? The set up came dozens of pages earlier.

Thelma and Louise are hitting the road and Thelma is packing her stuff. She reaches into her bedside table and pulls out a loaded revolver. Instead of flapping the chamber open and spinning the cylinder like a cop — making the audience go, "Jeepers! That's a fucking *gun*! Bet somebody shoots somebody with that bad boy before I go buy popcorn!" — Geena Davis daintily dangles the pistol by two fingers and drops it in her purse. The moment gets a big laugh and the audience forgets about the pistol! Until a ways down the road, when someone needs a pistol.

Make sure the set up and pay off are far enough apart for it to really work. You can't set something up and pay it off on the next page. You need a delicious time lag between the two. Even in *Meet the Parents*, which has a quick pay off after they establish the mother's ashes on the mantel, a bit of time does pass before the hapless hero ends up knocking the urn off the mantel with a champagne cork, accidentally turning Mom's ashes into cat litter.

In *Back to the Future*, a woman gives Marty a "Save the Clock Tower" flyer. Marty's girlfriend writes her phone number on it and Marty doesn't throw it away. Later, the flyer information comes in very, very handy.

One of the cleverest set ups ever is a four-parter, spread over many pages. In *The Apartment*, they establish that 1) Jack Lemmon tried to kill himself years ago (shot himself in the knee); 2) he still has the .45 automatic; 3) he's depressed, and is packing up to leave his apartment; and 4) he has an unopened bottle of champagne. Those puzzle pieces are the set up.

The pay off comes when Shirley MacLaine decides she is in love with Jack and forsakes Fred MacMurray. She sprints to Jack's apartment. As she's running up his stairs, she hears a gunshot. We know he's killed himself! She screams to his door, pounding it frantically — and he opens the door, with an overflowing bottle of champagne. Perfection!

Don't give us a zeppelin-size set up, either. The audience will smell the pay off a mile away. e.g., don't give a cop this clichéd speech: "I've got two weeks left until I retire. Want to see pictures of my family?" A ten-year-old can tell you what's going to happen to *that* guy! How about the one from every WWII movie: "Here's a snapshot of my gal. Ain't she swell? We're getting hitched when I get back." Guess who's about to catch a bullet? It's the old Star Trek problem. Kirk says "Spock, Bones, Scotty and Ensign Cannonfodder, we're beaming down to the planet." You KNOW the new nobody character is going to get killed. Anything they spoofed in *Galaxy Quest*, don't you do in your screenplay!

Check to see if you have any set ups that seem incredibly important, that are too pointed, that are obvious — and then have *no
pay off* — please, please don't do this! In *Toto Le Hero*, the main
character is abused and vilified by the boys at school. For his birth-
day his father spends all their savings to buy him a knife. Late in
the film the mean boys are chasing him across ice floes intent on
pounding him. We know the precious knife is in his pocket but
the clod never pulls it out to defend himself! Why? It ruins that
part of the story, and makes us think the character is stupid..

What if you *have* to have a set up, but it's one that everyone will
notice how can you establish it unobtrusively? In *Ask the Dust*,
Robert Towne camouflages the upcoming punch rather neatly:

> 1) Hero likes Girl but Girl is lusted after by leering Bartender.
> 2) Barely establish in a pile of other conversation about Bartender
> — he has TB.
> 3) While hero waits in car for Girl on foggy night, in background,
> we see Girl kiss Bartender. (last time we see Bartender as he's done
> his job as a plot device)
> 4) Hero and Girl have excellent sex. Somewhere during the fasci-
> nating to-ing and fro-ing, Girl coughs.
> CUT TO:
> An hour or so later in the movie, she croaks from tuberculosis.

The cleverest thing Towne did was have the girl cough during
sex. We're busy witnessing their passion and don't even notice the
cough. Until she gets sick. Then we remember it.

In *The Opposite of Sex*, by Don Roos, it's late at night in Christina
Ricci's white-trash home. She's packing in a hurry as she's about to
run away. As she's putting stuff into her bag, we notice a pistol.

```
                    DEDE (V.O.)
        Oh this part, where I take the gun, is
        like, "duh," important. It comes back
        later but I'm putting it in here for
        foreshadowing... which we covered when we
        did Dickens. If you're smart, you won't
        forget that I've got it.
```

Set up and pay off are closely tied to hiding exposition. Nice
segue!

☐ 29. You haven't buried exposition like Jimmy Hoffa!

Exposition is like, well, it's like Dr. Basil Exposition in *Austin Powers*. He's there to give you crucial information, but you need to keep him mostly hidden in your XK-E glove compartment.

Another way to describe it is "explaino." Information you have to get across to the reader, but you don't really want her to notice she's getting it. Do your best to hide exposition: in an argument, with a joke, by trimming it to the bone. Un-subtle, blatant exposition is an obvious sign of a newbie writer and makes readers cringe.

First draft, exposition is blatant. On the nose and in your face. Why are they telling us stuff that the characters would already know?

TOM
Hey, Ronnie, it's me, Tom.

RONNIE
Long time no hear from, mate. I need you to steal two cars. Expensive ones. Like Range Rovers.

TOM
I don't want to work for Mr. Franks again. Don't like him.

RONNIE
It's none of your business who it's for. Just be at the Rolling Nickel Saloon at five.

TOM
That's on Fifteenth Street, idn't it?

RONNIE
Yeah, like always, Fifteenth Street. And mind you don't leave your wallet in the car like you did last time, eh?

TOM
I was drunk. I won't be drinking this time. Me sister Fawn's in town. She hates it when I'm drinking, you know.

```
                    RONNIE
          Mr. Franks is always happy when your
          sister Fawn's in town. She keeps you out
          of trouble.
```

Second draft, exposition is less obvious, but the information is there. Anything that's not nailed down now, will be revealed later on. Like who Fawn is and what she does for Tom…

```
                    TOM
          You called, fathead?

                    RONNIE
          The Nick, at five.

                    TOM
          Not if it's for Franks.

                    RONNIE
          It's two Range Rovers. And since when do
          you get to be picky, Mr. Wallet In The
          Stolen Car Boozehound?

                    TOM
          No worries. Fawn's in town.

                    RONNIE
          Upon hearing that delightful news, Mr.
          Franks will be delighted.
```

My favorite example of hiding exposition, ever, is in Chapter 4 (Initial Contact — CRS) of *The Game*, by John D. Brancato & Michael Ferris. Michael Douglas comes to a bustling office, applying to play an elaborate real-life role-playing game. The place is chaotic, with employees milling around and workmen putting finishing touches on wiring, etc.

A character named Feingold pays a delivery guy for Chinese food and welcomes Nicholas, our hero, to take his information. It's almost a struggle to get to Feingold's office, with the bag of Chinese food dripping all the way. There's conversation about Nicholas's brother, who already played the game and did really well. At one point, Feingold asks Nicholas, "Sure you're not hungry at all? Tung Hoy, best in Chinatown." Nicholas isn't hungry.

The scene surges on and Nicholas gets irritated with Feingold and all the tests he's supposed to take, but — buried deep in the multi-page scene is *the* crucial sliver of exposition: "Tung Hoy, best in Chinatown" — tucked in a bit of business with a bag of gloppy food, and a lot of discussion about the game Nicholas is registering for.

Oh, they hid it so incredibly well! You'll deftly hide your exposition too, when you rewrite your screenplay!

It's virtually invisible, unnoticed in a lot of conflict. Later, when all is lost and Nicholas has absolutely nothing, it is the solitary clue that enables him to fight back. The interesting thing is that, an hour later, when he remembers the name of the restaurant, you remember exactly where he heard it.

Rent the movie. Study the scene. It's a brilliant piece of work.

☐ 30. You don't withhold surprises until as late as possible!

Do you withhold information from your reader, or do you deliver it all at once? If you hold back secrets and surprises, it makes the read delicious.

William Froug, legendary head of the UCLA filmic writing program, put it like this. "If you're a little old man, sitting in the park, and you want to feed the pigeons a bag of bird seed, how do you do it? If you dump the whole bag out, the pigeons will cluster around you in a frenzy for 45 seconds, eat all the bird seed, and disappear. However, if you throw out a little seed at a time, the pigeons will stay there all day."

The longer it takes for you to give them what they want, the longer they're going to stay interested.

As a screenwriter, you're not holding back bird seed, but secrets and surprises. They are some of your most important storytelling weapons. Deploy them with care.

At the beginning of the novel on which *Notes From a Scandal* was based, we know the Cate Blanchett character had an affair with one of her students. The first scene of the book is press people crammed around her house, baying for blood. It's a great way to open the story, but gives away the biggest secret, right at the get-go. Patrick Marber decided to keep that little bit of bird seed in his pocket as long as possible — revealing it later in the story and giving this important secret the maximum possible impact on the audience.

William Goldman did this in *Butch Cassidy and the Sundance Kid*. When he sat down to write, because he'd done his homework, he knew a few interesting facts about his characters. Did Butch open the movie saying, "Hi there, Sundance. My name's Robert Leroy Parker. I'm from New Jersey and I've never shot a man in my life. How 'bout a brewski?" He did not. Goldman saved these surprises until late in the story, revealing them when they would have the most power.

Fairly deep in the movie, when he and Sundance are drinking and talking about their pasts, we learn Butch is from New Jersey. Sundance is surprised, as he didn't know.

The more interesting reveal comes later, when they are payroll guards in Bolivia. Their boss gets shot and they hide behind some rocks. They end up in a face off, with Butch and Sundance holding pistols on a double handful of fearsome looking bandits.

BUTCH
Kid, there's something I ought to tell
you. I never shot anybody before.

SUNDANCE
One hell of a time to tell me.

A great way to reveal important information, and, in a crowded theater, it got a gigantic laugh.

Scenes

☐ 31. You haven't pounded each scene enough!

After acts and sequences, scenes are the smallest building blocks in story construction. Each scene is a little movie all unto itself, with the same structural rules as a screenplay: beginning, middle, and end.

> *"People may or may not say what they mean... but they always say something designed to get what they want."*
> David Mamet

A scene should:

1) **Advance the story**. If the scene begins with a young couple about to buy their first home and ends with their breaking up, the story has moved forward! If the scene starts with a woman drinking a milkshake and, at the end, she's finished it... the story has not moved forward... unless she gets super powers from the milkshake.

2) **Increase dramatic tension**. Dramatic tension means making the reader more nervous that she was at the beginning of the scene. Tighten those thumbscrews!

3) **Tell something about the characters**. If we learn that Sadie cries at weddings because her fiancé spontaneously combusted at their wedding, that's something new about her character.

The best scenes do all three: story, tension, character. Generally, "advancing the story" is the only reason to have a scene. In the editing room, the character stuff will get cut. If a scene only increases the tension, it's probably going to get cut too. If it moves the plot forward, the editor will keep it.

Unless, of course, it's funny. If a scene makes us laugh, we don't care about that other stuff. When we're chuckling, it's impossible to be bored. Funny scenes don't get cut.

Start with some action.

> I mean START with action. If you have to open with Dave sitting at a table, at least have him drinking his martini. Don't wait for the scene to get going before you slam a little action the reader's way. Movies are about movement. Have some!

Make us curious.

> In college, I had a fraternity brother who carried a cloth bag everywhere. It had something heavy in it. He was the IM team's place kicker, and he'd stand on the sidelines with that bag, set it down, go in, kick, and come back and pick up the bag.

> Start a scene like that, drive us crazy!

> Want me to tell you what was in the bag? Say, "Pretty please." You're dying to know, aren't you? See, curiosity is a good thing for a reader! Okay, it was a .45 automatic. He thought his bookie had a contract on him for welshing on a bet. Of course, it was two frat brothers who'd written a fake letter. They told him the truth before someone got killed.

Make sure every scene is as short as possible.

> Less is a lot more. It's amazing how much you can do without. You want as much power in the scene as possible, and a lot of that energy comes from speed and brevity. You can outline each scene beforehand, or you can just start writing. However you get the words down is your call. Once you've got a complete draft of your script, go back and start slicing away. Often, a scene becomes more powerful when you trim it.

> Scenes are half a page. Rarely, rarely four pages. Look at recent screenplays. The scenes are tiny little jewels that shove forward into the next tiny little jewel. Say it and get out before they get antsy.

Get into the scene as late as possible, get out as early as possible.

One thing to cut is the beginning. Another is the end. Hit the ground running and get out before they're bored. Avoid all set up at the top of the scene. Don't show the guy walking up the stairs and going into the bedroom — start with him already in the bedroom.

Cut scenes that can *be cut and not destroy your story.*

If it can go, it's gone. Because you do not want your reader to be bored for a nanosecond, lose any scene you can. The litmus test is, if you cut a scene and your story doesn't collapse like a house of cards, that scene needed to go. If the scene is crucial to the story — if the ending will change if it's missing, keep it.

The more you write, the easier it is to lose material, because you will learn that cutting makes what's left, stronger. At first though, it feels like you're hacking off an arm. Hey, writing is a game for masochists. Get used to it!

Combine scenes.

If you do something in Scene #21 and something else in Scene #34, there's a chance you can put those two pieces of storytelling into one, better scene. Your story gets shorter and the new scene has more going on.

Cut dialogue. Then cut it again. Then again. Less is best.

You need SO LITTLE dialogue to get to the bottom of the scene. It's mind-boggling how little. Try to see if you can get your point across if each character says only five words before the next one speaks. Watch movies and see HOW LITTLE they say!

Have you got heaps and heaps of juicy conflict?

Some scenes lay there like beached whales and are hard to write and impossible to read because there is no conflict. Add some! If you have some, add more!

You need two characters for conflict. Like George and Elaine. Or Jerry and Newman. Or Kramer and... anybody.

Events must be unexpected, but not unbelievable.

If a guy is walking down his grubby apartment hallway, and suddenly his landlady opens her door, pulls a shotgun and starts BLASTING, that's unbelievable. If however, like in *The Mask*, the guy is walking down the hall and sees a Do Not Disturb sign on a door — he tiptoes, but a RINGING alarm clock hops out of his pocket! He pulls out a giant mallet and SMASHES it. The landlady opens her door and SCREAMS. His eyes bug out at her, *then* she pulls her shotgun and tries to ventilate him!

You believe it then, because it fits with the rest of the scene.

Most scenes should push us into the next scene.

"You should look for your mother's sister." CUT TO: He's pumping his grandfather for information.

"I'm really hungry now." CUT TO: She's cooking dinner.

"Omigod! Jason Bourne is in the building!" CUT TO: Security guys running.

Don't be boring.

You are trying to entertain a reader, a person you have never met. Assume their attention span is that of a "16-year-old speed freak" and you'll be okay. That quote, legendarily framed at a studio that turned down *Jaws*, is from the coverage. The reader saw it as a bad thing. You should not.

What bores the unseen reader may not bore you, so give your script to friends to read and hope some have a low boredom threshold. Also hope they'll tell you the truth!

Keep character in the forefront.

In every scene, ask, "How do the characters, especially the main character, react during this scene? How are they feeling *now*? Is the scene correctly reflecting how they would feel at this moment based on what is going on in the story?"

If the reader feels your hero should be reacting in a certain way and the character does something else, you're distancing your reader from the emotion you intend to get across.

I cannot stress this enough.

Make characters as different as you can possibly imagine!

It makes the scene soooooo easy to write. Imagine opportunities for conflict between Katharine Hepburn and Humphrey Bogart in *The African Queen*. He's a drunk and she's a missionary. He's an unshaven slob and she wears white lace. He curses and thinks about sex. She's a prim spinster. On every possible level, they are *worlds apart* — which makes every scene a picnic to write.

"And awaaaaay we go!"
Jackie Gleason

What's going on in your character's interior?

Be interested less in the action than the interior.

Allow yourself to discover things about your characters.

Take away preconceived ideas. Don't decide at the start that he is X, she is Y and he is Z. It's writing! It's supposed to be fluid. JUST BECAUSE IT'S IN YOUR OUTLINE DOESN'T MEAN THEY HAVE TO DO IT!

Did your character do _____ that was unexpected? Did the new situation bring something out in your character that you didn't intend? Cool!

In my Saigon screenplay, as the city collapses around him, the main character is out at night looking frantically for his girlfriend. He's miserable because he's married, but is in love with this NBC reporter. I was writing along, minding my own business, having McKillop call her name and I had him stop by a telephone pole to regroup. Suddenly, my fingers were writing that he yanked off his wedding ring and threw it down the street! McKillop sagged against the pole, exhausted and grieving. I didn't write that, he did.

That was a wonderful moment in writing. I wanted to crow from the rooftop how I'd learned something new about the character. For me, it's the most intense scene in the movie.

They'll probably cut it.

☐ 32. Your scenes don't turn the action!

Each scene should end at a different place from where it began, or it serves no purpose.

Does each scene, or most scenes, have an initial direction, the direction we think the scene is headed, and then change direction so that we come out in a new place than we were before? If this doesn't happen most of the time, you've got no forward plot motion.

Every scene should tell us something about the characters, or advance the plot, or be funny, or be cut.

Jim Boyle was my first writing teacher. He taught my class things, back in the Pleistocene Era, that I use every day in my writing and every day in my teaching. This is one. We all called it a "Boyle Sheet."

Scene _____

BRIDGING IN
sets the stage, who it is

INTENTION / INITIAL DIRECTION OF SCENE
it is going to be about _____. It will lead to the conflict.

CONFLICT
a difference of opinion, friction

EXPOSITION
information plot needs to move forward

CHARACTERIZATION
both visual and in dialogue, a revelation about them

REVERSAL OR CLIMAX
A or B win, or there is an outside force

FOLLOW UP & BRIDGING OUT
What the next scene is about.

Fill out a Boyle Sheet for each scene, then light the engines.

My favorite "turning the action" moment is in *The 40-Year-Old Virgin.*

What Jim Boyle calls "bridging in" is what pushed us from the previous scene. Now we're here. It should be as short as possible, barely enough to get us into the meat and potatoes. In *The 40-Year-Old Virgin*, written by Judd Apatow and Steve Carell, Andy and Trish are in her bedroom, boxing up his action figures to ship off to buyers. She thinks he might make enough money to open a store.

"Initial direction" is what we think the scene will be about. As you may recall, they had a pact not to have sex until their twentieth date. Trish says, "It's our twentieth date." Woo hoo! They start kissing on the bed. She says she thinks she's falling for him. The initial direction, where they seem headed like a rocket sled on rails, is toward making whoopee.

"Conflict" comes when they lay back on the bed and accidentally knock some of the action figures on the floor — still in their original packaging. He wants to pick them up. Trish, since they're about to make love, doesn't want him to. He disagrees. Strongly!

"Exposition" is our learning about his plans for his collection. Andy would rather tidy up the boxes than be with Trish, as he feels the original integrity of the box is very important. Trish, however, feels terrible because she's throwing herself at him, and they're just toys — and that makes Andy mad.

Character info time! We learn that Andy, metaphorically, is just like his toys — still in the box. He can't come out to play. Trish *wants* to play, and really likes him, but he's *stuck* and can't venture into the unknown. This is his Need, which he must address by the end of the story. We learn that he feels she is forcing him to sell his action figures and quit his job and change. She defends herself by saying that she likes him and wants to help him grow up. Then she attacks him for riding a bike to work. She tells him she'll do anything he wants so he'll have sex with her. She worries it's because she's a grandmother and he tells her that she's a hot grandma.

Now comes the "reversal." Initially, we thought they would make love. Now, at the scene's climax, they break up! It's unexpected, but by now, we believe it. Andy burns out the door and she is alone with his collection, unlaid and miserable.

"Bridging out" gets us out of the scene. Andy gets on his bike and, grumping to himself, bikes away from her house — nearly getting hit by five cars. It's quick, to the point, and pushes into the next scene — where he gets drunk with his friends at a bar.

* * *

I understand drawings better, so here's a high-tech visual demonstration. Feel free to copy it in your notebook. Way back when, your fifth grade English teacher drew this on the board to represent a story:

Familiar? Rising action, climax, *denouement*. You've seen it a thousand times. Problem is, a story looks like this:

And, the important part, where the scene changes direction:

This is the key to understanding a scene. Andy and Trish start out, going in some direction:

You expect them to end up here:

But, suddenly the scene changes direction and ends up where you least expect!

Do that in every scene and thank Jim Boyle when you see him.

☐ 33. You don't have enough reversals!

There is a difference between "change in initial direction of the scene" and a "reversal." Change in scene direction is a plot development and moves the story forward. Reversal is a surprise.

In *The Wild Bunch*, by Walon Green and Sam Peckinpah, one heck of a reversal comes after the amazing fantastic colossal shoot-out robbery. They get away and, lucky to be alive, sit down to enjoy their loot. Everyone (including us) expects cash or gold. Nope. They open the bags, and:

```
          LYLE GORCH
     Washers. Washers. We shot our way out of
     that town for a dollar's worth of steel
     holes!
```

Actually, that's probably a reversal AND a plot development.

Do you have plenty of reversals? That's when you set the audience up to think one thing will happen, and then, something else happens and you surprise them. It's one of the main foundations of storytelling.

A classic reversal in a horror movie is where the beautiful girl is in the big four-poster canopy bed and she's terrified and she has the covers drawn up to her chin and, from the hallway, there's a light under the door. CUT TO: her terrified face. CUT TO: the light under the door and you see shadows of footsteps. CUT TO: her, completely afraid, and then the doorknob turns... CUT TO: The girl, about to faint from fear — and the door finally opens and CUT TO: the reversal: her little old Aunt Tilly, bringing tea and cake for a late night snack!

There's a second reversal when Aunt Tilly leaves, the door closes, the girl calmly munches on her treat, and CUT TO: the Hooded Claw drops from the canopy and chops her into *steak tartare*.

Watch a movie. Write down every reversal you see. You'll be amazed how many times they do it to you!

My favorite scene in *Knocked Up* is when the gorgeous girl and her older, married, less-sexy sister come up to the night club for the second time. Earlier, they sailed past the doorman and velvet rope. This time, Katherine Heigl (the girl) is pregnant and the sister's husband is probably banging somebody else. They aren't feeling so sexy. The doorman, a gigantic scary black man, stops them cold. He firmly says to wait at the end of the line because the club is full. Then, two young hot babes prance up and he lets them go right in! Leslie Mann explodes. She screams and screams at this guy. And screams some more.

You think the guy's about to take her head off! Then comes the reversal. Whoa! The doorman, Craig Robinson, tells her in the softest voice imaginable that he hates keeping people out, the stress makes him sick, he thinks she's incredibly sexy, and that he'd love to — well, never mind what he'd love to do.

Delightful reversal. Best scene in the movie.

☐ 34. You have not shouted at each scene, "How can I jack up the conflict?!"

"People come over. We start to drink. We start to cook. We continue to drink. And then something terrible *happens."*
Beverly Lowry on dinner parties in Greenville, Mississippi

"Every scene is an argument."
David Mamet

This is major. Listen up.

The simplest way to keep the reader reading is conflict. If a scene has no conflict, reading it is worse that watching paint dry. Every single scene has to have some form of conflict, or needs to be rewritten.

What Mamet said, is the golden rule. Everybody needs to be "arguing" about *something*, all the time. Watch *The Odd Couple*. Under "conflict" in Webster's *Unabridged*, there's a picture of Felix and Oscar.

Characters should have:

Conflict with other people.	His spouse. Her cousin. Satan. Her cousin, Satan.
Conflict with the world.	Society, the environment, government, etc.
Conflict with self.	Internal struggle over guilt, sin, fear, the past, etc.

Characters who get along beautifully can still be in conflict. Imagine a honeymoon couple, so in love — soulmates — in a cabin in the mountains. Blissed out on happiness, dinner is over, they're quaffing champagne and it's time for bed. How could they ever argue? Well, it just so happens that he wants to make love on the polar bear rug in front of the fireplace. She wants to retire to the bedroom and that California King waterbed. Ooopsie, conflict! Suddenly, the honeymoon is more interesting.

Is everything as emotionally intense as you can make it? Can you heighten existing conflict? Can you add conflict to scenes that do not have it? Otherwise, what on earth helps us turn the pages?

If conflict does not come easily to you in real life, now's your chance to go wild and inflict it on your characters. Once you know you must have it, you can inject it everywhere.

Are your good guy and bad guy in conflict with each other as often as possible? If not the main bad guy, then at least his lieutenant. In *The Godfather*, the bad guy was Barzini; his lieutenant was Solozzo. Sent by Barzini, Solozzo came to the Godfather to tempt him into the drug business. He battles the Corleones every time he's on screen. Even when he's smiling, he's "arguing."

While it's easy to imagine Michael Corleone in conflict with Solozzo, you can also have your sweet grandmother character do "battle" with her sweet husband over what flavor gherkins to have with supper tonight.

Conflict is all. You don't even need two people.

I saw a short film about a girl who hated the ugly sweater her grandmother had knitted her. Her mother made her put it on, and she hurried back to her room to take off the loathsome thing. She pulled it over her head and it got stuck on her glasses and her hair. She couldn't get it off! Then, as she stumbled around, arms in the air, blinded by the damn sweater, she stepped on something and nearly fell. She was only in conflict *with a sweater*, but it was beautifully conceived and gave us something to watch! She could have come back from yelling at her mom, yanked off the sweater and tossed it on the bed, but it would not have been remotely memorable.

Conflict is everywhere. If not, make it so.

☐ 35. You have not used the incredible power of rhyming scenes to your advantage!

A rhyming scene is a moment that repeats. Via the repetition, and a change, we learn something about the characters.

In *Reds*, when Eugene O'Neill comes to Louise Bryant's apartment and asks for a drink, he is interested in having an affair. Her beau, Jack Reed, is out of town. They have a long, flirty scene that centers around her pouring Eugene a drink from a whiskey bottle. There is a bit of byplay where she asks if he wants a glass, and at last, she brings him one. At one point, she asks if he is nervous, because, as she pours, his hand is shaking. Finally, by the end of the scene, it is clear they will have a romance.

And they do. A stemwinder of a romance.

Many scenes later: Louise Bryant is moving into a house outside New York. Eugene is there and asks, as the moving men are coming in and out with heavy trunks, if she has any whiskey. She's nervous and rummages through the boxes for a glass. She finds a teacup, but that's not good enough. He insists on a glass. She finds one. As we watch the scene, we remember the first time, with the whiskey and the glass. We remember that their love affair started at a moment like this. This time, as she pours, it's her hand which shakes. All the little elements in the scene rhyme with the ones that came before, but it's the differences that make us take note.

With this scene, their romance ends.

But the writer doesn't give the actors any dialogue to the effect of "Wow, it was great when we started and we had such a grand time together. What a pity it must end this way." The writer lets the viewer make those connections by presenting the information in a rhyming scene.

Another rhyming scene is in *Kramer vs. Kramer*. It's really a rhyming shot, but it moves the story forward by leaps and bounds.

Dustin Hoffman's wife left him. He knows nothing about being a father to his young son. The first of the two rhyming shots is of him beating eggs in a bowl. He's terrible at it. He thumps the fork around the bowl, banging it on the sides like a complete klutz.

Time passes. He gets better at being a father.

Back to the kitchen. He's making scrambled eggs, but this time, he's an egg-beating whiz! His hand, with a fork in the same bowl, twirls like a *Cordon Bleu* chef. The guy is fantastic at cooking, and by analogy, at being a dad. No one tells you this. You get it because of the rhyming scene.

A wonderful way to move the story forward. Powerful and visual.

Rhyming scenes. Great arrows in your quiver.

☐ 36. You haven't cut the first and last lines from as many scenes as possible!

In an interview, Quentin Tarantino said, "When you're rewriting a scene, cut the last two lines of dialogue." He is SO right. Go through your whole script *only looking* at the last few lines of dialogue in each scene. Now, cut them and watch what happens!

We're fifty miles west of Saigon. Peterson is searching for his wife, who is Vietnamese. In the jungle, he happens upon an abandoned tea plantation and an elderly Frenchman who has lived in Vietnam for decades. Croyère offers him a bath.

EXT. FRONT LAWN   DUSK

Peterson comes out, bandaged and bathed, wearing old
fashioned but comfortable clothes of Croyère's.

>   CROYÈRE
>   Mr. Peterson. You seem much recovered. Tea?

>   PETERSON
>   I'd be most grateful.

The butler serves.

>   CROYÈRE
>   Eh bien. Now perhaps you will tell me
>   what has caused you to... go for a stroll
>   in the jungle.

>   PETERSON
>   (tastes it)
>   Your tea?

>   CROYÈRE
>   You know it?

>   PETERSON
>   My wife...

>   CROYÈRE
>   She is Vietnamese? Where is she?

>   PETERSON
>   (growing weaker)
>   Dunno. Went to Xuan Loc to find her,
>   but was a hair late. If she bails out
>   of Saigon before I get there, I don't
>   know... I just have to get there, that's
>   all.

>   CROYÈRE
>   (with compassion)
>   What will happen if you do not find her?

Peterson clearly hasn't considered this.

The scene ends with a good moment for the actor. The reader gets
to do the work, imagining Peterson's face when Croyère mentions
the unimaginable thought that Peterson might not find his wife.
It's a strong ending.

Now. Here's my *first* draft. Notice how, after "Peterson clearly hasn't considered this" it sort of wallows on, a tad aimlessly. Imagine yourself, writing the scene, reading it aloud, and then slicing off the last bit and exclaiming at how much better the scene is without the last few lines. When you trim the fat at the end, the good writing, already there, rises to the top.

```
INT./EXT. MANSION / FRONT LAWN      DUSK

MUSIC draws the silent Aussie through the luxurious house
to the front veranda. On the front lawn, an elegant old
gentleman sits before two huge loudspeakers. CROYERE is a
French tea planter.

A BUTLER brings Peterson a chair. The SONG ends.

                    CROYERE
                (French accent)
            Bertrand Croyère. How do you do?

                    PETERSON
                (weak and confused)
            G'day... I'm Peterson...

                    CROYERE
            Tea?

                    PETERSON
            Sure. Why not?

The butler serves.

                    PETERSON
                (tastes it)
            Your tea?

                    CROYERE
            You know it?

                    PETERSON
            My wife...

                    CROYERE
            She is Vietnamese? Where is she?

                    PETERSON
                (growing weaker)
            Dunno. Went to Xuan Loc to find her,
            but was a hair late. If she bails out
            of Saigon before I get there, I don't
```

> know... I just have to get there, that's
> all.
>
>   CROYERE
>   (with compassion)
>   What will happen if you don't find
>   her?
>
> Peterson clearly hasn't considered this.
>
>   PETERSON
>   Bloody hell, mate. What a question.
>   (beat)
>   I appreciate the tea and conversation,
>   but the clock's running and if it's not
>   too much trouble, me shoulder and me
>   would like a little beauty sleep before
>   the hike to Saigon.
>
>   CROYERE
>   I trust you will find the accommodations
>   to your liking.
>
> Croyère rings a silver BELL. Two SERVANTS appear, help
> Peterson up the wide front steps.

All that palaver about getting beauty sleep is wasted. When it's put back in, the power of the earlier ending is apparent.

Imagine your scene as a hydrofoil, slapping at top speed across the ocean — massive power and forward motion. By dropping the last couple of lines, you'll end the scene with the hydrofoil still banging forward! But, if you hold on to those lines, the air leaks out from under the skirt and the whole magillah sags flat.

This also works if you chop the *first* part of a scene. Start *in medias res*, as late as possible. Kill all set-up in favor of opening with action.

Here's the first draft. Take note, the beginning is about to get cut!

> INT. LUXURIOUS LIBRARY   NIGHT
>
> The quietest place in Saigon. Van Cao fidgets in an Empire
> chair. He glances around with apprehension.
>
>   SERVANT
>   Mister Ling will be with you in a moment.

Startled, Van Cao watches as the SERVANT leaves a tea tray,
vanishes. Long stillness. We hear measured FOOTFALLS. A
somber CHINAMAN glides into the library.

> VAN CAO
> Mister Ling.

> CHINAMAN
> Doan Van Cao. You are here to sell
> your café.

He strolls to the window, admires his well-tended garden.

> VAN CAO
> It is difficult to put a price on
> something so-—

> CHINAMAN
> --Nevertheless, you have.

> VAN CAO
> (resigned)
> Eight million piastres.

> CHINAMAN
> It is worth only one third that.

> VAN CAO
> It is worth fifteen.

The Chinaman slowly pours their tea. He sits at his desk.

> CHINAMAN
> These are troubled times. I can offer you
> four.

> VAN CAO
> (angry)
> Never.

> CHINAMAN
> If you do not sell to me, you will not
> sell...

> VAN CAO
> (deciding)
> Then it is not for sale.

> CHINAMAN
> For reasons we both know, Mister Doan Van
> Cao, you are not going to want to be here
> when our friends from the North arrive.
> You have precious little time in which to

reconsider this rash decision. I will be
here when you do so.

The Chinaman sips his tea.

Now, the rewritten version. The first few lines are gone. It also
changed from a library to a temple, because it was cheaper to
shoot in a temple. I loved the opening bit, but once it was gone,
I never thought about it again. What is left, is stronger. I added
the Chinaman saying, "If you do not sell La Coupole to me..."
so the reader will understand what Van Cao is trying to sell.

INT. CHINESE TEMPLE   NIGHT

Incense smoke drifts through the quietest place in Saigon.
Van Cao drinks tea with a somber CHINAMAN. Van Cao doesn't
want to name a price... finally must...

                    VAN CAO
               (resigned)
          Eight million piastres.

                    CHINAMAN
          It is worth only one third that.

                    VAN CAO
          It is worth fifteen.

The Chinaman slowly pours their tea, leans on his cushion.

                    CHINAMAN
          These are troubled times. I can offer you
          four.

                    VAN CAO
               (angry)
          Never.

                    CHINAMAN
          If you do not sell La Coupole to me, you
          will not sell...

                    VAN CAO
               (deciding)
          Then it is not for sale.

                    CHINAMAN
          For reasons we both know, Mister Doan Van
          Cao, you are not going to want to be here
          when our friends from the North arrive.

```
          You have precious little time in which to
          reconsider this rash decision. I will be
          here when you do so.

The Chinaman sips his tea.
```

Without the opening bit, the scene is tighter, starts with the characters already in the middle of the conflict — it's just *better*.

One last example. You can also trim the middle!

```
INT. GRAHAM'S SEVEN PAINTINGS

Huge, nearly abstract canvases of bloody, dead, eviscerated
animals. Road kill under a layer of sloppy handwriting.
Graham poses with Magda, more photos.

Magda departs. Camilla approaches.

                    CAMILLA
          I'm Camilla Warren. Nice night.

They shake, slowly. She is very appealing.

                    GRAHAM
          Buying, or watching?

                    CAMILLA
          Watching.

She inspects him.

                    CAMILLA
          Sold anything?

                    GRAHAM
          I will.

                    CAMILLA
          When you do, find me.

And she's gone.
```

Here's the same scene, with the cut marked:

```
INT. GRAHAM'S SEVEN PAINTINGS

Huge, nearly abstract canvases of bloody, dead, eviscerated
animals. Road kill under a layer of sloppy handwriting.
Graham poses with Magda, more photos.

Magda departs. Camilla approaches.
```

~~CAMILLA~~
~~I'm Camilla Warren. Nice night.~~

~~They shake, slowly. She is very appealing.~~

~~GRAHAM~~
~~Buying, or watching?~~

~~CAMILLA~~
~~Watching.~~

~~She inspects him.~~

                    CAMILLA
          Sold anything?

                    GRAHAM
          I will.

                    CAMILLA
          When you do, find me.

Now she's gone.

Now the final product:

INT. GRAHAM'S SEVEN PAINTINGS

Huge, nearly abstract canvases of bloody, dead, eviscerated
animals. Road kill under a layer of sloppy handwriting.
Graham poses with Magda, more photos.

Magda departs. Camilla approaches.

                    CAMILLA
          Sold anything?

                    GRAHAM
          I will.

                    CAMILLA
          When you do, find me.

And she's gone.

Cut stuff. Make what's left, stronger.

☐ 37. Your character does research when she could be talking to somebody!

You know the scene. We've seen it a hundred times (which should be a tip off anyway!). The intrepid heroine needs to find out about what happened in the past, so she goes to her local library and zips through old newspapers on microfilm, until she discovers... something... important....

And it's soooo boring.

Eliminate old bound newspapers, dusty archives, files, libraries, and computer records in favor of conversations between actual people. Have her track down the town's old, crotchety historian to find out about the plane crash that killed her parents. If your character must go to a library, at least your heroine and the clerk can argue, have conflict, react to each other.

Write a scene that is memorable! There's nothing memorable about a microfilm reader, unless it falls on her. Remember in *Chinatown* where Jack Nicholson has to deal with a smarmy, officious clerk?

```
              CLERK
          (quietly snotty)
      Sir, this is not a lending library,
      it's the Hall of Records.

              GITTES
      Well, then -- how about a ruler?

              CLERK
      A ruler? What for?

              GITTES
      The print's pretty fine. I forgot
      my glasses. I'd like to be able
      to read across.
```

What a great scene! Because the hero *talks* to somebody!

If nothing else, you can provide employment for the actor who will play the doddering, oddball, strange historian. He'll get his health insurance. You'll feel good about giving him work and the producers will save money not renting a microfilm machine.

Face to face conflict with an interesting person is way more fun than dusty old newspapers.

☐ 38. Your characters talk on the phone too much!

This is like the "anti-microfilm" rule.

Don't have characters talk on the phone when they could be face to face. It's better for the actors, certainly, and it's also more interesting for the reader when characters are in the same room. Characters face to face are more compelling than characters on the phone.

It will really loosen you up in terms of conflict and what can take place between the characters, because, when you stick them in a room together, interesting stuff can happen. They can throw skillets at each other, notice nuances of expression on each others' faces, cook a meal, or finger-paint together — none of which can happen if they're only on the phone.

☐ 39. You have not made every scene memorable!

Try to make *every* scene remarkable in some way. Ask yourself, "Is there anything about this scene that I can make — better?" Just because your first draft is a boring pan across a city skyline doesn't mean you can't rewrite it. Take the Jasper Johns approach.

> *"Take an object. Do something to it. Do something else to it. Do something else to it."*
> Jasper Johns

One of the finest writing lessons of all time.

It's the magic "what if." What if she doesn't leave now? What if she walks out on that line? Sometimes that will really help. Persistently asking "what if" will get you a piece of gold.

Another way to think about this is to give each scene a second layer, to make it more interesting.

Tom Schulman, who wrote *Dead Poets Society* and *What About Bob?*, tries to do that in every scene. He wrote an opening "let's meet Bob" scene. In the end, it didn't make it into the film, but you'll see what I'm talking about.

First draft: Bob is standing in his bathroom brushing his teeth. Okay. That's fine. Nice. We see Bob. We see his bathroom. We'll learn about him from the way he moves or smiles at himself in the mirror. But it's nothing to write home about. Then Schulman started wondering what he could do to make the scene remarkable.

Schulman said, "I knew we had to be ahead of the audience about this guy Bob, so in the rewrite, I put in a title card before the bathroom scene. The card read: 'There have been 2,567 recorded cases of people swallowing their toothbrushes... The world record holder was a patient in a Russian insane asylum. In his lifetime, he had 121 toothbrushes removed from his stomach.' *Now*, you cut to Bob brushing his teeth..."

Now what do you think about the scene?

The audience feels totally different just because the title card was added. The shot of Bob is the same, but not really, because we're anticipating — *something*. Then he swallows his toothbrush! He's panicked and takes a deep breath, manages to calm himself, opens his cabinet and inside — there are *20 more brushes*. He gets another one and finishes brushing his teeth.

THAT is a character introduction! *That* is a memorable scene. And it only appeared because the writer took an existing scene and did something to it.

Why wasn't such a fantastic scene in the movie, you ask? Bill Murray couldn't swallow the candy toothbrush without throwing up.

Let's pay a visit to Francis Coppola's stunning *Apocalypse Now*. In the "Mr. Clean's Death" scene, imagine the writer doing the first draft. They're chugging up the Nung river, Lance having fun with a purple haze smoke bomb and all of a sudden, tracer bullets stream out of the jungle, there's a vicious firefight, and Clean is dead. Chef is torn apart by his buddy's death and the scene ends with him in agony, hold his dead shipmate's body.

It's a good scene, but as the writer, you must always think about going back for a second dip. What can you do to make the scene *more* memorable for the audience? How can you make the already harrowing scene even worse? How can you make the reader/viewer *worry* more?

For the second layer, we get the element of everybody getting mail from home.

Chef is up front, reading a "Dear John" letter from his girlfriend, 13,000 miles away and Clean is in the stern, listening to a cassette tape "letter" from his mother. While Lance is playing with the smoke bomb, Clean's mom tells him the family is going to buy him a car, but that he has to keep it their secret. Then, the firefight breaks out and Clean is killed. Now, this time, with the second layer in place, when Chef holds Clean's dead body, the writer twists us on the emotional gaff as the mother's cassette player voice continues lovingly in the background, "bring your hiney home all in one piece, cause we love you very much. Love, Mom."

I have no idea if the writers planned it that way or added it as a second layer, but it's gut-wrenching.

Dialogue

☐ 40. You don't keep a log of overheard dialogue!

You've got to learn to write great dialogue. Actors want to say cool stuff. You're writing this movie so actors will attach themselves to it. There's nothing more exciting than knowing somebody really talented loves your dialogue and wants to say it on the big screen. But that takes a lot of time, work, effort — blood, tears, and sweat.

One way to improve is to write down dialogue you hear.

Keeping a log of overheard dialogue is a crucial step in the process of becoming a better writer, and it's a habit you should maintain for the rest of your writing life.

Listen to what people say on buses, in line at movies, at the market, anywhere — and keep a notebook in your pocket. Or write it in your laptop. Or BlackBerry. Or on your hand. It's a pity we no longer have paper cuffs and collars. Think what great notepaper they'd make!

First of all, it's fun to eavesdrop.

Second, it's delicious training for your ear. The more real dialogue you listen to and copy down, the more you're going to understand how people talk. They interrupt each other. They step on each other's words. They don't speak in complete sentences. Depending where they're from, they have specific word order, rhythm, syntax, and vocabulary. Read Mamet's dialogue, you'll see what I mean.

Check out *www.overheardinnewyork.com* for some swell examples.

If you write down overheard dialogue and ceaselessly plunder your notebooks, your characters will have a deeper level of reality than if you don't write down what you hear people say. Plus, it's mind blowing what you'll hear.

Top this one! I heard it in a restaurant. Man to his girlfriend: "I don't *care* what your doctor says. I'm telling you, you don't have cancer, bitch!"

Hello! You could write a whole screenplay based on that.

☐ 41. You haven't separated the character's voices!

You know George Costanza, right? Seinfeld's overbearing buddy? Good. I'll get back to him in a minute.

Some years ago, I was on my way to a meeting in Hollywood. I was on Fountain, at the light at La Brea. I looked out my window and saw a woman walking up the sidewalk. She was tall and thin. She had on nine-inch platform shoes and a powder blue double-knit pants suit. Bellbottoms that were starched and rigid. She was deliberately putting one foot straight in front of the other, like she was walking on a wire, almost like a robot. Facing straight ahead, she stared stiffly at the horizon. Her dark hair was pulled straight back, severely. It wound up, off the top of her head, in a narrow cone that went up to a foot-high point, like a unicorn. She was odd.

The light changed and I drove off. I got to my meeting and had this two-sentence conversation. When you think about it, an astonishing conversation.

Me: "I just saw the strangest person I've ever seen in Los Angeles."
Karl: "I know who it is."

Whoa. Then Karl said, "And I know where she *lives*." Double whoa. After the meeting, I went south on Detroit, just below Melrose. On a corner, was her house. It couldn't have belonged to anybody else. It was black. The whole house, roof, chimney, gutters, windows, walls and big rocks in the concrete yard were painted *black*. It was as if the entire house had been dipped in a giant bucket of paint.

Her name was Neptunia and I know one more thing about her. My friend Max was fascinated by her and her house. One fine day, bless her little heart, Max knocked on the black front door and asked to use her phone, as she'd lost her dog. Neptunia let her in, and here is what Max saw. "Everything in the house, and I mean everything, was covered in shag carpeting. The floor, the walls, the furniture. The carpet came up to the sofa, ran over the sofa and then back down across the floor." Max, who does not blow away easily, was properly blown away.

I've had students call from spring break screaming joyfully into their cell phones, "I'm in front of her house AND IT'S JUST LIKE YOU SAID!" However, sorry to say, before you pack up and pay a visit to Detroit south of Melrose, Neptunia's house has been remodeled. The black house is no more.

Okay, all that by way of introduction to separating out character's voices.

You can imagine how Neptunia would speak, right? You can hear her voice in your head. If she's calling the neighborhood store to have her groceries delivered, or if she's on the phone to the dentist, or talking to Max about a lost dog named Chloe, her strange, little high voice and her unusual but brilliant word choice is etched in your mind and flows into the keyboard so her dialogue sounds like Neptunia and no one else.

Remember George Costanza? You know how George talks. EVERYBODY knows how George talks: If you drop George on a desert island and he wanders over to borrow a cup of sugar from a headhunter, you know what George's use of language will be. Right?

Now, imagine George lives next door to Neptunia and his basketball just landed in her yard, but she won't give it back. You write dazzling dialogue for those two birds arguing. *If you cover up the names*, the reader will absolutely know if it's George or Neptunia speaking.

You separated the characters' voices. You're a champ.

This of tantamount importance. Readers pounce when you don't do it.

Character by character, check their dialogue to make sure:

1) All the way through, they always sound just like themselves.

Is their "voice" consistent and in keeping with where they're from and their morality and economic stratum and how they were raised, and everything *else* having to do with their character?

The speed at which they talk. The rhythm of their language. Choice of words. Do they use contractions a lot, seldom, never? Do they cuss a lot? Do they use big words, but don't know what they mean? Are they from North Dakota and does it show in their dialogue? Were they in the military? Are they shy?

How much can you teach us about each person, just by their personal use of language?

2) Their dialogue doesn't sound like any other character's.
3) They don't sound like you!

Separating out the voices holds true for minor characters because you're writing actor bait. Sure, you're interested in getting Mr. Mega Star to attach to play the male lead, but you also have to cast Pizza Delivery Dude. You write interesting, specific Pizza Delivery Dude dialogue, you're going to get a great actor to play Pizza Delivery Dude.

Here's some dialogue from my adaptation of *The Summer Fletcher Greel Loved Me* by Suzanne Kingsbury.

```
        MAN ON SODA MACHINE
          (auctioneer fast)
  I'm doing good. Annie May's on the
  phone this mornin, her son Walter
  he run around with that little
  Peterson boy. The Petersons, they
  can't hold theyselves together. Big
  James Earl Peterson, that boy's
  daddy, he gone shot himself through
  the mouth last month. Just last
  Sat'day, that little un done the
  same thing, .22 on his tongue, and
  pulled the trigger. Walter gone and
  have to watch it. He ten years old.


            RILEY
  Son of a bitch.


        MAN ON SODA MACHINE
  That boy's fat as a hog, too. Dead
  fat kid on a back porch in this
  heat's a Goddamn buttache.
```

Where do you think Man On Soda Machine is from? Vancouver? I don't think so. His voice is not remotely like this career diplomat who's disgusted with America for lying to the South Vietnamese:

```
          MCKILLOP
  I've been here five years...
      (looks at Ellen)
  This is my home... And now we're just
  running out...
      (this kills him)
  Nobody asked us to come here. We
  told these people we'd save them
  from the boogie man. And they
  trusted us... And now it's over...
  Just shot to pieces. We came in
  here with our "we wear coats and
  ties, we know what we're doing
  here folks" attitude, and... we
  didn't... And now... and now, we're
  going like a thief in the night...
  leaving them... in such a mess...
  and, and, and... I'm so ashamed
  and so sorry....
```

Trudy Mead doesn't sound like either McKillop or Man On Soda Machine.

I wrote this with Dub Cornett.

```
                TRUDY
I'm Trudy Mead. Call me Trudy. And you,
my dear, are going to be the first woman
to graduate from the Equine program. I
don't care if it kills you and me both,
we're going to get you through, darling.

                BARBARA
Thanks.

                TRUDY
I wanted to be an Equine vet. Twenty
years ago, there weren't even many girls
in the vet program at all, at Auburn,
much less in the large animal practice.
So I been stuck lancing boils on
poodles's asses hoping you'd come along
and make my life a little more worth
while. So don't let me down, kiddo!
```

Imagine a scene with these characters all on the same page. You would never need to read their names to know who's speaking. That is your goal. Every character's voice so distinctive that the reader, reading like the wind, won't have to waste time reading the character's name to know who's talking. Dialogue has to work like that, or they won't give your script to their boss.

☐ 42. You haven't worked your dialogue hard enough!

Dialogue is tough, but there are ways into it.

One option is to write dialogue for someone you know so your character sounds like your friend. Write for yourself, how you used to be at that age, but don't be autobiographical — channel your *feelings*. Always keep in mind each character's age and experience.

You can write for an actor whose voice you know well, but who might never end up in the movie, especially if they're dead. I once wrote a character and used Jack Nicholson's voice and speech pattern and rhythm. He never read the script and was too old for the part anyway, but it gave me a voice in my head. When you read the dialogue it sounds like *somebody*. No one ever said, "Hey, that sounds just like Jack Nicholson, you talentless clod," but it does sound like a character a reader can grab hold of.

Find the emotional core in every character, even if the experience isn't something that everyone will have, or could have, but making it human always encourages the reader to become involved.

Talk into a tape recorder until you get a solid handle on the character's voice. Try not to let your spouse's parents witness this.

Ask yourself: Is every smidgen of dialogue as good or funny or terse or interesting and as well-written as possible? Look at *every* line of dialogue and think how you could improve it, eliminate it, or how you could use it to move the story forward in a better more interesting way.

Just 'cause you wrote it doesn't mean you can't rewrite it! Or cut it!!

Take acting classes.

Make up your own rules: say, everyone in the lead character's family can speak with British syntax, even if they're all American.

Do a dialogue pass for each character. Type Ctrl F or Apple F, for FIND, set it for "match case" and then, in uppercase letters, a CHARACTER'S NAME. Go through the script one character at a time checking only *their* dialogue, making sure it always sounds like them and no one else. Even for Pizza Delivery Dude.

Have you put commas so it reads with the rhythm you intend? Are there periods where there should be periods? Is there no punctuation where there should be a comma, and so on and so on?

Go buy the children's book *Eats, Shoots and Leaves* by Lynne Truss. Read it to your kids and then sneak it over to your writing nook and gobble it up. It's about how commas matter. It's instructive, and hilarious. One example: a panda bear robs a bank, but has a snack first: he eats, shoots and leaves. OR at the zoo, what does a panda do for food: he eats shoots and leaves. Slightly different meaning, eh? Commas rock.

```
                    GITTES
          What can I tell you kid? You're
          right. When you're right you're
          right, and you're right.
```

In dialogue do you say "you are" when you actually mean "you're?" Make sure you have contractions where there should be contractions. People have a tendency to sound highly over-educated if they don't use contractions. Is that your point?

Remember, people interrupt each other and don't speak in complete sentences.

Sometimes, to get dialogue right, you have to do research.

If you're writing police dispatcher dialogue, find a real police dispatcher to help you. Television reporters don't talk like well-diggers. Take time to get it right. However, if you're looking for a Russian Grand Duchess to help you with dialogue research, you're probably going to have to make it up.

Know what language your character uses. If you're writing about Country music do you know what "girm" means? What about "blue steel" if your character is a prostitute? "Lapping" for con men, "rock solvent" for cavers, "crayon" for mountain bikers, "chibi" for a manga fan, and "bafflegab" for politicians. Do your homework.

Daniel Waters, who wrote *Heathers*, knew if he used current high school *patois,* that every single bit of teenage dialogue would soon be dated, so he made up his own. And, the stuff he made up became part of the language:

```
                    VERONICA SAWYER
          What is your damage, Heather?
```

And this classic...

```
                    HEATHER CHANDLER
          Well, fuck me gently with a
          chainsaw. Do I look like Mother
          Theresa?
```

Like "I'll be your huckleberry," from *Tombstone*, "Gosh!" from *Napoleon Dynamite*, and "I am McLovin," from *Superbad* — if you work your dialogue hard enough, it might enter the zeitgeist.

Daisy Foote, one of the finest playwrights of my generation, does the coolest thing to get her dialogue right. If she's writing a play about someone from, say, Nova Scotia, she calls around to her friends, finds someone who knows someone who lives in Nova Scotia who's willing to help, mails them a tape recorder and a bunch of tapes, and asks them to record their family having dinner. She doesn't care what they talk about, but she's interested in their use of language, the rhythm of their speech, and how they say what they say. The results are spot-on accurate. Daisy writes some of the finest dialogue I've ever heard.

You can too.

☐ 43. You didn't A-B the dialogue!

Jim Boyle taught me this superb technique.

It's difficult to keep two character's voices separate when you're writing a scene. It's also crucial. To insure the people in a scene have their own distinct voices, A - B the dialogue.

Write character A's dialogue first. Just *their* dialogue. Not the other guy's. If he's from Brooklyn (and you're not), it's going to take you a while to get into his voice. The language he uses, rhythm of speech, word order — everything that makes a shop keeper from Brooklyn sound like he's a shop keeper from Brooklyn.

You already have a general idea of what you want to do in the scene, so writing half the dialogue isn't that difficult, actually. You have a goal, where the scene is headed, and you write in that direction.

And you write and write and write — *only* Character A's dialogue. You don't have to write the other person's dialogue yet, so don't worry about it. Just be a guy from Brooklyn, and let 'er rip.

Pretty soon, you're going to hear his voice in your head, and the dialogue will flow. And it will sound like a grocer from the heart of Brooklyn. Finally, you will exhaust all the possibilities of dialogue for that scene from Mr. Brooklyn, and now it's time to work on Character B, a little old lady from Alabama.

So, you start to write Character B's dialogue, just her half of the same scene, and lo and behold, when you start, it sounds a lot like your little old lady is from — Brooklyn. After a while, though, you'll shed the trappings of Brooklyn, and will enter into the world of doilies, red clay, and Bear Bryant. You'll be able to concentrate on her world, her problems, her diction, her speech patterns — all the way to the bottom of the scene.

When you're done, print it.

Get a highlighter and mark all the swell dialogue that Mr. Brooklyn said, and all the good stuff that Mrs. Alabama said, bouncing back and forth between them until you have a real conversation. Cut and paste and you have a conversation between two people who sound nothing like each other!

Bingo. Screenwriting's biggest problem solved with a minimum of effort.

You're welcome.

☐ 44. You have Q & A dialogue!

The worst, most godawful dialogue on the planet is in hometown television spots for furniture stores.

> Sally: Say, Bob, what's this gorgeous piece of furniture?!
> Bob: Hey, thank you Sally. It *is* a gorgeous piece of furniture, isn't it?!
> Sally: Sure is, Bob. Can you tell me a little bit about it?!

Bob: Well, Sal, I certainly *can* tell you a little bit about it! It's a solid mahogany Broyhill chest of drawers with brass fittings and dovetail construction!
Sally: Wow, Bob! Dovetail construction? It sure looks expensive! How can I possibly afford a solid mahogany Broyhill chest of drawers with brass fittings and dovetail construction?!
Bob: It does look expensive, Sally, but, hey, it's surprisingly affordable!

ARRGGGGGGGGHHHHHHHH! I can't stand to type one more word of that garbage!

She asks a question. Q.
He answers it. A.
Barf.

Question:

> SAM
> You're kidding me.

Answer:

> ANGELO
> ~~I'm not kidding you.~~ I don't joke
> about money.

Q & A dialogue is like quicksand. It stops all forward motion. Then it drowns you. If you've got Q & A dialogue, take heart. It's just a first draft. You haven't sent your script to an agent yet. I hope.

Good dialogue answers the question, but leapfrogs OVER the obvious answer and gives us new information — while still answering the question. This from *The Devil's Own*:

> HARRISON FORD
> Did they catch the fuckers?

> BRAD PITT
> They were the fuckers.

Always move us forward:

> DIANE
> She boozing these days?

```
                    FRANKLIN
          Still on the wagon.

                    DIANE
          Are you going to the party?

                    FRANKLIN
          I'd rather die.

                    DIANE
          Why not?

                    FRANKLIN
          You've met Nan.
```

Rent *Playing By Heart* with Angelina Jolie. Amazing dialogue. Then check out the 1935 Randolph Scott version of *She*. Some of the worst Q&A dialogue, ever!

☐ 45. You have characters speaking text but not subtext!

Subtext is unspoken text. It's what they mean, but don't say.

If two fifty-year-old men are talking to each other on a Saturday night, and one says, "What are you going to do tonight?" and his buddy answers, "Nothing. What are you going to do?" you know what the writer wants you to know without either guy saying it: "my life is so miserable because I don't have a girlfriend."

The unspoken text is subtext.

At one point in *Reds*, John Reed (Warren Beatty) and Louise Bryant (Diane Keaton) are married, but estranged. They're in Russia, working and living together, but not sleeping together. While it's not the arrangement he wants, it's the best he can get and there's always hope. Up to now, every single time he's ever given her criticism on her writing, which she has always asked for, she's gotten angry and rejected it. *This* time (nice rhyming!) he tells her what's wrong with her piece, and she listens! She tells him he's right. This is a sea change for her character. He's stunned.

So are we. Then she says, as she's getting into bed, "You've been right about something else, too."

Now comes the subtext. Camera is on him. He's looking at her and we *know* he's hoping that she's changed her mind, and wants to have sex. We KNOW it. We don't have to be told. It's not in dialogue, but we *get* it.

Then she says, "The Bolsheviks will take Russia out of the war." And he says, "Good-night." He doesn't say, "Gee, honey, I thought you wanted me to come to bed with you." He may have said that in the first draft, or the ninth, but he doesn't say it in the one they shot. They take what the character is thinking, the subtext, and they bury it.

Here's some rather on-the-nose text:

```
              MYRIAM
     You are so mean to me. Our life together
     has been such a sham. You are so hateful.
     You don't understand me or my needs and
     our marriage is definitely on the rocks.
     If you treat me badly just one more time,
     I swear, I'm leaving you and your sorry
     Packers fan drinking buddies. Is that
     clear?
          (a moment)
     Are you even listening?
```

Here's my favorite example of subtext. This is from *Bandits*, written by Harley Peyton.

Redheaded Cate Blanchett sings along with "I Need A Hero" while she cooks dinner. She nearly does a striptease, she's so into the song. You get a huge sense of her fiery personality as she uses the sprayer hose as a microphone, drumming on a colander, chopping vegetables, tossing flour around, etc. Then, they cut to wide in the stunning kitchen, with an incredible view of a distant river, and you realize the whole thing was a fantasy. She imagined herself singing and dancing. Now, she's standing there, having cooked an amazing meal and her husband walks in:

```
                    HUSBAND
             (thinks it's great)
       What is that smell?
```

She goes into great detail telling about this stellar meal she cooked. She's quite sexy about it, too. Then he tells her he's got dinner tonight, with clients. She covers the hurt by saying that she cooked the meal just for fun.

Right there, you know their marriage is on the rocks. He doesn't have a clue who she is. She's taken all this trouble and he doesn't notice. When she says, "It's just for fun," you know that's not what she means. So he leaves. She's standing there alone, shell shocked, and then he comes back.

```
                    HUSBAND
       Sweetheart?

                    WIFE
             (thrilled)
       Yeah!?

                    HUSBAND
       Why don't you go see a movie?
```

He goes. She's enraged. The next thing she does is slam out of the house, leaving him.

When she says, "Yeah!?" we *know* she wants him to say, "Sweetheart, why don't you come with me and have dinner." Or, "I'll cancel dinner with the clients and we can eat here together." We get all her hope and desire, all that subtext, from *one single word of dialogue*.

His next text is, "Why don't you go see a movie." The subtext is "our marriage stinks and I have no respect for you."

But the screenwriter doesn't write that. He lets you figure it out.

☐ 46. You did *too much* research!

William M. Akers' First Law of Research: Don't do much!

But, conversely...

☐ 47. You didn't do *enough* research!

Gee, how confusing!

> *"Do I ice her? Do I marry her? Which of dese?"*
> Charley Partanna in *Prizzi's Honor* by
> Richard Condon and Janet Roach

Research can kill your story, so watch out. Beware. Run away! On the other hand, research can save your story, so dig in deep!

Here's my theory on research. Do only as much as you need to write your script, and no more. Especially at the front end, before you have a draft. Find your story, *then* do the research.

My script about the fall of Saigon is currently under option to a Hollywood studio, so it's probably not crap. When I first sat down, I had only the vaguest idea of the story I wanted to tell, but I was wise enough to know that research is like a rattlesnake coiled to bite.

Before I wrote the first draft, I read one book about the fall of Saigon. I interviewed a CIA guy who had been there, and I read a month of *New York Times* articles leading up to the last day of the collapse. That was it. It took a few days. But I knew enough to get started. I figured out my characters and story. I wrote my script. When I got done, the characters were okay, the story was okay, and I had lots of facts wrong. No biggie. I went back to my man from the CIA, some Vietnamese people, an Air Force pilot, and I read some more books. Because I had a completed draft, *I knew where I needed help.*

Slowly, but surely, my mistakes were corrected. When finished, the script was so accurate that when I'd go into meetings, people thought I'd been in the Vietnam war.

After I had that first pass, any research I did was pointed, direct, and *only applied to my story*. I wasted no time wandering in the woods lost.

Research can destroy your story.

Face it, research is often more fun than writing. It's always more interesting to talk to cool people and read fascinating books than it is to sit there in front of your computer trying to figure out why your story and your life are going down the drain.

The most dangerous part of research is the "kitchen sink" morass. You find out something juicy and you say, "Oh, cool! I can put this in!" And, in that one moment, you have torpedoed your story and don't even know it. Only when you have your story and characters locked down and tucked in, can you go do research, safe and content that you won't "throw in" extraneous garbage that seemed fascinating when you learned it, but only weakens your story.

You can know too many facts. Your core story can be buried under mounds of "great stuff" until it is lost forever.

I say "beware the evils of research" to every class I teach, and one night after class a woman came up with tears in her eyes, saying, "I wish I'd heard you say this before I wasted three years researching before I sat down to write, and then I couldn't tell my story." It was so sad. So, even if you learn nothing else, this book just paid for itself.

* * *

William M. Akers' Second Law of Research: What you have, get right!

If you're writing about something you know nothing about, it is easy to find experts willing to share their knowledge to get your writing correct. Whatever you do, don't send something out with mistakes, because your reader will ferret them out and loathe you.

At a writers conference, I once heard an author read a short story about quail hunting. He mentioned that the character's shotgun had a telescopic sight. Shotguns don't have telescopic sights. I knew instantly he was full of bull and dismissed his entire story. Don't let this happen to you. Get it right.

A small thing. A little later in this book, I mention a quote I overheard at the Los Angeles Farmers Market. I first wrote it "Farmer's Market," then realized I wasn't sure of the spelling. I went on line, found it, and corrected the mistake.

```
FADE IN:

SERIES OF SHOTS -- L.A. LANDMARKS

L.A. skyline. Hollywood sign. Movie posters. Palm trees.
Rodeo Drive. Everything and everyone sunny and happy.
```

The above scene description was written by one of my students. She's never been to Los Angeles. Her L.A. landmarks are okay, but show no knowledge of the city. I gave her a smidgen of color.

```
FADE IN:

SERIES OF SHOTS -- L.A. LANDMARKS

L.A. skyline. Angelyne billboard. Palm trees. Rodeo Drive.
Everything and everyone sunny and happy.
```

If you've done time in L.A., you know who Angelyne is. She gives the scene description a little pizzazz. The reader will say, "Hey, this writer knows her stuff."

However, *obvious* research makes you look like a clown. The same as if your petticoat shows. Don't put something in just because you know it, especially if it's show-offy. By the last rewrite of my Saigon screenplay, I knew so much stuff about the fall of Saigon and the kinds of helicopters and the safari jackets the cops wore and a zillion other things. I found myself going through the script and taking out cool research that didn't help tell the story. Just because I found out the Ambassador's dog was named Nitnoy, didn't mean I had to have the Ambassador call his poodle by name!

* * *

William M. Akers' First Law of Research — Contradiction: The right research can get you an Academy Award nomination.

Will Rokos, co-writer of *Monster's Ball*, and a lovely guy, came to my class. He had had a screenplay idea about a guy who worked on death row. From his research, he learned prison guard jobs often run in families. If you've seen the film (and you should, because it's really good and has a "wow" first act ending), you'll realize that, without that key piece of information found during his research, he'd never have written the script he did.

* * *

Enough about storytelling. Let's move on to Act II and the part of writing no one talks about.

Stephen King once had a conversation with Amy Tan. At Q&As after writer's talks, wannabe authors always ask "Where do you get your ideas," and "How can I get an agent," and "Would you take a look at my work and tell me if you think I should quit?" Mr. King asked Ms. Tan what question she is never asked. She said, "No one ever asks about the language."

It's what writers really love — the writing — and no one mentions it. For sure, no one ever taught me anything about how to put words on a page.

FADE OUT.

ACT II:

Physical Writing

Just because you wrote it,
doesn't mean you have to keep it.

<pre>
                    CECELIE
You can't write one word because that word
has to be oh so perfect. But you have
no idea what the oh so perfect word is,
because you haven't barfed your heart out
onto the page and sorted through to find
the chunks of brilliance.
</pre>
Melissa Scrivner, on writer's block

"Of the needs a book has, the chief need
is that it be readable."
Anthony Trollope

"I leave out the parts that people skip."
Elmore Leonard

"Works of imagination should be written in
very plain language; the more purely imaginative
they are the more necessary it is to be plain."
Samuel Taylor Coleridge

"Only the hand that erases can write the true thing."
Meister Eckhart

FADE IN:

"The first draft of everything is shit."
Ernest Hemingway

When you get to the bottom of your first draft, congratulations, you're about 1/10th of the way done! The real writing, which is rewriting, will now commence.

Hemingway, charming as ever, was totally correct. Everybody's first draft is shit. Even his. Yours too! You have to rewrite and rewrite and rewrite until you get it right. Then you stop. The good news is, you can fix just about anything. It only takes elbow grease and time.

You have to have a great story, true. But you must also communicate it to someone else — on paper. If they can't get it off your page, your story is worthless. The words on the page must explain to the reader the movie in your head. It's way more complex than you might think.

"All they read is the dialogue."
Overheard at the Farmers Market, Los Angeles

Untrue. Believe this at your peril. If the guy who said that were a working writer, he'd be in an office on the Universal lot instead of sucking down coffee at the Farmers Market in the middle of the afternoon.

Good writing matters. Not to everyone, but to enough readers, producers, actors, and directors to make it worth your while to pay attention. Readers who appreciate good writing will notice your scene description. If it's sloppy, they're going to head toward the door. By the end of the first page, they can't tell if you know what a reversal is, but they will certainly know if you can write a decent sentence.

Physical writing. Nobody ever talks about this stuff.

Well, Stephen King does.

This is something I spend a *lot* of time on with my students. Much of what I laboriously figured out on my own is included in King's superb book, *On Writing*. I wish it had existed when I started.

Welcome to Writing

☐ 48. You aren't educated in your chosen storytelling medium!

How are you going to figure out this most bizarre of writing forms if you're not reading lots and lots and lots of screenplays? Are you nuts?

Do you go to movies?
Do you rent movies?
Do you read screenplays?
Do you read?
Aw, come on!

You have no doubt taken writing classes. Or more fancypants: Creative Writing. You know, by now, having done it since the third grade, how to write a short story. Or a novel, or a business letter, or a dazzlingly wicked Email. But, if you've bought this book, you are not a big time screenwriter, and you had better be reading all kinds of screenplays, all the time.

No successful writer got where they are without reading *all the time.* If you spend half your writing time reading and half writing, you're moving forward faster than the writer who only works on her own stuff.

You learn more. You get out of your head. You see what other people have done when faced with the same problems.

When I started to write, the only book I could find with pages that looked like screenplay pages was *Five Screenplays by Preston*

Sturges. It's still on my bookshelf, right in arm's reach. The fact that they were written before 1950 didn't affect the format. It's still the same.

I invoke the amazing *www.script-o-rama.com*. Go there and rejoice! Read a script every day. Pretend you're a development person. Read three scripts a day! Pretend you're Johnny Depp. Only read scripts with offers attached.

But read scripts. Bookstores and libraries have them. I'm a big fan of libraries because they are free. And, if they're free, you'll read more screenplays. The more you read, the better a writer you will be.

Read, read, read.

However, there's a good chance your screenplay will suck — if *all you read is screenplays!* Don't you dare say, "I'm a screenwriter, dude. I'm not interested in writing a novel."

Read it *all*. Read EVERYTHING you can get your hands on. Scripts. Plays. Blogs. Journalism. Short stories. Comic strips. Comic books. Fiction. Non fiction. Memoirs. Backs of cereal boxes. Books by guys who didn't write in English. The articles in Playboy, ha ha ha. Books by dead men. Books by dead women. Anything that's good. Anything. It will help you like you won't believe.

If you read Thomas McGuane, it will help you understand something about your own writing… even if you're not writing about a rancher in Montana. Dickens can teach you a ton about comedy. Shakespeare's good.

So are these writers: Suzanne Kingsbury, Terry Kay, David McCullough, Nadine Gordimer, Joyce Carol Oates, James Jones, George V. Higgins, Bruce Feiler, Ernest Hemingway, Irwin Shaw, Zadie Smith, Camille Paglia, Guy de Maupassant, Jane Austen, Anton Chekov, Edgar Allan Poe, Tobias Wolff, Anne Tyler, Lee Smith, Roald Dahl, Jack London, A.S. Byatt, Jesse Hill Ford,

Calvin Trillin, Donald Bartheleme, Jim Thompson, Flannery O'Connor, Elmore Leonard, Isabel Allende, Carl Hiaasen, Patricia Highsmith, Jamaica Kinkaid, Jay McInerney, Richard Ford, Jeffrey Lent, Tim Gautreaux, and on and on…

Ask your friends to tell you names of the best writers they've ever read. Ask your parents. Ask your parents' friends! Perhaps one will suggest Richard Brautigan. He was my favorite writer when I was in college and only one of my students has ever heard of him. Read his watershed novel, *The Abortion*. It sure has a voice. So does *The Catcher In The Rye*. Read *that* and tell me with a straight face that a writer has to sound like every other writer.

Your screenplay sucks because you don't read scripts written before you were born. If you can't talk about Preston Sturges, Samson Raphaelson and Joe Mankiewicz in the same breathless tone you ooh and ahh about Charlie Kaufman, you still have some learning to do.

And finally, your screenplay sucks because *you don't watch movies*!

Every class, I ask my students what movies they've seen that week. Sometimes the answer is zero. Every single week I see at least one movie in a theater and watch three or more on DVD. In a year, that's a lot of movies. And I already know how to write a screenplay! How many movies do you see in a year?

Do you know about Netflix (*www.netflix.com*)? They mail DVDs to you. At last count, they had around 85,000 titles.

However you do it, educate yourself in this wonderful storytelling medium. It will pay off in the long run.

☐ 49. You're using the wrong writing instrument!

Let's start with basics: paper, pencil, pen, computer, typewriter, different brand of pen.

How you get the words on the page will affect your writing. Do you like paper with lines? Your style will change if you move from pencil to computer. Hemingway wrote longhand, except for dialogue, which he did on a typewriter.

This also applies to where you write. Your bed (where Woody Allen writes, in longhand), an office, the front passenger seat of your car, a picnic table at a playground, your kitchen, a coffee shop, or wherever.

Each combination of writing instrument and locale will affect your writing. You have to find the cocktail that works.

If you're having trouble getting your thoughts out, change the method by which you put words on the page. Some people dictate and then type it later. When I have to do something crucial, I write in pencil. My brain connects to the page more directly when I use a pencil. The great thing about a pencil is that it's slower than a computer, and I have a tendency to leave out as many words as possible — which tightens up the writing nicely.

Any way you can get it on the page: Willard Carroll, who wrote and directed *Playing By Heart*, told my class he is a very undisciplined writer. He spent months taking walks, thinking about his characters and their stories. Once he'd finished working it out in his head, *then* he wrote his script — in eight days.

What do you think the production budget was for *this* cast?

Nastassja Kinski, Dennis Quaid, Patricia Clarkson, Gena Rowlands, Sean Connery, Gillian Anderson, Madeleine Stowe, Anthony Edwards, Ellen Burstyn, Jay Mohr, Jon Stewart, Ryan Phillippe, Amanda Peet, and Angelina Jolie!!

He got THAT cast and made the movie for five million dollars. Because he writes actor bait.

Karl Schaefer, who created the legendary television series, *Eerie, Indiana*, writes his first draft on a computer, then makes corrections on a hard copy, and then retypes the entire draft into the computer. Retyping the whole script is such a pain that he instantly leaves out anything he doesn't *have* to type. Again, tighter writing, automatically.

Keeping in mind that the reader doesn't want to read your script, leaving out unnecessary crud is a superb idea. So, just because you own a computer, doesn't mean you have to use it!

☐ 50. Your prose is not CRYSTAL CLEAR!

Make sure your reader understand what you *hope* they do.

The path from the image in your head to the reader's brain is, sadly, not a hard-wired main circuit line. The meaning of each sentence isn't beamed from your tinfoil-wrapped head to the reader's.

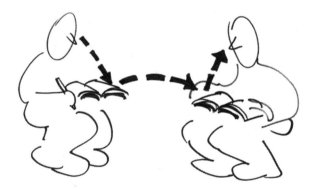

What you write goes from your mind, through your fingers, to the page, and only then up to the reader's tiny pea-brain. Along that treacherous journey, there's enormous room for (scary music here!) *confusion*.

When you write a sentence, you are asking someone to take a trip inside your scrambled little head, and what *they* get from the page may not be what *you* imagine to be on the page. Woefully, unfairly, but truthfully, if your writing is misunderstood, it's not the reader's fault. Tie does not go to the runner.

Once you've got a draft, it is incumbent on you to weed through any potential "errors in transmission." You must continually ask, "Is what I think I mean here, actually what they are going to understand when they read it?" Difficult question.

When I was a little shaver in my first filmmaking class, I made a romantic film, set in Italy (if you can believe it) and I used Sinatra's "Strangers In The Night" on the soundtrack. On the soundtrack of my life, it was one of the most important songs, ever. It was powerful. It could reduce me to jelly. I put it in the soundtrack of my 8mm autobiographical film. When I played it for the class, when that scene came on, I was all choked up. And guess what?

The class laughed.

It was a slit-your-wrists bleak moment for Yours Truly, but a hell of a lesson in filmmaking. The on screen image juxtaposed with the Sinatra song did not remotely mean the same thing to the audience as it did to me! I was sitting there, all teary-eyed with nostalgia for some girl I'd known, and they were howling at my idiotic choice of music.

Take a caution from my disastrous screening and agonizing pain of bygone years. Be sure that what you *think* the reader is going to feel, is what he is *really* going to feel.

This is true in the macro, for your whole story, and in the micro, for each moment.

For instance, don't have a character pick up their best friend and have you call it a "body" unless the friend is dead, because that's what we're going to think.

`Bob picks up the body.`

And this example: are the goons flanking Pastor Al or the entrance?

```
EXT. WINERY GATES - NIGHT

Pastor Al climbs out of his limo and approaches the
entrance flanked by his goons.
```

Here, we get the impression that Officer Tindel has been over-served. Your reader may not realize you only meant for Tindel to be sleeping.

```
EXT. WINERY GATES - NIGHT

Franklin squeezes out of the police cruiser and takes a
pull from his flask before wiping his mouth with a chubby
paw and heading for the party.

Inside the cruiser Tindel is passed out.
```

Here's some crummy writing, or at least a tad vague, from, er, me:

```
EXT. PARKING LOT     DAY

Loose Wrap spots the Nervous Man about to board a chopper.

                    LOOSE WRAP
          That him?

                    GIRLFRIEND
          It's my suitcase. I want it back.

                    LOOSE WRAP
          Wait with your brother.

He sprints over, wrests the suitcase away.

                    LOOSE WRAP
          You lose, motherfucker.

The angry man glares at Loose Wrap from the open door. The
Chinook LIFTS OFF.
```

This is picky, but it matters. In the first piece of scene description, the Nervous Man is "about to board" the chopper. That means he's not on it yet. He could be in line, five people away from the chopper. Next time we hear about him, he's glaring at Loose Wrap from the open door, and the helicopter flies away. The picture in our mind is murky. Was the guy standing near the door or was he *in* the helicopter? A tad confusing. And, please, pardon my use of a dirty word.

Here's the rewritten version. "About to board" has become "boarding."

```
EXT. PARKING LOT DAY

Loose Wrap spots the Nervous Man boarding a chopper.

                    LOOSE WRAP
          That him?

                    GIRLFRIEND
          It's my suitcase. I want it back.

                    LOOSE WRAP
          Wait with your brother.

He sprints over, wrests the suitcase away.

                    LOOSE WRAP
          You lose, motherfucker.

The angry man glares at Loose Wrap from the open door. The
CH-53 LIFTS OFF.
```

With that slight change, we get a better picture of the characters' geography. We create the image that the Nervous Man is not waiting around to be told where to go, but is actually *stepping onto* the helicopter. So, when the chopper flies away, we know the Nervous Man is *in* it.

After more research, I also changed it from "Chinook" to CH-53.

Be clear. For God's sake remember the poor reader, running across those lily pads, trying to make an image in her mind, trying to figure out what the heck it is you want her to understand is going on. If she doesn't get it, it's your fault.

Be clear. Don't write, "Frank dresses in nice-looking clothes," because we might think he's getting dressed. Instead, write "Frank wears nice-looking clothes," so we understand that he's a fashion plate. Make sure we understand the picture you're beaming into our brain.

Here is scene description, the final version:

```
He takes out his phone and dials. It RINGS without picking
up. He calls a different number.
```

Obvious that the guy makes two phone calls, one after the other, to different people. Now, the original. Remember: Confusing = Tearing of hair and gnashing of teeth.

```
He takes out his phone and dials. It RINGS without picking
up. He calls again.
```

We think he calls the same number twice. Because he doesn't, we're confused.

Be clear. Check every chunk of your scene description RIGHT NOW! This is a checklist, after all. Check some stuff off!

Look at this one. Yipes, I am one picky dude! Now I'm irritated about one cotton picking word! What do small rocks NOT do when they hit a pond?

```
EXT. POND    NIGHT

Kara and Travis cuddle under the stars next to a quiet
lake. The saw grass rustles in the wind. Travis's arms are
wrapped around Kara as she tosses small rocks and sticks
into the pond, shattering the night silence.
```

They don't "shatter" the night silence! A tractor trailer truck that end-over-ends from the freeway bridge, crashing down in Travis's pond, will "shatter the night silence," but for Pete's sake, not a "small rock." Boink! Off the lily pads!

How many times does Petey get hit by the ambulance?

```
TIME SLOWS DOWN as Mark stops on the sidewalk.

Lucy and Trey watch from inside the Tahoe.

Petey runs into the street. Is hit by the ambulance.


INT. TAHOE

The kids press their faces against the windows.
                    LUCY
          OH NO! PETEY!
```

```
                         TREY
          Oh shit.
```

INT. AMBULANCE

A THUD is heard and the ambulance stops. The DRIVER
scrambles out of the ambulance

```
                         DENISE
          What the hell was that?

                         EMT
          Oh shit.
```

Petey's mom begins to cough even harder.

EXT. STREET

Petey runs into the street. The ambulance lurches forward
as the siren begins to sound. It immediately stops as the
front bumps Petey, knocking him off balance and his head
hits the pavement.

This writer has Petey get hit three different times, when he only meant for him to be hit once.

This dialogue seems fine until you read it a couple of times:

```
                         SOOTHSAYER
          He has protection from a spirit.
```

Does this mean the spirit protects him from those trying to kill him, or does it mean he has an amulet that gives him protection from a spirit trying to do him harm? One sentence. Totally *opposite* possible meanings.

```
                         DEPUTY SHERIFF
          I heard her come in the Chrysler.
```

Which meaning did *that* writer intend?

Format

☐ 51. You don't understand screenplay format!

This seems so easy. For some reason, it's not.

Write in Hollywood approved screenplay format. Period. Don't do different and fun things because you're so "creative." They will pick up your script and notice your format. If it doesn't look like everyone else's, they'll use it to wrap fish.

If you buy Final Draft screenwriting software, it will be easier, but you can still make mistakes. So, listen up. About 95% of format questions are answered in the next few pages. Certainly enough to keep the reader reading.

```
In Final Draft, use Warner Bros. style.
```

Screenplays look the way they do for a reason. The first thing you see is a slugline, followed by scene description. Other than INT. and EXT., no periods in a slugline.

```
INT. HAUNTED HOUSE     NIGHT

The mysterious, howling, terrifying, awful wind tears through
the rotten dark yellow rickety shutters and scares Johnny
clean out of his L.L. Bean bright green rubber galoshes.
```

The slugline tells you where the camera crew is standing when shooting. It's at the far left of the page (plus a little extra margin for three hole punched paper) with scene description underneath, because it's what you see first. The visuals. The action. What they *do*. That's what movies are about. What happens. Not what they say. In plays, the dialogue margin is at the far left because plays are about words, not action. Not in movies.

Do not put a slugline at the bottom of a page unless there is at least one line of scene description with it. Never have a slugline anywhere without some description.

Almost never call camera angles. If the camera movement is *critical*, you can indicate it. HELICOPTER SHOT. RAPID DOLLY.

Here's a slugline for point of view. Things do not have points of view. Only people.

ELLEN'S POV - THE PISTOL

Scene that takes place in two places. Like a car riding down a street. On a porch. Through a window.

EXT./INT. PORCH/LIVING ROOM

Only in a slugline, do you use one hyphen alone. Everywhere else, use two.

Here's how I indicate a flashback:

FLASHBACK - EXT. EDGE OF CLIFF   DAY

Make sure sluglines are consistent. Don't say:

INT. JIMMY'S OFFICE   a few times and then
INT. OFFICE COMPLEX   and finally
INT. THE CUBE FARM

Pick one and keep with it. If you use Final Draft to break your script down, it can't do it accurately if the sluglines are not consistent. Also, back to my usual rant, it confuses your reader.

A character's name is in CAPITAL LETTERS every time he or she speaks. The character name is indented more than the dialogue. The character name is not centered on the page. All character names, short or long, have the same left margin.

                    JOHNNY
          Is that you mommy?

He hears nothing but the wind. He looks around for his favorite galoshes. They're history.

```
                                          DISSOLVE TO:
EXT. GRAVEYARD     NIGHT

The mysterious, howling, terrifying, awful wind rips between
the rotten, crumbling pitted marble headstones. ERNEST and
ABNER crouch on lovely pre-Raphaelite monuments.
```

Because we are meeting Ernest and Abner for the first time, their names are capitalized. They will never be capitalized again in scene description. If you're English, for some reason, you capitalize the CHARACTER NAME every time it appears in scene description. If you're not English, don't do it after the first time. SOUND EFFECTS and CAMERA MOVES and OPTICAL EFFECTS are also in caps in scene description.

```
The car EXPLODES. The phone RINGS. Harry and Sally KISS loudly.

We SEE the killer. DOLLY BACK with Frank. REVEAL the formula
on the table.

The schoolhouse is old and rotting. SUPERIMPOSE TITLE: FIVE
YEARS AGO.

                    ERNEST
          I just love to eat little high
          school kids that come up to the
          cemetery on a picnic.

                    ABNER
          Sounds like a swell way to spend an
          evening to me.

Ernest hits Abner in the face with a cream pie.
```

Notice that Ernest's name and Abner's name sit right down on top of their dialogue. There is no space between the character name and the dialogue.

If you have a two-part slugline, put a hyphen between the general part (the car dealership) and the specific. Always keep the same number of spaces between INT. and the location. Always maintain the same number of spaces between the end of your location and the DAY or NIGHT.

```
INT. CAR DEALERSHIP - SHOWROOM    DAY
```

Cream pie still dripping from his nose, Abner buys a Mercedes.

```
                    ABNER
                (wryly)
            I'll take this one.
```

The SMARMY SALESMAN licks his lips, thinks of his vacation.

The (wryly) is called a parenthetical or a wrylie. It gives the reader or actor a hint on how you want them to say the dialogue. It sits on the dialogue, and the character name sits on it. Never any spaces between them. It always goes before the dialogue, never after, though it can separate two bits of dialogue.

```
                    SMARMY SALESMAN
            An excellent choice, sir.
                (smirks)
            Napkin?
```

Use parentheticals only when the dialogue's meaning might be unclear, i.e., only when the reader might misunderstand.

```
                    JOE
                (hates her guts)
            Darling, I love you more than life
            itself. I can't bear to be away
            from you for even an hour.
```

Always write in present tense. You're describing events that unfold before the reader's eyes. It's happening right this second! Not like this:

Kate stares incredulously at Eisman. He just finished relating his understanding of the crime to Kate and the Chief.

Use three dots to show pause in speech and to connect speeches when action separates them to indicate continual dialogue.

```
                    NAN
            What is going on? This place...
```

```
                    ABNER
            I know my socks were here.
```

```
                    NAN
            ... is like a three ring circus.
```

Use two dashes to indicate interruption. At end of one character's speech, start of next character's speech.

                    ABNER
          Have you seen... my socks? It's--

                    NAN
          --Do I look like I care?

Use (MORE) for dialogue continued on next page, then use (CONT'D) on next page beside character name.

                    BARBARA
          I'm feeling just great here! Life is just
          like it was supposed to be
                    (MORE)
    _____ page break

                    BARBARA (CONT'D)
          and little Eddie is going to have his
          operation Tuesday. How nifty.

Don't use (MORE) if it takes up the same space as it would to complete the speech on one page. Avoid (MORE) whenever possible.

For some reason, phone calls are a toughie for beginning writers. I see this a lot:

                    NICK
               (on the phone)
          What do you want?

                    SALLY
               (on the phone)
          I want you to stop being so nosey.

                    NICK
               (on the phone)
          You're the one going through my
          garbage!

                    SALLY
               (on the phone)
          Only because you threw away my
          love letters!

To have someone talk on a phone, set up the first person's location and then they talk to the other person:

```
INT. BEACH HOUSE     DAY

Sarah picks up the phone. Dials.

                    SARAH
          Mister Smith? Is that you?

                    MR. SMITH (O.S.)
          Are you going to pay me or not?
```

Once you've established the first character in the first location, go to:

```
EXT. CONSTRUCTION SITE     DAY
```

and in that scene description say: INTERCUT TELEPHONE CONVERSATION or INTERCUT SCENES. After that, just run the dialogue as though they were standing there talking to each other.

```
EXT. CONSTRUCTION SITE     DAY

Mr. Smith is darn irritated. INTERCUT SCENES.

                    MR. SMITH
          You owe me money, girly girl.

                    SARAH
          Liar, liar, pants on fire!
```

(V.O.) is voice over. It is either a narrator or dialogue from another part of the movie that is laid over the scene we are watching.

(O.S.) is off screen. A character is in the other room or off camera when we hear them speak.

```
                    BENEDICT (O.S.)
          Honey, have you seen my socks?

                    NARRATOR (V.O.)
          He was destined never to find them.
```

Never hyphenate a word at the end of a line of dialogue unless the word has a hyphen in it anyway.

Underline key words in scene description (rarely) so the reader will be sure to see them.

```
Oswald picks up the high powered rifle.
```

Don't do it with CAPS.

```
Worn out, Gary and Ed survey the reborn course. They both
look like they've found a long lost love. A high ROCK WALL's
left of the fairway.
```

Don't use italics. They're too hard to see.

```
                    CHERRIE
          It's you that I love. For me there
          can be no other. Ever.
```

The speed at which these people read, you need to give them all the help you can. In dialogue, underline words that need emphasis. And don't do it a lot, either.

```
                    CHERRIE
          It's you that I love. For me there
          can be no other. Ever.
```

Dots. No space before three dots. One space after.

```
                    DARTH
          Luke... I... am... your father.
```

To familiarize yourself with format, copy ten pages of a screenplay you admire by typing it into your computer — every single word. First, you'll really nail down the format, and second, you will see how few words actually go on a page of screenplay. You'll get a feel for writing that will carry over into your own work. Hunter S. Thompson typed up page after page of F. Scott Fitzgerald when he was learning to write. Seems like a swell idea for you, too.

At one page per minute, more or less, pace is controlled by the visual look of your page. The fewer words, the faster the reader's eye moves down the page. A page filled with solid scene description will be more majestic or filled with long takes.

Here is a page from *Children of Men*. It has wide dialogue margins, which I counsel against. Lots of white space, though. Notice the scene description, one line, a space and then two lines. Quick, to the point, breaking up the dialogue. Rarely do you see just dialogue on a page. Longest piece of dialogue is four lines. Most is far less.

This is solid dialogue from *The 40-Year-Old Virgin*. Narrower margins speed up the read. One piece of dialogue is eight lines, but it's a dialogue heavy script. One line of scene description only.

And *Alien.*

That dialogue is short, staccato, and moves quickly. Most dialogue is one-line only. Terse scene description. One paragraph of which is only one word!

Back to *Children of Men*. This page combines dialogue and scene description. No paragraph of description is more than three lines. No parentheticals. Longest piece of dialogue is four lines.

The 40-Year-Old Virgin dialogue / action page has more dialogue, but still the scene description paragraphs are short. No more than two lines!

The *Alien* page looks totally different from the first two. I marked sluglines with double lines so you can see them. VERY short bursts of scene description. Only one bit of dialogue is two lines long. The rest are one. Imagine how quickly that page will read!

Now, a page of action from *Children of Men*. Some dialogue breaks it up, but not much. The page is solid scene description, but no paragraph is longer than four lines. Short paragraphs insure the reader will pause at each one, take in the brief amount of information, and continue.

Action in *The 40-Year-Old Virgin* looks different. More white space. Less emphasis on the description, more speed. No dialogue at all. Six sluglines, six scenes on one page. They are moving on along!

Wrapping up with a page of action from *Alien*. Seven sluglines. No paragraph longer than one line. This is a speed-of-light read. Still, enough to get the point across.

Which page would a reader rather read!? Hmmm?

If you want to know more about format, get *Formatting Your Screenplay* by Rick Reichman or *The Hollywood Standard* by Chris Riley.

You don't have to write in Final Draft. You can use Microsoft Word. Word offers lots of opportunity for growth. Who needs it?

In Word, use Courier Regular font, not Courier New.

Final Draft knows when you want to write a character name, and it lines up the dialogue margins for you. You can do that in Word, but it's a pain. Here's how: go to *www.tennscreen.com*, the Tennessee Screenwriting Association's website, and click on "Writing Tips" and then "Screenplay Formatting: Word as a Screenwriting Processor." It will take you through the steps.

If you can afford Final Draft, use Final Draft.

☐ 52. You have naked sluglines or no sluglines at all!

Final Draft calls it a Scene Heading. Everybody else calls it a slugline. It tells the crew where to stand. It tells you where your feet are, too. I call a slugline with no scene description with it a "naked slugline" — and you shouldn't do it.

```
EXT. NORTHERN FOOTHILLS     NIGHT

                    BOB
          Look out fellas! It's the fifty
          foot lady!
```

Always include scene description — it tells us what's going on:

```
EXT. NORTHERN FOOTHILLS     NIGHT

What in the wide, wide world of sports is that?!

                    BOB
          Look out fellas! It's the fifty
          foot lady!
```

Give us a bit o' the ole scene description after LA SORBONNE
DORMITORY:

SERIES OF SHOTS - DAWN

Sun rises. Paris. Eiffel tower. Opera house.

Fouquet's café. On the sidewalk, a GRUBBY BUM scares people
with a rubber rat.

EXT. LA SORBONNE DORMITORY - DAY

INT. JEAN MICHEL'S DORM ROOM - DAY

Jean Michel wakes up, makes coffee. What a cool guy!

Don't have spaces where there shouldn't be spaces. The reader
knows you didn't proofread and you look like a doofus. Check
out "in the along!" Double doofus.

EXT. ROSABAL'S ENCOUNTER - NIGHT

Rosabal is walking with Vega in the along the road home
as he is encountered by the rural guard who approach in a
jeep.

Too many spaces and poor proofreading here, too:

                    DRIVER
          Come inside, Colonel.

EXT. THE FOOTHILLS

Che climbs down form the tallest tree in the area and joins
the group.

Also be careful to give us sluglines whenever we need them. Don't
have a block of scene description that takes us several places without adding the requisite sluglines to show us where we are. Here,
Nic walks outside and we don't get a slugline.

Nic sees a mirror nearby and walks over to it. He examines
his wounded lip and notices there are drops of blood on
his white shirt. He frowns and walks out the door. He calls

Joseph from outside.YOU NEED A NEW SLUGLINE HERE, AS HE'S
WALKED OUTSIDE THE BAR. ADD: EXT. BAR   NIGHT

A handful of missing sluglines here:

INT. XN FRAT HOUSE   DAY

Brothers sit around watching TV. Some play beer pong. Pledges
dressed in silly costumes carry on with chores. Jesse lies
in bed in his second story room.

BANGING on the door. Brothers pay little attention. Jesse looks
out the window to see chief of campus police MITCH ROCKNY
nailing a flyer to the door in Martin Luther fashion. Identical
papers cling to other frat houses.

Don't put us in the living room and then, like *I Dream of Jeannie* — *blink!* to Jesse in his room, a whole floor away. Then, blinking again, we're at the front door. Then, back up to Jesse's room, looking out his window to the cop nailing a flyer to the door, then, exhausted and confused, to other frat houses, elsewhere.

With the right sluglines, the above scene would look like:

INT. XN FRAT HOUSE - LIVING ROOM   DAY

Brothers sit around watching TV. Some play beer pong.
Pledges dressed in silly costumes carry on with chores.

INT. JESSE'S ROOM   DAY

Jesse lies in bed in his second story room.

INT. XN FRAT HOUSE - LIVING ROOM   DAY

BANGING on the door. Brothers pay little attention.

INT. JESSE'S ROOM   DAY

Jesse looks out the window to see chief of campus police
MITCH ROCKNY nailing a flyer to the door in Martin Luther
fashion.

```
EXT. VARIOUS FRAT HOUSES     DAY

Identical papers cling to other frat houses.
```

It takes up more room, but the action is clear. Endeavor to be clear.

☐ 53. You over-direct your actors!

Don't tell us everything that happens in the movie in your head. Edit.

```
She turns to the ringmaster, picks up her megaphone and
hands it to him.
```

The director tells the actors how to move. You don't. Or, the actors figure it out for themselves. Don't tell the reader that the actor turns, then reaches into his wallet for his business card, what expression is on his face, etc.

```
She hands the ringmaster her megaphone.
```

Here's some over-direction of actors. Here, too, are a pair of proofreading mistakes.

```
Kristin looks up, stares at Jean, then at her wristwatch, and
then back at Jean. She stand up, walks over to the car, and
gets in, but doesn't make any more looks towards her mother.

Jean walks to the refrigerator, pulls out a martini pitcher,
and pours herself a glass.

Jean finally walks over and looks at Allen's shoulder and
then up at his terrified, frustrated face.

Jean walks in and stands as few feet behind and to the right
of Wilson.

CNBC goes to commercial. Wilson turns around to face Jean.
```

Way too much detail here:

```
He pulls her towards him, caressing her cheek with his other
hand.

He first wraps his hands on her forearm then slides down to
her hands, cupping them, then stroking them.
```

```
                    KIM
          My father complained about the ring
          earlier.

Looking down at the ring, Thanh slides his thumb and
pointer finger over the gem.
```

This one has two sins: over direction of actors and incorrect use of a parenthetical.

```
                    LURCH
          (Lurch turns) You rang...?
```

So, while we're on the subject:

☐ 54. You use parentheticals wrong!

Don't feel rained on. Nearly every student I've ever had uses parentheticals incorrectly. Maybe I'm a lousy teacher. Be careful with them because they can cry out "Format mistake!" to the producer the instant he opens your script to check the page count.

Only use a parenthetical if the meaning of the dialogue is not already clear.

```
                    JIMMY
               (relieved)
          Whew. Thank God!
```

We know he's relieved, so you don't need to tell us twice.

```
                    JIMMY
          Whew. Thank God!
```

You need one here:

```
                    CLEO
               (loathes him)
          I love you.
```

Also, despite what you see in screenplays you buy at a bookstore or read on the Internet, you should not give action in a parenthetical.

```
                    CARUSO
               (lighting cigarette)
          I am having trouble with my tonsils.
```

You see it a lot, but you're not supposed to do it. Well, maybe a little.

A parenthetical is not a sentence. No capital letter at the start, no period at the end. What's next is wrong!

```
                    ELWOOD
              (Looks at cigarettes.)
         Gimme one, Jake.
```

Don't micromanage your "actors," because meaning and gestures should come across in dialogue. Go through your script and take out any parentheticals that tell the actors what to do. Do it now. Right now. Go on. I'll wait.

```
                    RALPHIE
              (swipes hand across brow)
         Zowee! I thought you were serious.


                    ANNE
              (shoots him a look)
         You gotta be nuts.
```

No need for parentheticals here:

```
                    MATT
              (looking around)
         Who? Where?


                    ALBERTINA
              (pointing)
         Over there, with Lucy. See?
```

Don't use the word "interrupting."

```
                    DAVID
         What time is dinner honey?


                    MAGGIE
              (interrupting)
         I want a divorce.
```

Do this, with dashes:

```
                    DAVID
         What time is dinner honey--


                    MAGGIE
         --I want a divorce.
```

Don't do this:

```
          ROBERT
     (laughs)
Oddly, I'm Robert Donn...

          CANDY
     (surprised, interrupts him)
Donnely. You're supposed to be putting
the new avionics in my plane. Is that
right?
```

Do this, with dashes:

```
          ROBERT
     (laughs)
Oddly, I'm Robert Donn--

          CANDY
     (surprised)
--Donnely. You're supposed to be putting
the new avionics in my plane. Is that
right?
```

Basically, eliminate every parenthetical you can by making the meaning clear in the dialogue. Also, the parenthetical sits on the dialogue. Not vice versa.

```
          ROBERT
That's the most amazing thing
I've ever seen in my entire life!
     (as he levitates)
```

That was wrong. Please do it right.

Generally, they need to be one line only. And not often, either. Think Tabasco — just a tad, now and then. It's tempting to tell the reader exactly how you want her to imagine your scene, but leave a little to her imagination. These are too wordy and inserted too often:

```
          FRANCIS
     (loudly, with concern
     and tenderness)
My friends, I am Brother Francis
of the Franciscan Order, and our
Lord Jesus would never be so
greedy as to demand the gift of
salvation back from us.
```

```
                    OFFICIANT
            (wincing at "Lord
            Jesus" and
            interrupting, slick)
        Brother, I no longer use that name, though
        I assure you that I am he.

                    FRANCIS
            (puzzled and with
            deepening concern)
        My friend, I am afraid that you are
        a heretic at best and a blasphemer at
        worst...

                    OFFICIANT
            (livid, but speaking
            slowly with
            authority and
            control)
        Silence! Look upon me and know
        that I am your master. Leave now
        while I punish this infidel.
```

Finally, don't use parentheticals that repeat what we already know:

```
                    ARNOLD
        Where did their money come from?

                    RITA
        Search me. Rob a gas station?
            (frustrated, yelling)
        Where the fuck did that money come
        from?!

                    ELOISE (O.S.)
            (yelling)
        Maybe they saved it, you fool.
```

Try this:

```
                    ARNOLD
        Where did their money come from?

                    RITA
        Search me. Rob a gas station?
            (frustrated)
        WHERE THE FUCK DID THAT MONEY COME FROM?!

                    ELOISE (O.S.)
        MAYBE THEY SAVED IT, YOU FOOL.
```

Parentheticals are evil Sirens, tempting you down the path of wickedness. Resist their insidious song!

Characters

☐ 55. You change character names on us!

Make sure character names stay consistent. If a woman is called Glam-Fab Woman, don't call her Skinny Glam Woman in the next chunk of scene description. If he's called Major Humphreys in scene description, call him Major Humphreys when he speaks — don't call him Hap.

```
EXT. FRANKLIN'S HOUSE     DAY

Peter's wife, GRACIE, welcomes David inside.
```

If the hero is David, and his buddy is Peter Franklin, whom everyone calls Peter, but you call it "Franklin's House" in the slugline, then you've confused the readers. Just for a moment, they misstep as they race down the lily pads floating in the swamp. Then they recover, but you've made them a little jittery.

Pick a character name and stick with it. If all his friends call him Peter, you call him Peter when he has dialogue.

```
                DAVID
        Coffee, Peter?

                PETER
        I'll have sugar with that, please.
```

Don't do this:

```
                DAVID
        Well, Peter, that sugar's finally
        gonna kill ya.

                FRANKLIN
        Not if I kill it first. Ha ha ha.
```

Horrible dialogue. My own. But, you wouldn't believe 1) how confusing this is, and 2) how many times I see this mistake.

And so, when you take us to his house, call it PETER'S HOUSE. Please.

☐ 56. Too many of your characters have names!

From page 1, your reader is trying to emotionally attach to your characters. When she meets someone named JOSEPH, she will start to learn about him and devote energy to remembering who he is. If he dies two pages after he was introduced, the reader has wasted her energy getting to know Joseph, when he should have been called NERVOUS STOCK BROKER.

Or perhaps: OBESE POLICEMAN, CALM WAITRESS, HENCHMAN, SMILING PRIEST, or, like in *Animal House*, my personal favorite set of non-name character names:

BIG DUDE

    BIGGER DUDE

        GIGANTIC DUDE

I've written a bunch of screenplays and I made this mistake in the first draft of the last adaptation I did, so don't feel bad if you do it too.

A reader can absorb about eight names. After that, they're drowning.

HALEY, FLETCHER, RILEY, CRYSTAL, BO, HANNAFORD, GYWN, DADDY are the ones I settled on, because they are the main characters. We see them a lot and need to know their names.

Stupidly, in my first draft, I also used the novel's names for (among others!) ELSA, LETCHY, MAMA HATCHEY, SPIER, GYPSY, JOY DOUGLAS, CALLEY PEARL, JUDGE GREEL, BIG BERTHA and LEAN. To keep it straight, I would have needed to hand out a *dramatis personae* to each reader. "You can't tell the players without a scorecard!" What a bonehead I was.

Eventually I woke up and smelled the coffee. I changed those names to: STORE LADY, GUY IN LEG BRACES, BBQ LADY, THE BARBER, GWYN'S SISTER, JOY THE DIVORCEE, WORTHLESS BROTHER, FLETCHER'S FATHER, CHICKEN LADY, and MAN ON SODA MACHINE.

After I got rid of so many names, someone who has *not* read the novel could read the screenplay and know what's going on. It's less confusing. You do it too!

☐ 57. Character names begin with the same letter! Or WORSE, they RHYME!

It's uncanny how many beginning writers do this. Check to make sure you're not one of them! If not, pat yourself on the back. If so, read on:

Daniel Waters, author of *Heathers*, writes down the entire alphabet and gives each character a name beginning with a different letter. So can you.

Aloysius
Bertram
Conrad
Delilah
Ethan
Fergus
Grace
Helen
Irene
Jenkinson
Klup
Lance
Mariah
Norbert
Oscar
Petunia
Quincy
Rosslyn
Stagger Lee
Terrence
Uriah
Victoire
Washington
Xavier

Yancy
Zoe (except every girl in every script these days is called Zoe!)

There must be some sort of innate muscle twitch that makes writers want to use names that are similar. I see it all the time in my students' scripts. Don't do this:

DAN
DALE
DICK
DON
DAVE

Or this:

> CHAD and CHRIS
> LENA and LYLE
> TONYA and TREVOR

Or, from a script by a friend of mine...

> GINA and GWEN

Gina is the daughter, heroine of the story. Gwen is the hated mother. I was reading along, and couldn't figure out why the despised mother had been invited to the son's house for dinner. I had to flip back and figure out that, no, Gina is the good guy and Gwen is the harridan. I was totally confused. I like to pretend that I'm not stupid, and so too does your reader. Make them feel intelligent:

Do this:

DAN
ALGERNON
FRANKIE
ZAP
SCARY CURMUDGEON

Please, please, please, oh dear Lord, don't make them rhyme:

DANNY
BILLY

```
WILLIE
CALLIE
BOBBY
ROBBY
SALLY
LENNY
VINNIE
```

Or, for pity's sake, names that are the same length:

```
TOM
BOB
TIM
JOE
SUE
PAT
ANN
```

I had one student use JEN, JON, and JESSIE in one script, in one scene, on the same page! Arggghhh!

Some writers delight in giving male names to female characters. Why do people do this!? It's a mystery. Are you *trying* to confuse us?

```
Sam. Alex. Tracy. Jesse. Sandy. Chris. Jackie. Madison.
Cary. Cameron. Stacy. Terry. Billy. Whitney. Dylan. Tyler.
Leslie. Lindsay. Ryan. Jules. Stevie. Sean. Pat. Jamie.
Meredith. Blair. Kim. Ashley. Beverly. Drew. Blake. Andy.
Bryce. Hayden. Riley. Jody. Kelly. Reese. Logan. Peyton.
Nicky. Lane. Kerry. Jo. Bret. Max. Douglass. Taylor. Etc.,
```
ad nauseam.

Even though Shirley is also a man's name, you'd never name a man *that* in your script, would you? So please, please, please don't call your main female character Alex or Sam.

```
                    MR. JANSEN
          Am I getting through to you, Mr. Biel?
```

Even people who know what they're doing make this mistake. I am currently reading the sequel to the book *The Player*, by Michael Tolkin. It has these wrenchingly confusing names:

> Lisa
> Willa
> Jessa

all of which rhyme and are the same length: one is the second wife, one is the first wife's child, and one is the second wife's child.

> June

is the first wife and mother of Jessa, which is confusing because they both are short names and both start with "J." And, finally, there are two other characters:

> Eli
> Ethan

ARGGGGHHHH. I'm halfway through the book and keep flipping to the front to see which children Griffin Mill had by which wife.

You're a writer. Be original! Think harder! Buy a baby name book. Use names from history, use the names of old football players or Formula 1 drivers or kids you were in fourth grade with. If nothing else, look at *www.imdb.com* and combine names from cast and crew lists. Check out *Harold and Maude*. Look at the amazing names! Bud Cort, Vivian Pickles, Cyril Cusack, Charles Tyner, Eric Christmas, Tom Skerritt, Gordon Devol, Harvey Brumfield, Hal Ashby, Lynn Stalmaster, Charles Mulvihill, and Buddy Joe Hooker.

Stealing from *Harold And Maude*, I came up with some pretty cool names.

```
Vivian Devol
Cyril Stalmaster
Bud Mulvihill
Gordon Tyner
Hal Cusack
Buddy Joe Christmas
Charles Pickles
Eric Skerritt
```

```
Tom Brumfield
Harvey Cort
```

Make up names like Charles Dickens did. His names help describe the characters. You can do that too!

```
Pumblechook
Sally Brass
Josiah Bounderby
Abel Magwitch
Henrietta Boffin
Jane Murdstone
Thomas Plornish
Sophie Wackles
```

Do check your character names on imdb.com to make sure they've never been used before. You're young. "George Bailey" and "Alexis Carrington" may not pop out to you, but will to the producer.

Is the reader pronouncing the name in his head the way you intend? If you've got an odd name for a character, perhaps rethink it. Peter Dubchek can be pronounced "Doobcheck" or "Dub check." Don't confuse your reader.

Remember, in cowboy movies, the good guy wears the white hat. The bad guy wears a black hat. Easy to tell them apart. Now imagine if the filmmaker had given everybody white hats? No way *you'd* make a mistake that silly. Right? Riiight.

☐ 58. You do not describe main characters with a concise, telling, two (or so) sentence character description!

Tell us a wee bit about the character we've just met. You only have one chance to talk directly to the reader about who these people are. Don't miss it.

This writer needs to tell us more about her main female character:

MURIEL REED, a grounds keeper, captivates Gary. She fills the sprayer with soda and mists brown over the grass.

Tell about their personality, their character, their foibles or flaws, but no physical details unless it's incredibly important. Like, if they're seven feet tall. Try to leave race out of it, as well as height, weight, hair color, eye color, etc. If you describe a character who could only be Jude Law, and Tom Cruise reads it (as if!) and wants to be in it, but thinks he's wrong for the part, imagine how high a building you're going to jump off!

Be as vague as vague can be about your character's age. "30s" is much better than "32." Again, always give any actor a way to be in your film.

A friend of mine was adapting a novel. The character in the novel is 52. She put that in the script. Mr. Major Actor didn't feel he could play someone who was 52. He was 47. He'd have agreed to play the role if it had said, "Late 40s." Oh well.

Study what these folks do, and do likewise. From *Good Will Hunting* by Matt Damon & Ben Affleck:

The guy holding court is CHUCKIE SULLIVAN, 20, and the largest of the bunch. He is loud, boisterous, a born entertainer. Next to him is WILL HUNTING, 20, handsome and confident, a soft-spoken leader. On Will's right sits BILLY MCBRIDE, 22, heavy, quiet, someone you definitely wouldn't want to tangle with. Finally there is MORGAN O'MALLY, 19, smaller than the other guys. Wiry and anxious, Morgan listens to Chuckie's horror stories with eager disgust.

Requiem for a Dream by Darren Aronofsky and Hubert Selby

ON THE TV -

- is Tappy Tibbons, America's favorite television personality. His charismatic personality shines for the entire world to see.

Rocky by Sylvester Stallone

In the ring are two heavyweights, one white the other black. The white fighter is ROCKY BALBOA. He is thirty years old. His face is scarred and thick around the nose... His black hair shines and hangs in his eyes. Rocky fights in a plodding,

machine-like style. The BLACK FIGHTER dances and bangs
combinations into Rocky's face with great accuracy. But the
punches do not even cause Rocky to blink... He grins at his
opponent and keeps grinding ahead.

Fight Club by Jim Uhls

TYLER has one arm around Jack's shoulder; the other hand holds
a HANDGUN with the barrel lodged in JACK'S MOUTH. Tyler is
sitting in Jack's lap. They are both sweating and disheveled,
both around 30; Tyler is blond, handsome; and Jack, brunette,
is appealing in a dry sort of way. Tyler looks at his watch.

American Beauty by Alan Ball

CAROLYN BURNHAM tends her rose bushes in front of the Burnham
house. A very well-put together woman of forty, she wears
color-coordinated gardening togs and has lots of useful and
expensive tools.

Ghostbusters by Harold Ramis & Dan Ackroyd. Nice example of "most important word at the end of the sentence":

DR. PETER VENKMAN is administering an ESP test to two student
volunteers, a boy and a girl, who sit across the table from
him separated from each other by a screen. Venkman is an
associate professor but his rumpled suit and the manic gleam
in his eyes indicate an underlying instability in his nature.
However, while a little short on academic credentials,
Venkman is long on confidence, charm and salesmanship.

This one's my favorite! This writing is FANTASTIC. What a way to introduce a character! *The Big Lebowski* by Joel & Ethan Coen:

It is late, the supermarket all but deserted. We are tracking
in on a fortyish man in Bermuda shorts and sunglasses at
the dairy case. He is the Dude. His rumpled look and relaxed
manner suggest a man in whom casualness runs deep.

Scene Description

☐ 59. You use novelistic language!

The quickest tip is the word "realize."

Seems so innocuous, that little word. Like termites, it's a sign of serious trouble — novelistic writing. Be monumentally careful not to use language that puts the reader *in the character's mind*. On the big screen, you can't see the light bulb over Teddy's head:

```
Teddy is surprised to see Freddy, and realizes he hasn't
seen him in several years.
```

(Were you confused because the names Teddy and Freddy were so similar? Ha! Now you know why readers hate it when screenwriters use names that rhyme or are spelled alike!)

In your writing, since third grade, it's been the most natural thing in the world to say, "Susan remembers with fond nostalgia the fun she had in college." It works in a short story just fine. *You can't do it in a screenplay*. In a movie, we can't sense a character's thoughts like we can in a novel. We only see what they *do* and hear what they *say*. We can't see them think! In prose, it's so easy to go into the character's mind — but don't. *If the camera can't see it, you can't write it.*

How do we *see* these two "interior thought" processes? We don't.

```
NOISE and nervous chatter from the curious guests pour from the
winery as the realization that the ring is missing sets in.
```

```
Dave realizes that Carolyn is actually Martin's love child
with Princess Queenock of the planet Zectron.
```

This is a major *bête noire* for some readers. They hate "getting inside the character's head" and will loathe your script if you do it.

"Assume" is another word that alerts you to the fact you have entered the character's head.

```
Suddenly, she turns toward the light. She assumes it's Paul.
```

Have her say, "Paul?"

You have to see it onscreen, or it doesn't exist. This is difficult to do. You must rigorously school yourself to notice when you've wandered across the line into novelistic writing. Search out "assume," "realize," "feels," "appears," and "think." Get rid of them. Find ways to *see* the action, the character, the tension, and the conflict on the page. *Show* us what is going on. *Write the scene like a silent movie.*

This is extraordinarily difficult and of colossal benefit. Force yourself to create moments that tell the reader what's going on by what the characters are *doing*, but not through dialogue. When you go back and add a smattering of dialogue, you won't need much. Eureka! Great writing! Rent *They All Laughed* and see how much the great Bogdanovich is able to get across with next to no dialogue. Or look at *The Triplets of Belleville*, which has *zero* dialogue.

But, gentle reader, do not despair.

Having put you on your guard and scared you silly about novelistic writing, let me softly whisper that it is sort of *semi*-legal to toss in a TEENSY LITTLE BIT of what characters are feeling. In *The Remains of the Day* screenplay, Emma Thompson asks about the book Anthony Hopkins is reading and we are told, "He feels threatened and she just wants to get close to him."

From time to time, you may give a wee bit of psychology for the actors. Sparingly.

Bob and Sgt. Watson exchange glances. Is their best soldier
losing his mind?

As panicked REFUGEES swirl around him, he pulls out Carter's
tape recorder. Thinks about throwing it away. Presses the
record button instead. Heartbroken.

Here's my favorite example of telling a character's emotions in
scene description. One of my students wrote it.

INT. MARK'S TAHOE

Mark is driving home as a slow love ballad plays. He speeds
down the highway, looking for anything to make him feel
anything.

Novelistic writing. Do it a little tiny bit or not at all. "Not at all"
is safer. Just like, for example, parachute jumping.

☐ 60. You poisoned your scene description with "to be"!

This is one of the most beneficial (and easiest) things you can do
to improve your writing. Even if you're not a great writer, losing
"to be" will make you look like you know what you're doing.

Mrs. Hale, my fifth grade teacher, always told me to use "active
verbs." I never had a clue what she meant. I do, however, understand how to get rid of "to be." Go through *every* line of scene
description, and if it has the verb "to be" in any form, rewrite it
so it is active.

INT. KITCHEN   DAY

The boys are eating a pile of pancakes. Syrup is all over
everything. Dottie hovers over pans of sizzling bacon, sausage,
and scrambled eggs. Jimbo is reading the sport section of the
newspaper. Kara is helping Dottie distribute breakfast to several
plates. Grant enters still sleepy.

INT. MINDY'S ROOM   DAY

Mindy is taking a shower. Water is heard running in the bathroom
in her room. Her bathroom is cracked. Christian picks up the
chair next to the bed and carries it towards Austin.

INT. JIMBO'S TRUCK   DAY

Country music is playing softly inside of Jimbo's massive cab.
Grant is sleeping in the back of the cab. Bo is finishing the
last of fast-food burger as Jimbo slurps the last of his drink.

EXT. URBAN ELEMENTARY SCHOOL   MOMENTS LATER

Jimmy and Aaron are just arriving at the playground. There is
already a group of kinds assembled in the field. There are two
captains and the rest of the boys are lined up to be selected.
There is an odd number of boys.

INT. GYM   DAY

Samantha enters.

Boofy is using the treadmill, Anna is working her calves, and
Roxanne is doing her abs.

"To be" signals the reader on page one that you aren't an experienced writer, as "to be" is one of the first things to fall away as
you climb the ladder toward becoming William Goldman.

Dave runs to his car. The bumper's being held on with duct tape.

Dave runs to his car. The bumper held on with duct tape.

Of all the items on the *Your Screenplay Sucks!* checklist, this is the simplest and has the highest power-to-weight ratio. Your writing will improve by leaps and bounds if you follow this simple rule:

Get rid of "is."

Now you know.

"Is" isn't the only worty dird in the screenwriting canon.

☐ 61. You haven't cut as many "thes" and "thats" as possible!

If a reader sees "the" all over everywhere, they're going to know you're not a top writer. Same with "that."

Type "Ctrl F" or "Apple F" and search out "the" and "that" and get rid of a lot of them. It will tighten up your writing.

```
Alex just stares down and squeezes the meat out of a crab leg.
```

```
Alex just stares down and squeezes meat out of a crab leg.
```

Here is one sentence with five instances of "the." Ugh.

```
As the boat approaches the beach, the waves start breaking
off the bow on the nearby reefs.
```

```
As the boat approaches the beach, waves start breaking off
the bow on nearby reefs.
```

Do you want me to go on? Of course you do!

```
It is their oak tree strength as a couple, the inspirational
letters from his children, and his brother's devotion that
give Claus the strength he needs for the journey ahead.
```

```
We see that Detective Able is eavesdropping.
```

> *"Substitute damn every time you're inclined to write very; your editor will delete it and the writing will be just as it should be."*
> Mark Twain

Seven Deadly Sins of Screenwriting

Using Find (Ctrl F or Apple F) in your computer, chase down these words in any form you find them. Losing them or changing them will strengthen your work.

"Find" spaceisspace should find only the word you're looking for, not every "is" in your screenplay.

is He is grinning — **becomes** — He grins.

are The convicts are singing opera — The convicts sing opera.

the Nacho hightails it out of the town — Nacho hightails it out of town.

that Ralph can't tell that she's French — Ralph can't tell she's French.

then She laughs. She then looks at Alice — She laughs. She looks at Alice.

walk Tika walks down the hall — Tika prisses down the hall.

sit Sitting at the poker table, Doc deals the cards — At the poker table, Doc deals.

stand The surgeon stands at the operating table and works — At the operating table, the surgeon works.

look Cheryl is looking at Stephanie — Cheryl studies Stephanie.

just I am just totally exhausted — I am totally exhausted.

of the Tom sits by the entrance of the mall — Tom sits by the mall entrance.

begin The tape begins playing — The tape plays.

start She starts moving toward the den — She moves toward the den.

really   Betty is really pretty — Betty, hot as a two-dollar pistol, struts in.

very   The kids sing a very old song — The kids sing a traditional song. ("very" means the following word is weak)

ly   (as on the end of an adverb!) search for **ly**space Also search for **ly.** and **ly,** as **ly**space will not find an adverb at the end of a sentence, etc. Grade school writers go wild over adverbs. You're past that now. Use them, um, sparingly. If at all.

Change these words in whatever you write and the results will be tighter and stronger.

Okay, it's 16 deadly sins. So sue me.

☐ 62. You don't put the most important word at the end of the sentence!

Simple rules for better writing: Most important word at the end of the sentence. Most important sentence at the end of the paragraph.

```
I could hear the whistle of the axe already.

I could already hear the whistle of the axe.
```

The power in a sentence comes at the end. The last word. You can feel it when the sentence is done correctly. Ooompf! It's like every joke. The punch line is at the end, and the punch word is the last word of the joke. Until you hear the last word, the joke's not funny!

Leave your reader leaning forward in anticipation until the very... last... word — that's where the punch comes. Here's the first draft:

```
            MR. FITZBIGGON
    Well. That's all. You may expect swift
    litigation on behalf of the airline.
```

Now, rewrite it.

```
                MR. FITZBIGGON
        Well. That's all. On behalf of the
        airline, you may expect swift litigation.
```

This story had a recent run on the Internet. Notice how you don't know what's going to happen, literally until the very last word. You're wondering where the story's headed, anticipating the finish, and then they give you the *socko* rocket boost!

> Due to inherit a fortune when his sickly, widower father dies, Robert decided he needed a woman to enjoy it with. So he went to a singles bar and he searched until he spotted a woman whose beauty took his breath away. "Right now, I'm just an ordinary man," he said, walking up to her, "but within a month or two, my father will pass on. Then I will inherit over 20 million dollars." The woman went home with Robert, and four days later she became his stepmother.

If you have a friend who can't tell a joke, it's not because he or she can't tell a joke, it's because they can't remember the punch line. And it's most likely because they can't remember the word *order* in the punch line.

An off-color joke illustrates this point:

> What are the three stages of marital intercourse?
> Whole house sex. Bedroom sex. And hallway sex.
> Hallway sex is where you bump into each other and say, "Fuck you."

Okay, it's not the greatest joke on earth, but if you mess up the punch line it's not funny at all. Once, a friend came up, busting to lay one on me:

> "Didja hear, didja hear about the three stages of marital intercourse?!"
> "No, tell me."
> "Well, there's whole house sex, and there's bedroom sex and then there's hallway sex." Dramatic pause. "Hallway sex is where you say 'Fuck you' when you bump into each other."

It lay there like a dead dog in the sun and now I don't return his calls.

☐ 63. You describe dialogue in scene description!

If someone is talking, unless it's background walla, write the dialogue.

```
One boy grabs the Bully by the neck and head butts him,
bloodying his nose. The Bully starts crying for them to stop.
```

You have to write the Bully's dialogue.

This is background walla. It's okay in description:

```
The RIOTERS surge toward the factory gates, YOWLING and
SCREECHING at the scabs.
```

This is not walla. Buckle down and write her dialogue.

```
The Bratty Goth Kid won't stop dishing some lip.
```

Don't do this, either (and while you're at it, run your spell-check!):

```
Two nine-year-old twin boys, AUSTIN and CHRISTIAN, rush in
the kitchen like whirrling dervishes. Dottie stops them and
tells them to bring the tenderloin into the dining room.
```

If an actor is going to say it, write the dialogue.

```
A policeman comes into the commotion. It's Leo dressed as a
beat cop. Dale calls Leo over to inspect the contents of a
blue suitcase. Dale holds up bags of heroin.
```

Rewritten, this becomes:

```
A policeman comes into the commotion. It's Leo dressed as a
beat cop.

                         DALE
           Leo! Get a load of this blue suitcase!

Dale holds up bags of heroin.
```

The writer could have written "Dale waves Leo over to inspect the contents of a blue suitcase," and it would have been fine. No dialogue would have been implied.

This is a combination of "don't put dialogue in scene description," and "don't tell us in scene description and then again in dialogue."

```
BLACK CONTINUES... GREGORIAN CHANT... Flaming words begin
writing themselves across screen. A MAN'S VOICE with a French
Accent begins speaking, as if reading them.

                    THERON (V.O.)
          October 4, 1677. The memoirs of Theron,
          nephew of Innocent VII, Chapter Four:
          Concerning St. Francis of Assisi.
```

Cut the last sentence of scene description. Put (French accent) in a parenthetical and press on. Finally, change "VII" to a word an actor can say.

```
BLACK CONTINUES... GREGORIAN CHANT... Flaming words begin
writing themselves across screen... a MAN'S VOICE reads them.

                    THERON (V.O.)
                  (French accent)
          October 4, 1677. The memoirs of Theron,
          nephew of Innocent the Seventh, Chapter
          Four: Concerning St. Francis of Assisi.
```

☐ 64. You have not paid attention to image order in scene description!

As someone reads your scene description, they create images in their mind. Image after image pops into their head, telling your story — *in the order that they read it*. You have to give it to them in the right order, or they won't see it the way you imagine.

Here's an example of confusing image order: "During the American Revolution, Andrew Jackson was captured and wounded by British soldiers." Does that mean they grabbed him, handcuffed him, and *then* shot him? Probably not.

```
Laura and Dutch race monster trucks at a video arcade.
```

Here's how it appears in the reader's mind as he moves image by image through the sentence:

Laura and Dutch race monster trucks WOW, WHEN DID LAURA AND
HER GRANDPA BUY MONSTER TRUCKS?! I THOUGHT THEY ONLY RACED
HORSES... OH, WAIT, NOW I SEE... at a video arcade. I GET
IT. FINALLY. OOPSIE.

Say it this way:

At a video arcade, Laura and Dutch race monster trucks.

I think about the reader, standing beside the camera, their feet on
the edge of the frame, watching the story unfold, image after image.

THE STREET

Frantic Vietnamese drop from the struts as the Huey reaches
treetop height.

The first image is of Vietnamese dropping from helicopter struts.
But we don't know anything that allows us to place that image in
context. After rearranging, it makes better sense.

THE STREET

As the Huey reaches treetop height, frantic Vietnamese drop
from the struts.

If we don't know a helicopter has reached treetop height, it's confusing to prematurely talk about people dropping from the struts.

The best way to unearth this problem is to read your work out loud!

This counts in sluglines too. Tell us what we need to know as we
need to see it. Here's a mistake I made.

Original slugline:

EXT. CHAOTIC STREET - XUAN LOC ("SWAN LOCK")   NIGHT

REFUGEES stream past. The CREW rapidly sets up, The reporter,
ELLEN, exuberant, healthy, in her thirties, is a total pro.
One crew member, TU, is a young Vietnamese man.

And a slugline on the same page:

EXT. U.S. MARINE - SAIGON   AFTERNOON

A young black MARINE GUARD looks out unblinking from under
his white cap. He sweats with the heat.

Uhh, stupid.

I should have had the wide shot first, then the close up. Tell us we're in Xuan Loc and then say it's a crowded street. Tell us we're in Saigon, *then* tell us we're looking at a Marine.

```
EXT. XUAN LOC ("SWAN LOCK") - CHAOTIC STREET    NIGHT

REFUGEES stream past. The CREW rapidly sets up, The reporter,
ELLEN, exuberant, healthy, in her thirties, is a total pro.
One crew member, TU, is a young Vietnamese man.
```

And, on the same page:

```
EXT. SAIGON - U.S. MARINE      AFTERNOON

A young black MARINE GUARD looks out unblinking from under
his white cap. He sweats with the heat.
```

Makes more sense this way, and every little bit helps.

Remember, scene description is *only what the camera sees*. Don't say "a manila envelope filled with a stack of papers" until he opens it and you reveal to the camera that it's a stack of papers. You can say "a bulging envelope," but you can't tell us what's inside unless the camera can see it.

Here is an example of incorrect image order:

```
EXT. SIDEWALK     DAY

American Gothic-like Gary and the SOD SQUAD are on a billboard
reading, "Got Grass? Grassguru.com".
```

Interesting writing problem here. When you re-read what you have written, you have to keep the readers in mind. The first words they see will be the first picture they put in their head. "American Gothic-like, Gary" makes me imagine that Gary is standing up straight on the sidewalk with a pitchfork. Then I see the words "sod squad." I am thinking he is standing next to a bunch of people, all of them on the sidewalk. Then, and only then, do I see the word "billboard." Suddenly, I have to rearrange the picture in my mind. This is confusing. You must be aware of the picture you're creating for the reader. The reader can only get information in the order you give it.

```
EXT. SIDEWALK    DAY

High above them, on a billboard, Gary and the SOD SQUAD,
American Gothic-like. "Got Grass? Grassguru.com."
```

Final example:

```
The stake hits the rock floor as Francis rolls out of the way.
```

Francis has to roll out of the way FIRST. Then the stake can hit the floor. Don't make us imagine the stake hitting the floor and then try to conjure up Francis rolling out of its path. If it's hit the floor, why does he have to roll anywhere?

Image order. It matters!

Again, and not for the last time, read your stuff out loud!

☐ 65. You haven't cut scene description to the bone!

If screenwriting is closer to poetry than it is to novel writing (it is), then great screenwriting is next door to haiku. Your new personal deity should be Walter Hill, the Zen master of "less is more" in the words-on-the-page department. He wrote *Hard Times*, *48 Hrs*, and a goodly chunk of *Alien*.

Here's my stab at the Walter Hill style. Almost no words. Everybody can take a giant step in this minimalist direction.

```
ANGLE ON PARKED CAR

Dark interior.

A cigarette glows.

Safe and quiet, Bake Martucci smiles.

In the back seat, Mutt Masso.

Mutt gives a paper sack to a SKINNY BLACK MAN.
```

EXT. CEMETERY   DAY

Potter's Field. Pathetic.

PREACHER and MOURNERS sing a Baptist HYMN.

T-Money's FAMILY. His mom cries.

Vanessa with Isley. Isley's real hurt.

N.O.D. looks on, sad, but disgusted.

Kids wearing tee shirts with T-Money's face.

In b.g., WHITE POLITICO oozes for a TV camera.

The hymn grinds to a close.

                    PREACHER
          Let us now take a moment to remember all of
          our family members who are in jail.

Isley catches N.O.D.'s eye.

Everyone prays.

EXT. CANAL STREET   DAY

Bus pulls up.

Isley gets off. Careworn.

EXT. BROADMOOR - SMALL HOUSE   DAY

Tidy house, lawn.

Isley picks up the paper and mail.

Pit bull spots Isley. Alert.

Isley stops.

Showdown.

Pit bull steps forward, fierce... then wags his butt off.

                    ISLEY
          Hey, Zulu. You lookin' after my momma,
          girl?

Isley is licked to death.

Choose your words with extreme care and use only the exact precise ones. Imagine your pencil weighs 50 pounds, and be reluctant to use it. It's not as easy as it looks, but it's well worth trying.

If you read the *Alien* screenplay at *www.script-o-rama.com* and watch the DVD at the same time, it's fascinating how the script is EXACTLY like the movie, but with few words. This is the ideal page for the Hollywood reader. Clear action in his head and almost no words!

Terse is good. Blabby is, well, doom.

When you go to a new location, introduce it with a slugline and a bit of scene description, and then get on with it. Do not go into lengthy, dense, interior decoration–laden detail. That's for novelists. Create an image in our mind and press on. This is my all time favorite scene description:

```
INT. BOB'S APARTMENT    NIGHT

A shitty room.
```

It makes an instant picture for the reader. Your picture and my picture will not be the same, but more or less, *we get it.* And we get it economically. I don't remember where I read that the first time, but I wish I'd written it.

If, however, there is something they *must* know, you have to tell them.

```
INT. BOB'S APARTMENT    NIGHT

A shitty room. Behind the sofa, nine HUNGRY MARTIANS.
```

Five lines of scene description, per paragraph, maximum. Four is better. Childish, isn't it? So is Hollywood. Scene description paragraphs in *Cinderella Man* by Cliff Hollingsworth and Akiva Goldsman are *two lines long.* Never more. Boy, is that a quick read!

Long paragraphs make us miss the important stuff. Also, and worse, readers tend to skip them.

```
There are other chairs in the room, but Conner sits alone. He
types on the computer with a pile of papers in his lap for
filing. He looks out the window at PEOPLE relaxing on the lawn.
Couples, some of them sleeping. He sighs. The humdrum of his
life. His phone RINGS, he answers with an enthusiastic smile.
```

That's a lot of description. First time I read it, I missed the part about his phone ringing. Bust up paragraphs into shorter chunks that have their own meaning. The first paragraph becomes about the world of his ratty office. The second paragraph moves the story forward by discussing something completely different. As it's crucial for us to understand that the phone rings, give it its own paragraph.

```
There are other chairs in the room, but Conner sits alone. He
types on the computer with a pile of papers in his lap for
filing. He looks out the window at PEOPLE relaxing on the lawn.
Couples, some of them sleeping. He sighs. The humdrum of his
life.

His phone RINGS, he answers with an enthusiastic smile.
```

See, isn't that better? Sadly, it's longer, but we live in an imperfect world.

Your scene description must convey the meaning you want with as few words as possible.

```
In his rearview mirror, Jimmy sees a cop car, lights blazing,
right behind him.

Jimmy sees a cop car, lights blazing, in his rearview.
```

We still get it. It's quicker. We see a better image that takes less time to read. Here's a first draft sentence.

```
The lawn has beer bottles and a rolled up "Slip n' Slide"
scattered about.
```

This becomes:

```
Beer bottles and a rolled up "Slip n' Slide" scattered about
the lawn.
```

A stronger sentence. Ends on a better word, and, hey!, it's shorter! The third draft improves it even more:

```
Scattered about the lawn... beer bottles and a rolled up "Slip
n' Slide."
```

Cut for the speed of the read as well as the reader's understanding of what you're trying to get across. Don't hide the meaning of your image by piling on tons of words. You're no longer an English major, getting paid by the pound. Think minimalism. Remember, unless the reader is your boyfriend, he doesn't really want to read your material in the first place, so make it as painless as possible. White space on the page = reader keeps going.

Have you saved a line as often as you can?

```
Jimmy slows down and pulls one lane to the right. The cop
speeds by.
```

```
Jimmy slows and pulls over. The cop speeds by.
```

Remembering the reader, make the entire script as tight as possible, and, remember your page count. Go through the entire script and see if you can pull up one or two words and save a line.

```
                    SERENA
          I've met your mother; she
          doesn't really seem like the
          type.


                    CONNER
          She knows her views are not
          welcome in the mainstream,
          bourgeois society. She fears
          reprisals.
```

You can cheat with Final Draft, pull up that last word, and save a line! Yee ha!

Put the cursor at "she" and click and hold on the little home-plate-shaped-thing at the top of the page. A vertical line will appear. Slide it to the right. The margin for that chunk of dialogue will widen. Move up "welcome" and you save a line. It's only stretched one space past the actual margin, and no one will notice. But you, clever chap, saved a line! Wheeee. Do it again for the next side of dialogue.

> SERENA
> I've met your mother; she doesn't
> really seem like the type.

> CONNER
> She knows her views are not welcome
> in the mainstream, bourgeois
> society. She fears reprisals.

Save a line 55 times and you save a page! Pathetic, I know, but this is the career you've chosen.

Lucy frowns, packs the sliced fruit pieces, heads down hallway.

> SECURITY OFFICER
> It's okay. He likes things sliced
> up.

It also works for scene description. Pull the margins over and no one will notice — yee ha!

Lucy frowns, re-packs the sliced up fruit pieces, heads down hallway.

> SECURITY OFFICER
> It's okay. He likes things sliced up.

Why cut "in her power?" Because, if Dr. Forstman can do it at all, it's in her power! Don't be redundant.

From here on in, Dr. Forstman will do anything in her power to obstruct Walter.

From here on in, Dr. Forstman will do anything to obstruct Walter.

And don't tell us the same thing twice (ha!).

She heaves: throwing up in Sean's lap.

She heaves in Sean's lap.

"Failing" means "failing to perform."

```
Just when it looks like it will work the computer fails to
perform.
```

```
Just when it appears to work, the computer fails.
```

This one is interesting. Can you guess why I added the "as" between the two sentences? It has to do with clarity of meaning and the image the language creates. This is picky, picky stuff, but you're asking for tons of money, so you'd best be a nitpicker to the extreme. Why is the "as" there?

```
Ten tons of rubble collapse. Walter and his team claw their
way to the surface, but the crucial artifacts are smashed to
powder.
```

```
Ten tons of rubble collapse as Walter and his team claw their
way to the surface, but the crucial artifacts are smashed to
powder.
```

I only found this on about the fifth read, but it's still wrong. If the ceiling collapses, it will to smash Walter and his team to smithereens. How can he climb if he's squished? Putting the "as" there makes the two actions, ceiling falling and Walter climbing the ladder, *simultaneous*. If they're happening at the same time, Indiana Jones makes it to the top without dying! Picky, yes. True, also yes.

So, shorter is generally better.

```
We begin to hear the sounds of a man and woman making love.
We begin to hear a man and woman making love.
We begin to hear lovemaking.
We hear lovemaking.
```

```
A CLICK is heard.
CLICK.
```

```
Sam eats his eggs like a total PIG. He stuffs his face and
slurps his coffee.
Sam eats like a total PIG. He slurps his coffee.
```

```
He is instantly alert. He asks what is going on.
He is instantly alert, asks what is going on.
Instantly alert, he asks what is going on.
```

Here's another one where you have to read it a bunch of times to find the problem, but your reader may trip over it on his first try!

```
Mr. Peterson knows someday he's got to hand the reins over to
Gavin, but giving up control tears him apart.
```

```
Mr. Peterson knows someday he's got to hand the reins over to
Gavin, but giving up control rips him apart.
```

The word "tears" can be pronounced two ways. Like tearing something in half, but also like tears trickling down a cheek. I changed it to "rips" to avoid the slightest hint of the possibility of confusion.

This one's obvious! You're getting the hang of it now!

```
No one will change their vote and no one knows which one is
the one who abstained.
```

```
No one will change their vote and no one knows who abstained.
```

It can get to be a mania. Shorter, clearer, swifter is BETTER. Tape this to your monitor: *Length. Abhor it.*

Readers and producers and directors actually care about this stuff. If your description impresses them as someone who understands good writing, it will make your writing stand out from the pack and glorious, golden doors will open for you. Make your scene description sing!

Make the prose as vivid as possible. Spielberg did, in *Close Encounters of the Third Kind*:

```
The truck swapped paint with the fencepost.
```

Show us, don't tell us! Use words to create exciting images. Don't be boring. Don't be so creative the reader is confused, but make each scene a little movie for the reader — and make it a good one!

190

Never tell us something we do not absolutely *have* to know. If you *can* cut it, it's gone. Move the story forward or die. No idle banter. No cute use of language.

Here's some nice scene description. No fat. Good images.

```
Benji tosses the ball into a slimy dumpster. The Winnebago
rolls off, leaving the boy in a cloud of soot.

CARMINE "THE EAR" DiBENEDETTO (70) steps out. Spry as a fox
and tough as a buzzard's beak, there's something off-kilter
about the guy. Maybe it's his '70s leisure suit. Maybe it's
because his right ear is much bigger than his left.

Benji spits, then frantically tidies the trailer, tossing
dirty clothes into the bathroom. He opens the front door.

The Hippie Chick walks over and French kisses Sam, blowing
pot smoke into his mouth. Sam holds the smoke and smiles.

She grabs him in a bone-crunching bear hug. Mukesh whimpers.
```

Be clear:

```
                    DAVE
          He was here every other night.
```

What do you mean? He was here every night, but the night of the murder, or he visited regularly, every two nights?

Don't say "the" something if we've not seen that something yet. "The walking track encircles the police station" should be "A walking track." After we've seen it the first time, you can say "the."

Don't use (beat) unless it's CRITICAL! Your idea of timing and Russell Crowe's may be different. Go through your script and take them out.

Don't use the word "walk." If at all possible: shamble, shuffle, strut, oil, stroll, hurry, amble, cut, move, dash, meander, glide, ease. Get your scene description to make a useful image in the reader's mind. Here's some first-draft writing:

```
Susanna enters the room.
```

Give us more! Tell us about her character and emotions by showing how she walks.

```
Susanna breezes into the room.
Susanna oozes into the room.
Susanna marches into the room.
Susanna flounces into the room.
Susanna slinks into the room.
Susanna grumps into the room.
```

What's wrong here?

```
On last seat sits a pretty YOUNG GIRL - 20s, straggly
blonde hair. Her head rests wearily on the window glass,
dozing off.
```

Don't be redundant. We know the window is glass. Also, proofreading is a jolly idea.

```
On the last seat sits a pretty YOUNG GIRL - 20s, straggly
blonde hair. Her head rests wearily on the window, dozing
off.
```

Be clear. The window is not dozing off, nor is her head.

```
On last seat sits a pretty YOUNG GIRL - 20s, straggly blonde
hair. Her head rests wearily on the window. She dozes off.
```

You can also lose the word "sits." If it's a seat, we assume she's
sitting.

```
Last seat, a pretty YOUNG GIRL - 20s, straggly blonde hair.
Her head rests wearily on the window. She dozes off.
```

If she's young, don't tell her age. You also save an entire line!
Whoopee!

```
Last seat, a pretty YOUNG GIRL, straggly blonde hair. Her
head rests wearily on the window. She dozes off.
```

I repeat: Don't tell us anything we don't have to know. Here's a
first draft:

```
EXT. NORMAN ROAD - JUST BEFORE SUNRISE

Theron makes camp, unburdening and picketing his horse,
spreading a bedroll and lying down.
```

```
EXT. THERON'S CAMP - DAY
```

```
A small WEASEL rummages through Theron's packs, which have
been carelessly tossed aside. It rummages through the
wineskins. Theron snores a short distance away.
```

```
EXT. THERON'S CAMP - EARLY EVENING
```

```
Theron awakes, and begins getting his gear together for the
next night's travel. He finds his wineskins strewn about,
chewed to bits, with dried blood covering all. He curses and
rummages through the mess, finally finding one last undamaged
skin. He signs and uncorks it, drinks blood from it.
```

What happens in the above scenes is interesting, and compelling. But the meat of the scene is hidden by stuff the writer doesn't have to have. After the trims:

```
EXT. NORMAN ROAD - JUST BEFORE SUNRISE
```

```
Theron makes camp.
```

```
EXT. THERON'S CAMP - DAY
```

```
A WEASEL rummages through Theron's packs. He snores a short
distance away.
```

```
EXT. THERON'S CAMP - EARLY EVENING
```

```
Theron awakes, and finds his wineskins chewed to bits, with
dried blood covering all. He curses and finally finds one
undamaged skin. He drinks blood from it.
```

Compare the two. What was lost in nuance is made up for in speed, length, and clarity. Try to figure out why I cut what I cut. Did I go too far? Sometimes I do.

Check out this doozy — it desperately cried out to be broken into short, intense paragraphs. When the writer finished his rewrite, his page *should* have looked like this, all cuddly and reader friendly:

```
HRE. KTSDMFSDLL SSI
```

```
Olk sroir djdjs enn jfjskjjdskj lksk ekslks qeuruhs edj jedjs
smd. Slkdlsk mcx, mcskhedfdlka sdlds sdkjds skjdks ejeiogtl
dk kkzs jkmxlk ddj flflroeiu djd jjsja vmfndn sllslsss.
```

Yiyiy fjfjd fk wwir fngnfh ssss, ktjrh ssbxvs gkhkk dkdkkcjcj
kg, cmcmcc. Fjdjs ssik dssgsgs yuigmkinecxct. Xtdxd drd r
rxr rx.

Uskekss secttctc in ininin n I ni mojin plmohtf. Seazxrc knm
mtcrsx kmijx ftx.

Instead, he submitted:

EXT. AUDITORIUM DAY

On a saggy sofa just outside the auditorium doors are Jeff
and Sally. Sally is a quiet nerdy thing while Jeff is more
goth-weird. He wears a grubby jacket that no one can stand,
but he's not a stoner. Obviously from their dress, neither
would be popular in a normal high school. Both are sharing
a drippy hamburger. Jeff sips a diet Coke while Sally is
drinking a Perrier. It is boiling hot today, so it's a good
thing for them, the sofa is under some trees which provide
shade. A silent moment between them. Sally sees that Jeff
is staring blankly into space.

If you did this in an early draft, it's all right, because it's not too
late to fix it. So, fix it. Welcome to…

Rewriting

☐ 66. Don't repeat! Anything! *Ever!*

Rewrite like Jack Sparrow! Cut, slash, gouge, trim, hack away the putrid parts!

> *"I write it. I read it. If it sounds like writing, I rewrite it."*
> Elmore Leonard

What's wrong with this?

```
INT. MR. FITZGIBBON'S OFFICE - DAY

A plush office. Sweeping views of the city through floor-to-
ceiling glass windows.
```

We know windows are made of glass. Don't tell us ANYthing we already know. Ever, ever, ever. Sometimes it's hard to realize we already know stuff. That's why you read your work out loud.

```
All listen intently except Cam. He grows restless. Shifts
noticeably.

Matthew falls to the floor with an expressionless face.

Matthew falls to the floor, expressionless.
```

If something is understood in the story don't repeat it. In other words, don't tell us what we already know. Don't be redundant. Be sure not to say the same thing twice. Always be on your best behavior not to tell us something that we already know. If it's something that the audience previously understands to be true, always be on your best behavior and remind yourself not to tell us something that we already are aware of.

Ha ha. Get it?

```
Austin and Christian squint their eyes as if summing up Mindy.

They hug. Alice gets in the back seat of the cab and drives
off.

Melody rushes out of her office.
```

The simplest example of this is if someone's asleep in the bed, just tell us that he's asleep. This guy's in a hospital:

```
Louie's sleeping in bed, hooked up to a ventilator.

Louie's sleeping, hooked to a ventilator.
```

Or this one:

```
He looks at the clock on the wall.
```

You don't need to know the clock is on the wall, because most clocks are on walls. If a girl dives into a swimming pool, then we know until she gets *out* of the pool that she's *in* the pool, so don't tell us for the rest of the scene that she's in the pool. Don't say "she swims across the pool." Be entertaining. Say "she splashes to the deep end."

```
He looks at Stephanie with a huge grin on his face.

He looks at Stephanie with a huge grin.
```

No one grins with their elbow. You could trim it one more time, of course.

```
He grins at Stephanie.
```

If the characters just heard a big KERANK KERANK noise:

```
                    TRAVIS
          Yeah! What?

                    KARA
          That was Grant's car. I know that noise.
```

Don't repeat noticeable words in the same neighborhood. Don't mention a girl's "toned physique" twice on a page. This writer also left out a period:

EXT. BEACH   DAWN

SHOT of the back of MADISON (MAD) GREENSPUN'S toned physique running.

SHOT of sunrise

INT. BATHROOM   DAY

Body hops out of shower and towels off.

INT. KITCHEN   DAY

Wheat bread pops from the toaster. Hand spreads jelly onto it.

EXT. PARKING LOT   DAY

Mad pulls up in a 1974 brown Chevy pick-up. She parallel parks in an obviously tight spot, bumping the car in front and behind her in order to fit.

She hops out of her car, grabs her backpack, a brown lunch bag, and a bouquet of sunflowers from below the passenger seat.

Her petite, toned physique sports scrubs and black converse. She starts towards the hospital and turns back towards her truck.

Don't use the same word often:

Kate turns around and begins marking points on the map with a large red marker.

Then two lines later, don't say this:

She pulls out a different marker and begins marking the old murder sites.

Readers notice this stuff. They won't hire you if they think you're lazy. Once you tell us a girl's hot, stop.

A hand taps Mark on the shoulder. He turns. Standing there is ALICIA SASSY, a 23 year-old Barbie doll with ~~platinum blonde hair, a Playboy centerfold rack, and~~ curves Beyonce envies.

Don't repeat information you just told us in the slugline:

```
INT. ST. JAMES INFIRMARY     DAY

Inside of the St. James Infirmary.
```

```
INT. FERRARI - MORNING

Dunn has slowed ~~the car~~ to normal driving speed.
```

Don't tell us something in description and again in dialogue.

```
INT. STAGE RIGHT / BENEFIT - NIGHT

Various performances take place throughout the production
as Eve and Rudy look on from backstage. Finally, it is time
for the finale.

                    EVE
          It's time for the finale.
```

Or here:

```
INT. BAR TV     NIGHT

The story about David finding the kidnapped boy is still on
the TV. ~~The evening news is retelling it~~.

                    NEWS REPORTER:
          the kidnapper's, reputed to be the Hedges
          gang, got away after DAVID, a local man,
          saw the child at the mall and intervened.
```

While you're at it, find the grammar mistakes that writer made in the above dialogue. I found two. Plus two format errors.

Don't tell us something twice in dialogue, either. Everyone who works at the hospital already knows about the intercom girl.

```
                    RECEPTIONIST
          Wait a sec, you're the intercom girl?
          ~~The one who spoke every morning over the~~
          ~~intercom~~.
```

"It's" is used wrong. Also, "the table" is here twice:

```
INT. PETE AND SAM'S

The Italian restaurant appears lifted straight out of the
Godfather. It's atmosphere is dark, it's food is old school
Italian, and all there are regular customers. The mood is
jubilant. The table in the corner is not.

At a small table in the corner sits MARK and MR. BRIDGERS.
```

Not repeating is quicker and cleaner. Do it!

☐ 67. You rewrite while you write!

Do not, while you're writing your first draft, go back and rewrite what you've written. This is the Big Blue Screen of Death.

At the end of each writing session, print the pages you did that day, stack them on the pages you did yesterday and go have a drink or take a walk or read a magazine.

Next time you sit down to write (the very *next* day!), read the pages you wrote the day before, make a few notes about things you might want to change, and begin writing today's pages. Do not read the day-before-yesterday's pages. Do not look back to the beginning. If you rewrite now, YOU WILL NEVER FINISH YOUR SCREENPLAY!

Going back will reveal hitherto unseen problems. Going back will jack up your angst. Because your script will be revealed to be inadequate, imperfect, and not Zaillian-esque, going back tends to be monumentally depressing. So depressing that you may just decide it's better to — give up and *start another script*. Do not play into this sucker's game.

Write every day. Add to that slim pile of pages. After a couple of weeks, it will be a less-slim pile of pages. A month into it, your pile will be quite impressive. You have a lot to be proud of. Keep writing. When you finish your first pass, go have two drinks.

Take some time off. From that story, not from writing. Noodle around a few ideas. Work on a character for your next script.

Pound on an outline. After some time off, the script will be cold in your mind. Come back to your screenplay fresh, happy you have finished a 110-page opus. *Now*, now that you have a draft, it's time to rewrite.

But not before. Trust me on this.

☐ 68. You do a rewrite by reading the whole script at once!

Ixnay. Eathday.

You say, "What do you mean, don't read the whole script? How else can you do it?"

If you grab a red pen and say, "Hey, time for a rewrite. I think I'll sit down with some strong coffee and churn through this puppy," you are in deep quicksand. Don't just read the script from top to bottom; go in there like laser surgery. I mean, you *can* read the script from start to finish, and it's a good idea to do now and again, but I heartily recommend you have *a specific agenda for each read-through*.

I imagine a script as a nine-foot wad of chewing gum, floating in front of me, like a gooey pink planet. If you try to see the whole thing at once, it's impossible. But if you take a core sample, you can study that small part and actually understand what you're looking at. If you read with a laser scalpel instead of a blunderbuss, each read will serve you better.

A few examples:

Read it to look at *only* the murder mystery detective story (or the _____ aspect to the plot, whatever). If it's hard for you not to think about the rest of the script while you're checking out the murder plot, print those specific pages. Read and rework that 15-page stack, over and over and over until you're happy that slice of your story tracks as smooth as ice on ice. Then stick those pages back in and do another laser-beam read.

Check out the love story between your two main characters. All the Bob and Carol scenes. Just the Bob and Carol scenes. You'll get a fantastic idea what's going on in *that* part of your story and mistakes will leap out at you. Like rats on fire, they'll leap out at you. Later, study only the Ted and Alice scenes. Then, Bob and Alice, and then Carol and Ted. You'll be amazed what you find: like, for example, that Alice vanishes from the script for 30 pages and you had no idea!

Read just the sluglines. Are they doing for you what you want them to?

Go through the script and check for logic flaws.

Read it to check out Parson Elton Smithers' dialogue. (By the way, this is true for *every* character's dialogue.) Does he talk exactly like he's supposed to *the whole way through*? Does he ever sound English when he's supposed to be Scottish? Does he always sound like he's nearly 100 years old? Does he ever say things that he might not actually say, like "Yo, bro, where's my Escalade?"

Read it one time for typos and proofreading errors. Not story, just spelling.

Read just to check on emotion in each scene. Is it where you want it?

Read only scene description, no dialogue. Is it smooth? Have you gotten rid of "to be" in all its nasty little variations? Is the image order correct? Have you cut every single possible word? Did you go through the *Seven Deadly Sins of Screenwriting* and massage your scene description until it glows? Is your scene description witty and interesting? Have you broken it into short paragraphs?

Go through the script to check that every DAY and NIGHT is consistent and tracks correctly.

> *"Et cetera, et cetera, et cetera!"*
> King of Siam, in *The King and I*

The laser-beam read is a helpful tool, as these little parts add up to a unified whole and any flawed piece can be a real problem when they get around to making your film. However; if you don't *care* if anyone will actually make your movie because you're only writing the script so you can get with your writing partner to cheat on your spouse, heck, skip this whole step.

I am glad you bought the book, though. Nice touch.

☐ 69. You don't have a killer first page!

A reader can tell if you know what you're doing by reading about half a page. If your stuff is really great or really awful, he can probably tell at the end of the first sentence. For sure, the reader will know if you can write by the end of the first page.

That's sort of depressing, isn't it?

Or, exhilarating. Because, if you have a swell first page, you're going to launch them into page two, then five, and ten and thirty and whoooooooosh, like an otter on a mudslide, straight to page 110! All it takes is one great page! What could be easier?!

Things to think about on page one:

As little dialogue as possible. This is the only chance you have to set a mood, so take your time and do a little actual writing here. Tell us where we are. Tell us what it feels like. Tell us what it looks like. Give us a sense of the world.

Do we meet either the good guy or the bad guy?
Do we get a sense of the place, time period, and genre?
If you've got typos or grammar mistakes, you're dead.
If you use "to be" more than just a teeny bit, you're dead.

A reader's antennae are out, alert for signs that your writing is anything but stellar. The reader and, later on, the actor, is praying you know what you're doing. All you have to do is keep him on the lily pads and you have no worries.

Have you hooked the reader? Is there something on page 1 that will force them to turn to page 2? Check out the opening of *Love Story*. A guy is sitting by himself on a cold day. In V.O., he says, "What do you say about a girl who died." That's a grabber.

Are FADE IN and FADE OUT in the right place? Nothing advertises that you don't know what you're doing like this whopper, and on the very top of the very first page, no less.

FADE IN.

INT. CAR WASH   DAY

Bob's Car Wash is beloved by all who live in Perriwinkle Falls.

It's supposed to be like this. Notice that FADE IN: has a colon after it.

FADE IN:

INT. CAR WASH   DAY

Bob's Car Wash is beloved by all who live in Perriwinkle Falls.

Also take a gander at the fact that FADE IN: has one space underneath it. If you're like me and you have two spaces above every slugline (or "Scene Heading" in Final Draft) then you'll need to adjust the very first slugline so FADE IN: only has one space below it.

Do this, in Final Draft, by putting your cursor to the left of the very first slugline. Click Format / Elements / Scene Heading / Paragraph / Space Before / 1

It should look like this:

FADE IN:

EXT. COLD DARKNESS OF OUTER SPACE   ETERNAL NIGHT

CAROL HACKENSACKER, a great looking housewife and astronaut, files her fingernails while on a thrilling spacewalk.

Not like this:

```
FADE IN:


INT. STURBRIDGE FAMILY KITCHEN      DAY

A calico cat walks daintily through the debris of last night's
argument and plate-throwing contest.
```

This is also true after optical effects. Not like this:

```
                                              DISSOLVE TO:



INT. YOAKUM BEDROOM      NIGHT

The young married couple has unenthusiastic sex. It's painful
to watch. What a waste.
```

One space above a slugline after an optical effect (which Final Draft calls a Transition.) Like this:

```
                                              DISSOLVE TO:

INT. CIRCUS TENT      NIGHT

Timmy, laughing, jerks his mom's sleeve, points out the clown
with no pants.
```

Of course, what you do with FADE OUT doesn't matter so much. By then they've decided to buy your screenplay, give you a limo and a driver, and pay for your kids to go to college. Some people put a period after FADE OUT. Some put nothing. But, because the story is not beginning here, no colon.

FADE IN: goes on the left margin, because that's where your eye is when you start reading. FADE OUT is on the right margin because that's where your eye is when you finish reading.

```
FADE IN:


                                              FADE OUT.
```

If you buy screenplays or see them on the Internet, they often have scene numbers, little numbers in the margins, right beside the sluglines.

51   **EXT. BRIDGE - FROM HIGH ABOVE   DUSK**   51

The van stops, doors open. Several THUGS unload the bodies
of Brevard and Leverett.

They are dropped in the river. Oily water swallows them.

Scene numbers, which you can tell Final Draft to put in, are
helpful when you're rewriting, but when it's time to send that
puppy out, get rid of the numbers.

Scene numbers are for the Production Manager when she pre-
pares a budget, etc. She will do the numbering. You should be
so lucky that they call and ask for a Final Draft copy so they can
number it. Otherwise, spec material has no numbers because it
hasn't been bought yet. Don't do it. They'll take points off!

Get your reader comfortable as quickly as possible. Don't make her
wonder, "I wonder when this takes place?" Remove all prickly feelings she may have, the first of which is "When and where am I?"

FADE IN:

INT. DARK KITCHEN   (PRESENT DAY)

INT. SPACE STATION   (A.D. 5035)

INT. FRILLY BOUDOIR   (LONG, LONG AGO)

EXT. SMALL WYOMING TOWN   (1857)

Look at the next two first pages. Both students have a good grasp
of format, but this first page has enough hiccups to make the
reader worry about the upcoming 109.

FADE IN:

EXT. TALLAWASSESE, ALABAMA   NIGHT

Twilight. Canopy of pine trees.

TILT DOWN to a modest, two-story house sits atop a rolling
lawn. Three muddy pick-up trucks are stalled in the front yard,
next to a shiny yellow VW and a Mini-van. The sun is setting on
the typical middle-class American home.

INT. KITCHEN   EVENING

DOTTIE FISHER, 46, in shape, well-kept, maternal figure,
frantically doctoring a pork tenderloin in her luxurious, but
messy kitchen. Fine China piled high on the counter. A pot of
rice boils over on the stove. Fresh cut vegetables are encased
by a battle field of GI Joes.

Microwave is slimed with a solidified goop. Four pitchers of
freshly brewed sweet tea rest on an island amidst pieces of
corn husk hair. Auburn dish towels and pot holders strewn
throughout kitchen. Door frame covered in lines of children's
heights.

                    DOTTIE
Jimbo, I need your help!

JIMBO FISHER, 55, Dottie's husband, muscular, tired, and
masculine man poke his head in the kitchen.

                    JIMBO
What?

Dottie beigns to fix a salad.

                    JIMBO (CONT'D)
I just not a people person and Bo is which means, his family is
probably freakishly friendly. I'm not freaking out. It's just a
long weekend. I'll be out of here by Tuesday. Tuesday...

INT. DOTTIE'S KITCHEN   NIGHT

Dottie pours sweet tea into glasses. She wipes sweat. A LARGE
ROAR from the den.

Now, my concerns about moments that might give a reader pause:

FADE IN: should have one space below it, instead of two.

You have not told us the time period.

Third sentence has a grammar mistake. Should be "house that sits atop."

In the second paragraph, "to be" appears twice.

Are the pickup trucks actually "stalled?" How do we see that? Are they simply parked?

The house is described as "modest" but the kitchen, "luxurious." Is that a logic flaw?

Any time you say "typical" about something, we wonder why this family is worth our effort.

Dottie is described by physical appearance, but nothing about her personality.

You're better off saying "40s" instead of nailing down her age.

I'm unclear what is meant by "maternal figure." Is this a fancy way of saying "mom?" or are you commenting on her body?

Don't repeat. "In shape" and "well kept" are basically the same.

"Doctoring" should be "doctors." Maybe not.

The rice is boiling over. Does Dottie do anything about it?

Battlefield is one word.

"encased by a battle field of GI Joes." I have no idea what this image means.

Is four pitchers of tea realistic? Seems excessive. May be fine.

"Corn husk hair" is fine. You don't need "pieces" as the hair has not been cut up.

Auburn is a color to many people. Say "Auburn University" the first time.

Don't repeat: If Jimbo is muscular, we assume masculine. If he's her husband, we know he's a man. Don't tell us what we already know.

Again, we need some description of the character's character, not just physical appearance.

You don't need to say "begins." Just say "Dottie fixes a salad."

"Begins" and TALLAWASSEE are spelled wrong. *Permanent Fatal Error on page 1*!

Dottie asks Jimbo for help, then forgets she asked. Is this a logic flaw?

Need a comma after "Bo is" so we can feel the correct rhythm of the dialogue.
Probably, then, don't need a comma after "which means."
Do you mean for Jimbo to say "freak" twice?

"Dottie pours sweet tea." We've already been told the tea is sweet. From now on, just call it tea.
"Roar" is a sound. I'm not sure you can have a "large roar." That may be too nitpicky, though.
I have no sense of what kind of story we're in yet. Drama? Comedy?

There are enough vines, sticks, and slick spots on these lily pads to make the reader really slow down and watch his step. The "Dottie beigns to fix a salad." is, sadly, enough to cause the reader to fling the script into the swamp.

Here's another page 1:

TWO SNOWY WHITE DOVES   (PRESENT DAY)

Staring through the bars of a golden birdcage. Waiting for this wedding to end. Waiting for their shot at freedom.

INT. CROWDED SYNAGOGUE   DAY

SHOSHANNA GOLD, a young BRIDE-TO-BE walks down the aisle.

She's radiant. A well-heeled CROWD is enthralled.

BENJI SCHPALL, 25, her soon-to-be husband, soaks in her every move. Every step brings her closer. A life of happiness awaits. Their eyes lock. He tears up.

>   BENJI (V.O.)
>   You should probably know I was married before.
>   Almost.

As the bride reaches the halfway point, an ELDERLY BUSINESSMAN steps into the aisle, blocking her way. He takes hold of her hand and drops to one knee. He whispers to her.

She drops her bouquet, bursts into tears, and lays a passionate kiss on the Old Coot.

Benji recoils in horror. And falls backward off the stage.

>   BENJI (V.O.)
>   It didn't take.

INT. RECEPTION HALL

Paramedics work on Benji's broken leg. He's devastated.

SAM SCHPALL, 73, a rumpled lawyer with a terrific jew-fro, is engaged in a mighty struggle with the BRIDE'S FATHER. They're playing tug-of-war with a wedding gift.

>   BENJI (V.O.)
>   Ever heard of Sam Schpall? He was a famous
>   civil rights lawyer in the sixties. My father.

You can see the difference. The reader can sprint across those lily pads!

> There's no FADE IN: Maybe it doesn't matter.
> Interesting opening image. Good feel to "waiting for their shot at freedom."
>
> The choppy paragraphs are easy to read.
> Visual writing: we see the image with no effort.
> I'd like some character description of Shoshana, but I'm willing to bide my time.
> Benji's dialogue is good. Hooks us.
> I don't quite understand what the Old Coot kiss means, but, again, the writing is pulling me on, so I'll keep with it.
>
> "Paramedics" needs to be in CAPS.
> One space too many after "jew-fro," before "is"

We meet Benji under pressure, and there're a couple of funny moments on page one. The image of his father, the famous lawyer, tugging it out with the Bride's Father over a wedding gift, is a good character introduction. The V.O. is short and punchy. The scene description is nicely written and creates quick, telling pictures with few words. My favorite is "a life of happiness awaits." I can SEE the bride in white and slow motion, smiling at Benji.

The reader will turn the page and read on!

☐ 70. You blew your first ten pages! ARGGGGGHHHH!

Great first ten pages = life. Mediocre first ten pages = leprous sores, acid in your eyes, and boiling intestines for all eternity. This is critically important. So important! Reeeeeeally important. The first ten pages, and what you do with them, will make or break your script.

It's the only guarantee you've got, those pages. Some people will read to 20, others will stop at 30 if something major hasn't happened, but no matter what, they're going to read the first ten pages. They may chuck it in the rubbish bin halfway through page 11, but you've got a lock on at least ten! Yee ha!

Make 'em count.

The beginning is the point of attack, where something is already happening. There is *already* a problem. We may not know what it is, but the character knows, and we want to find out.

Daniel Woodrell's intense novel, *Winter's Bone*, opens on Ree Dolly, a young, hard-scrabble-poor woman up in the Ozark mountains, *way* up in the Ozarks, with two little children, a crazy mother, and a father who makes crystal meth. As soon as the author establishes *that* geography, a policeman drives up and tells Ree that her father's trial is in a week, but no one's seen him around lately. Then John Law tells her that, to go his bail, her father signed the note on her land and her house. If he doesn't show up for trial on Monday, Ree will lose her farm and have to move.

Now she's got to go find her daddy. The story starts off in a big hurry.

First ten pages. We don't know much about Ree when the story gets going, but we do know she's got ONE HELL OF A PROBLEM and it's a problem we're interested in.

You don't want set up.
You want a story that's already moving — with alacrity.

Show us the ordinary world — where and how the hero lives.
Introduce the main characters.
Make sure we know what genre we're in.
Tell us what the central conflict, premise, and theme are going to be.
Somewhere around page ten is the inciting incident.

How do you introduce your main character? Spend a lot of time with that one. Is their opening moment dramatic or telling or compelling or heartwarming? Is it the *right* intro? What can you do to improve it? Make it more dramatic?

Night of the Iguana opens with a rainy exterior of a clapboard church, the sermon's title on the sign. Then we slowly go inside, to see the pastor, Richard Burton, and his parishioners, jammed to the rafters, hungrily intent on watching him. Then (still in the first 45 seconds of the film), Burton goes nuts, excoriates his congregation, and totally loses control. That's an opening!

We desperately want to know who this guy is and why he's giving this frenzied sermon. He's tortured, obviously on the rack. We're intrigued by his problem. We want to find out what he did in his past, because he speaks of "appetites" that his relatives had, that he still has. The opening scene ends with his congregation pouring out of the church into the rain, like rats from a sinking ship. What a fascinating beginning, shoved forward by a character we want to learn more about. We want to turn the page and *keep reading*.

And, how do we meet the opponent? Same questions apply.

A quick look at first ten pages:

> *The Fugitive* — Hero's wife is murdered. He's arrested. The train he's being transported on crashes and he escapes.
> *Patton* — That amazing speech! (not the usual first ten pages, but a real grabber!)
> *Sleepless in Seattle* — His wife has died, and he moves to Seattle.
> *Tootsie* — Hero can't get an acting job. He goes with Teri Garr and she doesn't get the job, but the seed is planted for his eventual decision to dress like a woman.
> *True Romance* — The guy meets a girl and they spend the night together. She confesses his boss hired her to seduce him for his birthday. They realize they're in love.
> *The Graduate* — Party for Ben's graduation. He's told the future is "plastics." Mrs. Robinson asks for a ride home. In her sunroom, at *ten minutes into the story*, he says, "Mrs. Robinson, are you trying to seduce me?"

Look at how much ground they cover in the first ten minutes of *The Mask*. A lot! The hero is Stanley Ikpiss, nebbish. Despised by his landlady and disrespected by women.

1. After an undersea salvage accident, an ancient chest breaks open and the mask floats to the surface.

2. Stanley's female co-worker makes him give tickets that he'd bought for the two of them to her so she can take her friend to the concert. He's pathetic.

3. His buddy tells Stanley that he needs a change. They're going on a love safari! Lightning crackles.

4. A gorgeous girl comes out of the rain into the bank. Ignoring the buddy, she beelines for our hero, which surprises everybody.

5. Stanley wants to open a checking account for her, but struggles to get his desk drawer open. She dabs herself off with his Kleenex.

6. She pulls him toward her with his tie, sexy moment. His tie is supposed to make him feel powerful. She asks if it works.

7. He goes over all the types of accounts. We see she has a camera in her bag. Ho ho! CUT TO: The #2 Bad Guy and his Henchman. They talk about the bank's alarm system. They discuss the #1 Bad Guy.

8. #2 Bad Guy has ambition, wants to be number one. CUT TO: Stanley goes to a car repair shop.

9. The car repairmen treat Stanley like dirt, fleecing him for money. He gets the worse-than-awful "loaner" car.

10. Coco Bongo club. Stanley bumps up in the loaner to meet his buddy and two cute girls. #2 Bad Guy and his Henchman are outside the club. Stanley, again treated badly, is accidentally left outside the club.

We meet all the major players, including the mask and a photo of the #1 Bad Guy. We know the genre, which is modern-day comedy. We learn Stanley has no girlfriend and is basically a doormat for women, car repairmen, and everyone else he comes in contact with.

All that in ten minutes! I'm exhausted!

Right there in minute three, Stanley's buddy tells him he need a change — the whole point to the movie, laid out there in one line of dialogue. They do it in *The 40-Year-Old Virgin*, too!

```
                    DAVID
        You're like all of these action figures,
        hermetically sealed. You're all wound up.
```

Here are the first couple of pages from a script by two of my students.

CITY?

EXT.   URBAN NEIGHBORHOOD -- NIGHT   (PRESENT DAY)

A dingy city bus pulls up to a bus stop in a nondescript
downtown neighborhood. A YOUNG BLACK WOMAN gets off the bus
and pulls her jacket tightly around her as she steps onto the
cracked, uneven pavement. As the bus pulls away from the
curb, she surveys the nearly empty street and steps over to a
bench that has been tagged multiple time by rival gangs.
Setting her purse on the bench, she rummages around until she
produces a small mace keychain. Clutching the miniature
spray tightly in her hand, she slings her purse over her
shoulder and quickly makes her way down the sidewalk.

too long break into ¶s

INT. APARTMENT BUILDING LOBBY -- MOMENTS LATER

who cares?

Dark wood panelling and warm lighting give the lobby a sharp
contrast to unkempt state of the streets outside. The woman
yanks the door open and strides right past the bank of
mailboxes near the entrance. She heads straight for the
stairs and makes her ascent.

CLICHÉ = death
necessary?

ADD SLUG LINE

Upstairs, the environment isn't quite as welcoming, as the
wood panelling gives way to cinder block walls. The recessed
lighting in the hallway's ceiling is spaced far enough that
the walkway is a corridor dotted with sporadic spotlights.
With a quick jangle, the woman flips the mace to find her
housekey on the other side of the chain. She unlocks the
door and enters her unit.

too much detail

2 SPACES ABOVE SLUG LINE

INT. YOUNG WOMAN'S APARTMENT -- CONTINUOUS

necessary to plot?

hall

As the weak light from the hallway seeps into the apartment,
there is a small yip, followed by a tiny growl. The sound of
the dog tags jingle as the dog runs over.

                    YOUNG WOMAN
          Shhh, Oscar, it's just me.

The page must MOVE

The woman shuts the door behind her, while reaching down to
pet the Yorkshire Terrier that has come to greet her. She
flips a switch near the door, the one of the light bulbs goes
out with a pop and it startles her. The pitiful light in her
living room does little to dispel the night's inky darkness
in her home. With a short yip, Oscar trots back into the
other room, and the woman turns to set the series of locks on
her door.

Her weary, hunched body takes on a tense, alert posture as a
low, guttural growl rumbles from the other room.

                    YOUNG WOMAN (CONT'D)
          Oscar?

There is a short yip and a squeal, followed by a sickening
crack from the other room. The woman's eyes grow wide with

WAY WAY WAY too much detail — as SPLATTERING emanates
go through with a weedeater !!!

WAY too much DETAIL!
cut by ½ to ⅔

2.

the <u>sound of splattering noises</u> emanating from around the corner.

too much detail

                    YOUNG WOMAN (CONT'D)
          Os--   *is it agile... or not... word choice*   *and* *do this for entire script!*

~~She sees a large animal of some sort, soon revealed to be a~~
MAN-BEAST (lumber) ~~from the other room~~ on all fours from the
shadows of the hallway. It glares ~~at her as it~~ rears up ~~on
its hind legs, until it is standing upright~~, like a man.

                    YOUNG WOMAN (CONT'D)
                    (Fumbling with her
                    mace)
          Oh, fuck you mother fucker...   *realistic reaction?*

The creature emits a short snarl as it (walks) toward the woman.
Blood ~~spray~~ is smeared across its freakish ~~man-beast~~ face.

The woman, (no longer brave) drops her keys and fumbles with   *boring word*
the locks on her door, looking for an escape.

<u>As the creature approaches</u>, he reveals an 8-inch, jagged
blade in his hand. He smiles and licks his lips.   *why was she brave at all?*

                    YOUNG WOMAN (CONT'D)
                    (crying)
          God...Please...No...   *too much detail*

slows you down   (Finally,) as the man-beast towers over his helpless prey
brandishing his knife, he speaks in a low, guttural voice.

                    MAN-BEAST
          No prayers. No Mercy. Only slow
          blade. Only hell death.

EXT. APARTMENT BUILDING -- CONTINUOUS
                    A
~~A young woman's~~ (scream) ~~pierces~~ through the still night. Then
the sound of flesh being ripped. Then (whimpers). Then
silence.   *SOUND in CAPS*

                                        FADE OUT.

FADE IN:

INT. GOTHIC CATHEDRAL -- DAY   *Where? NYC?*

too much detail   The sparsely-populated Catholic church (is) currently holding
mass. Despite the sunlight visible through the stained glass
windows, a gloom hangs over the cathedral's interior.
Decades of candle smoke has collected on every surface. Even
the multicolored windows seem muted, overpowered by the stark
grey of the building's walls.

By now, you're beginning to see what I think is important. I'm not the only one.

□ 71. You haven't ripped out the first 20 pages!

"There is no backstory."
Walter Hill

Putting backstory in the first act is a mistake nearly everyone makes.

Beginning writers often take a long time to start a movie. There's no need to shilly shally around waiting for the engine to warm up. Your reader is dying to love your screenplay and you need to keep from disappointing her. When you have your first draft finished, see if ripping out the first 15–20 pages will help.

Movies are closer to short stories than novels, because it's all about brevity and how much information you give the audience. You have to be really picky and elegant about what you chose to tell them and what matters.

In the first 20 pages, find the tiny pieces of backstory that you absolutely *have* to have and salt them in on page 40, 62, and 93. Then toss the first 20. If the reader stops on page 20, but your story doesn't really get going until page 30, they will never see your story.

"I always try to find a place, how far into the story can I start
and still not confuse the audience... in 15 minutes, will they
have caught up?"
Peter Weir

Writers often take too long "setting up the story" when they should just get on with *telling* it. Don't explain who everyone is. Show us who they are by putting them in forward motion, doing stuff. A classic example:

Man wakes up in the morning.
Man showers and shaves.

> Man drives to the train station.
> Man buys a ticket.
> Man gets on the train. Train pulls out of station.
> It is revealed to audience that Man has a bomb in his suitcase.

Great reveal, but, even though there may have been lots of great character moments in those first scenes, the story doesn't get rocking until we find out about the bomb. "But I need to show you who this guy is!" you will say to me, plaintively, as I approach with my Big Fat Red Pen. I will say, "Ixnay! Put the guy on the train and let us find out who he is as the train is hurtling down the track."

Start with:

> Man gets on a train. Train pulls out of station.
> It is revealed to audience that Man has a bomb in his suitcase.

Later on, we find out he's divorced, hated by his children, etc. Learn stuff by having it squeezed out of the Man (who desperately needs a name that doesn't rhyme with anybody else's!) under great pressure.

Often, as you peruse your first 20 pages, you will find a scene that just *feels* like the opening scene of a movie; FADE IN: just naturally wants to go *there*. Listen to the little voice in your head. A lot of what you thought was important information can be thrown out, or replaced by just a little dialogue:

```
                CINDERELLA
      I had a tough childhood.
```

Whoosh! First 17 pages — gone!

☐ 72. You haven't cut every bit of extraneous action!

Have you eliminated as much dead wood as possible?

> *"You write and then you erase. You call that a profession?"*
> Saul Bellow's father

If a sultan says, "Bring the white stallion to our friend," do you show the servant walk to the stable, saddle the horse, and walk him across the parade ground to the throne room, or do you have the Sultan say, "Bring the white stallion to our friend," and CUT TO: our hero sitting astride the white stallion, rarin' back, ready to go?

Watching the DVD of *Le Samourai*, there were so many scenes of Alain Delon walking up and down long hallways and down streets and up streets and up staircases and down alleys, I finally gave up and zipped through those time-wasting scenes on Fast Forward. If you wrote scenes where characters burn shoe leather, the story will get tighter when you cut them. If the reader wishes she had a Fast Forward button, you're hurting.

Even *il grande Coppola* is not immune from the need for a little cosmetic surgery. In Chapter 13 of the *Apocalypse Now* DVD, the guys on the boat get their mail. They get shot at from shore. Clean gets killed. They pass a downed airplane and continue up river in fog. There's a cool shot of Willard on the left of a fog-shrouded frame, with his M-16. More fog and they get attacked from shore, only this time, it's arrows. Once they realize the arrows are harmless, everyone relaxes — and then Chief gets a spear through his chest, just like Mfumu in the source-material Conrad story, *Heart of Darkness*.

Neat. Tidy. One guy dies in a modern way; another guy dies in an old-fashioned way. The story moves forward like Peter Rabbit. Lippity lippity.

However, if you look at the same moment in Chapter 24 of *Apocalypse Now: Redux*: they chug up river, Clean gets killed, and, after they go under the downed airplane, there's the cool shot of Willard with his M-16 on the front of the boat in the fog — and then a Frenchman materializes from the fog and welcomes Willard to a pointless meal with irritable French people followed by boring sex with an older woman, then the French dude puts them back on the boat in the fog aaaaand we see the second half of the shot of Willard and his M-16. Well fed and well laid, at least, they head upriver for the arrow attack and Clean's death. Other than sex and a nice meal, that's all Willard gets. Nothing happens in the *entire* 25-minute (25 pages!) sequence that does anything to move Willard's story forward.

So, imagine this is your first draft — nicely done, but a little flabby:

```
REDUX


Chapter 23: "Mr. Clean's Death"
Chapter 24: "The French Plantation"
Chapter 25: "Clean's Funeral"
Chapter 26: "Dinner"
Chapter 27: "Les soldats perdus"
Chapter 28: "Arrow Attack"
```

In your rewrite, you ruthlessly cut stuff that doesn't shove your story ahead.

```
APOCALYPSE NOW


Chapter 13: "Mr. Clean's Death"
DISSOLVE IN THE FOG (Whoopsie! Where's the French
Plantation sequence?)
Chapter 14: "Arrow Attack"
```

An amazing lesson in screenwriting. Thank you, Mr. Coppola! Slice that dead wood and sell your script for a zillion dollars!

Trust me. It's better when it's shorter.

You can increase tension by cutting out the boring stuff. Cool, huh?

Each scene must crackle with forward motion. Good scenes shove ahead to the next one. When you read it, you can feel the *snap* at the end as it launches you relentlessly down the road. Your story should be moving like a freight train with no brakes.

First draft. This droops a bit at the end. It doesn't have to.

```
He jumps out of the cab before Carolyn can stop him. He
hauls ass down the street.

                     CAROLYN
          Come on man! Don't do this!
```

```
                    CAB DRIVER
          Where to?

Carolyn is silent.

                    CAB DRIVER
          Where to?

                    CAROLYN
          The laundromat.
```

If you cut the last little bit, you finish the scene with a "snap," keep the energy high, and push us forward.

```
He jumps out of the cab before Carolyn can stop him. He
hauls ass down the street.

                    CAROLYN
          Come on man! Don't do this!

                    CAB DRIVER
          Where to?

EXT. WISHY WASHY     DAY

The cab pulls in. Dave's inside, kicking the change
machine.
```

You can also drop out boring stuff in the middle:

```
"Daddy, my tummy hurts."
NEXT SCENE
Kid's in the hospital near death.
```

In *Tender Mercies*:

```
"You ever think about getting married?"
NEXT SCENE
They've been married for a while.
```

Cutting out the middle is ellipsis. It helps keep tension high. Use it to move your story forward. Just because stuff happens, doesn't mean you need to show us!

Here's a page from a script of mine, with my scribbles on it.

                         FATHER (V.O.)
                Matt. Matt. God am I lucky. Do
                you know that? I'm so proud
                you're my little boy...   ⌐

Matt is so lonely... ~~His reverie shatters~~ as LIGHTNING STRIKES
the oak tree. For an instant Matt sees a pirate hung from a
limb. ~~Then,~~ the apparition is gone. ~~Matt~~ sprints toward town.

                                                 He
EXT. DIRT ROAD ABOVE CORN FIELD   NIGHT
                              ⟨ok⟩
                                              nll
Matt ~~runs,~~ stumbles ~~at the road's edge.~~ Rocks ~~tumble~~ into the
corn field. <u>Matt hears a SPLASH.</u>   *Dirt clods*
⟨OK⟩
He ~~stops.~~ Heaves a rock ~~far into the dark field.~~ SPLASH.

Mystified, Matt stoops to climb down to the field. Then, in
the distance, FIREWORKS over the town.

~~EXT.~~ MATT'S P.O.V. - THE DISTANT TOWN

~~Ahead,~~ lit up like the 4th of July, ~~the Dalgleish Pirate~~
~~Festival is deliriously out of control.~~

ANGLE ON MATT / CORN FIELD   *more dirt*

His attention diverted, Matt runs toward ~~the~~ town. His feet *kick*
~~loosen more dirt, which slides~~ down the embankment. ~~Striking~~
the corn, ~~causing it~~ to <u>ripple like water.</u> Matt ~~didn't~~ see...
                                                    doesn't
~~EXT.~~ CITY LIMITS SIGN   NIGHT

"Welcome to Dalgleish -- Home of the Pirate Festival." Matt
flies ~~past,~~ into ~~the~~ town.

EXT. MAIN STREET / HARBOR

Banner across the street: Dalgleish Pirate Festival. Full
tilt pandemonium. ~~Swords and pistols and "Arrgghhhs" abound.~~
                      explores
Matt ~~wanders shyly through the streets.~~ No one notices.

At the harbor, Matt spots a trim brigantine among the pseudo-
pirate ships tied at the pier. "The Adventure." Dare he hope?

EXT. ALLEY   NIGHT
          passes
Matt walks ~~past~~ a dark alley. Hears WHISPERING.   *to*
     Well, laddie   *p.27*
                         DRUNK (O.S.)
          Have ye got me map, ~~lad?~~
~~Matt is~~ stupefied. *me hearty*
                         MATT
          Who's there?

Let's walk through what I did. Be forewarned. This will be boring.

I cut "his reverie shatters" because I'd already said he was lonely, and figured the reader would get that he was on to other things when lightning strikes the tree.

If he sees a pirate "for an instant" then we already know the "apparition is gone."

I changed "Matt" to "he" because I'd already used "Matt" twice in that paragraph.

"Rocks tumble" became "dirt clods roll" because it's a corn field. Not rocky.

"Matt hears a" is gone because SPLASH is a sound effect that he hears.

First I cut "far" because he heaved a rock into the field. Who cares how far? Then I cut "into the dark field" because we figure out where he heaved it from the context, so why repeat?

I trimmed the slugline all the way down to "THE TOWN." I actually put "DISTANT" back in the next draft. I liked the idea that the slugline helps create the image.

"Ahead" — we already know the town is in front of him.

The town is far away, so "lit up like the 4th of July" suffices, despite how much I love the line "the Dalgleish Pirate Festival is deliriously out of control." Don't repeat.

Don't need "ANGLE ON MATT." I'm not the director. Just tell us where the camera is.

"runs toward the town" Cut the "the." Interesting how, when it's gone, you never needed it.

"His feet kick more dirt down the embankment" is cleaner than what I had in the first draft.

Don't need "striking" the corn, once I said "causing the corn to ripple like water."

I made a mistake with "Matt didn't see," in that everything should be in present tense.

I dropped the EXT. because we know where we are by now.

"Matt flies ~~past~~, into ~~the~~ town." If he is running we know he's going to be passing the sign as he heads toward down. Also, another useless "the."

I'm still not sure I made the right decision here. "Swords and pistols and 'Argghhhs' abound" is a fun line. "Full tilt pandemonium" has fewer words, but may not be the best image.

First, I got rid of the adverb — "shyly" — then changed "wanders through the streets" to "explores." Far better word, as it tells more story than "wanders."

"Walks past" is the same as "passes" but takes up more space.

"Well, me hearty, have ye got me map?" ends with the most important word.

Clever me, I saved a line here by moving "stupefied" from scene description into a parenthetical. Looking at it today, I'd cut it.

* * *

In real life, instead of shouting, "The British are coming! The British are coming!" Paul Revere actually said, "The Regulars are out! The Regulars are out!" Which makes for better dialogue? The rewritten version, naturally.

Rewrite or perish.

☐ 73. You think your first (or ninth) draft is perfect!

Not what you want.

Pretend Judge Judy is looking at your draft, being an obnoxious critic — if you don't have a good answer for why something is there, she hammers you flat. You must turn into your own Judge Judy. This is not easy. If you love it when you write it and you love it when you read it, you're probably in trouble. Put it away for a while and ask tough questions when you drag it out for the rewrite.

Does this communicate what I wanted it to?

Do I start the story late enough?

Does the ending have enough emotion and power?

Do the characters behave like they should, and like they do in every other scene?

Do we care about the character and her problem?

Are the stakes high and do they go higher?

Will people who care about act breaks be able to find them?

Is ALL scene description terse and crystal clear?

Is every character's dialogue obviously being spoken by them and them alone? (the Thou Shalt Separate the Character's Dialogue commandment)

Do the pages look like they are supposed to?

Is the script really good or do I just hope it is?

Can I squeeze something more about the character from nearly every scene?

What can I do to make the scene better, more memorable, more interesting?

Have I done the *entire Your Screenplay Sucks!* checklist?

Rewriting is not only massaging the text to make the read easy. It also means changing the scene for any number of reasons. To make a character deeper, tweak dialogue, fix a structural problem, nuance a story beat — anything that makes the screenplay work better as a <u>story</u>.

You must keep reading and reading aloud and rewriting until everything is happening, not just the way you want it to, but in the best possible way for the characters and the story. It helps to have a critical eye. It helps not to love your writing too much.

Here's a scene I wrote.

FIRST VERSION:

INT. COMMERCIAL PHOTOGRAPHY STUDIO   DAY

MUSIC pounding. A rugged young PHOTOGRAPHER, half-dressed MODELS, HAIRDRESSERS, AGENCY TYPES, Marlene, a dozen HANGERS ON. The whole rock and roll enchilada.

The photographer shoots three women. Holding the legal papers, Robert blows in like Thor. The SLAMMING DOOR smacks everything to a sudden halt.

```
                    PHOTOGRAPHER
                (pissed at intrusion)
            This is professional.
```

Everyone watches, annoyed.

```
                      MARLENE
            Robert. I'm at work.

                      ROBERT
            So was I and I got served in the middle
            of a presentation!

                      MARLENE
            Get a grip.

                      ROBERT
            I thought we were working this out.

                    PHOTOGRAPHER
            Obviously you missed a memo.
```

Marlene hustles Robert out front. Behind them, silence.

In the first version, which I was totally happy with for a long time, Marlene, the wife who is divorcing Robert, is, um, not a nice person. After reading the script about a hundred times, I realized that if Marlene is a face-scratching harpie, then the reader will think Robert is an idiot for marrying her.

In the rewrite, she gets toned down. The entire scene gets toned down. The changes are subtle, but telling.

SECOND VERSION:

INT. COMMERCIAL PHOTOGRAPHY STUDIO   DAY

MUSIC pounding. Marlene, a rugged young PHOTOGRAPHER, half-dressed MODELS, HAIRDRESSERS, AGENCY TYPES, a dozen HANGERS ON. The whole rock and roll enchilada.

The photographer shoots three women.

Holding the legal papers, Robert slips in the back. What he doesn't count on is the door SLAMMING LIKE A THUNDERCLAP. Everything jerks to a halt.

```
                    PHOTOGRAPHER
                (pissed at intrusion)
            This is professional.
```

Everyone watches, amused.

                    MARLENE
          Robert. I'm at work.

                    ROBERT
               (wags papers)
          I got served in the middle of a
          presentation.

                    MARLENE
          Oh God. I'm sorry.

                    ROBERT
          I thought we were working this out.

                    PHOTOGRAPHER
          Obviously you missed a memo.

Marlene leads Robert out front. Behind them, gossip.

Marlene is kinder to him, not as biting. She no longer hustles him out. He doesn't seem like a fool for loving her.

Even seemingly insignificant changes like the ones above will have a long-term, cumulative effect. A change you make on page 48 will affect page 49 and 50 and 51 — every single page, all the way to 110. Imagine your story like a river flowing by. Every scene is downstream from the one before. If you make a change on page 48, like making Marlene a little nicer, it's as if you pour a bucket of blue dye into the river — as your story continues to flow, it will color everything downstream.

Picky, Picky, Picky

☐ 74. You don't know the meaning of every word in your script!

Readers care about this stuff. You may not in your real life, but in your "I'm a screenwriter life," you better get it right.

For instance, the word "cement." You probably use it wrong. Just because you heard someone say it doesn't mean it's correct. Cement is a powder that comes in bags. Concrete is a mixture of water, sand, stone, and cement. Driveways are not cement. Granny Clampett called it a "see mint pond" instead of a concrete swimming pool. But who cares, she wasn't trying to sell a screenplay.

> "He took out the mechanical pencil he always carried in his inside jacket pocket, and... made his characteristically neat proofreading marks on a sentence that said 'the book remains as fresh and unique as ever.' He changed it to read, 'remains unique and as fresh as ever.' 'There are no degrees of uniqueness,' Mr. Shawn said politely."
> Lillian Ross on William Shawn

Since you're probably online while you're writing, go ahead and use *www.dictionary.com* — a lot!

```
Dave and Timothy bang around the town, ecstatic and extremely
besotted.
```

First, lose the "the." If these guys are besotted with each other, are they drunk or perhaps in love? Which might it be?

Some landmines:

> affect, effect
> for all intents and purposes vs. (my favorite, after thirteen years teaching) "for all intensive purposes"
> your, you're
> there, their, they're
> mantle, mantel
> career vs. careen ("career" means hurry down the road, "careen" means to tilt over, like leaning a ship over on a beach to scrape barnacles)
> champing at the bit vs. chomping at the bit (Look it up. You only think you know.)
> get the hell out of Dodge (Dodge is a city, gets a capital letter.)
> She reigns him in. She rains him in. She reins him in. Which is correct? Go find out.
> unfazed
> Heroin. Heroine. Characters often want to shoot women into their veins. Odd.
> Peak. Peek. Pique. She was piqued when she couldn't get a peek of the peak.
> Site. Sight. Cite. Three words with vastly different meanings, used interchangeably by morons.

It's vs. its. Set your computer on search and search for every it's and make sure you've used it correctly. "It's" means it is. "Its" is possessive.

`The dog looks at its bowl. It's empty. The dog pouts.`

FYI, the "its, it's" glitch really pisses some readers off.

If somebody named Billy Ray says "I'm for it!" does it mean the same thing as someone named Nigel saying "I'm for it!"? Not hardly. Nigel, who is English, is in deep trouble and may end up in prison. Billy Ray just thinks "it" is a good idea. You have to know what you're writing.

Unless you are a sixth grader reading this book, and (fancy that!) working on your first term paper *and* first screenplay at the same time, you already know whether or not you have a decent command of the English language. For some people, grammar and spelling are terrible bugaboos. This is not a crime. It's akin to needing glasses. What's unforgivable is if you need glasses but don't wear them when you drive! Readers and producers will crucify you if you make mistakes in grammar, so, if your use of grammar is not what it should be, find a friend and get them to correct your mistakes. Sure, it's embarrassing to say, "My grammar is stinko," but it's worse to spend all that time on a screenplay and then waste a read because your prose is muddled, or worse, incomprehensible. Right?

This, of course, does not apply to dialogue. Not every character talks like Jane Austen. You're not supposed to use perfect grammar in dialogue. Duuh.

☐ 75. You use numbers instead of words!

Especially in dialogue.

```
              DAVE
    We have to be there at 5.

              CONNIE
    With all 135 kewpie dolls?

              DAVE
    It's 235, actually.
```

You are writing dialogue for an actor to say, and for a reader to read — the way *you* want it to sound. So, use words instead of numbers.

```
              DAVE
    We have to be there at five.

              CONNIE
    With all one hundred and thirty-five
    kewpie dolls?

              DAVE
    It's two thirty-five, actually.
```

This also applies to character names. It would be better to give them names that tell us something about them. COOL FRIEND.

ROMANTIC GUY. SWELL BABE. Use the available resources — tell us all you can, all the time.

```
                    FRIEND #1
          She's totally going to get dolled up
          right now.

                    FREIND #2
          Without a doubt. I would too. Hanks is so
          fucking dreamy.

                    FRIEND #3
          How bad ass would it be if Angie hooked
          up with him.

                    FRIEND #2
          She is the most balls-y o fall of us.
```

Do keep in mind, piss-poor proofreading pisses producers off! And do, sweet thing, do remember to RUN YOUR #$%@!&! SPELLCHECK!!! Unlike the above writer who failed to do both!

☐ 76. You call shots!

This one is pretty much common knowledge, but worth mentioning. If you've got a screenwriting teacher or book that tells you it's a clever idea to write sluglines like this:

```
INT. SUBMARINE - MEDIUM SHOT - BITSY AT THE HELM     NIGHT

EXT. WIDE SHOT - OLD McDONALD'S FARM     DAY

EXT. MEDIUM CLOSE UP - EINSTEIN'S PARAKEET
```

...put your book or your teacher out to pasture.

Never call a shot. That's not your department. They have movie directors and cinematographers who are well paid to figure out that stuff. Long ago, in Preston Sturges' time, scripts included camera angles. No more.

I said "never." I didn't quite mean it. You can, maybe two or three times in an entire screenplay, get away with calling a shot, but it better be diabolically important. For instance, if, for the reader to understand what is going on, the camera *has* to be high above the car that's about to explode, then you can give the camera angle.

But only once or twice. More than that, you're going to irritate someone, and why take that risk? However, you can still "place the camera" by how you write scene description.

```
EXT. GOLDEN GATE BRIDGE     DAY

A tiny figure, Tobias wavers at the center of the bridge.
```

Any semi-literate goofball gets the idea that this is a wide shot, and that Tobias is pretty small in frame. You don't need to tell us it's a WIDE SHOT. Furthermore, you don't need to do *this* to move us closer:

```
EXT. GOLDEN GATE BRIDGE     DAY

A tiny figure, Tobias wavers at the center of the bridge.
CAMERA DOLLYS IN from far far away to reveal that the
little fellow is crying.
```

You do it by controlling what you tell the reader:

```
EXT. GOLDEN GATE BRIDGE     DAY

A tiny figure, Tobias wavers at the center of the bridge.

A tear slides down his cheek.
```

Because you tell us about his cheek and a tear, we sense we are next to his face, hence, a CLOSE UP without actually using the dread camera description.

Use scene description to create a picture in the reader's mind — which is the same as calling camera angles, but you don't annoy the director. Or the reader.

☐ 77. You call specific songs!

Don't tell us what songs are playing unless you're going to cut your throat if they don't use that music. Even then, don't.

```
Conner sits next to a guy on the couch. He watches "Naked
Gun" but the sound doesn't carry over the MUSIC, "Wake Up"
by the Arcade Fire, in the background. He looks bored.
```

First of all, the reader may not know what "Wake Up" by Arcade Fire sounds like. I sure didn't. Second, a producer may think you'll be difficult to deal with because you're going to fight to the death for that one song. Third, they may fear the song is prohibitively expensive. Just say, "A romantic ballad" or "hard-edged punk" or "balls-to-the-wall blues number" or something that tells us what the music sounds like without actually calling the song.

That's the director's job, anyway.

The guy who wrote *Reservoir Dogs* didn't call "Stuck in the Middle With You" by Stealers Wheel for the ear-cutting-off scene. He left that up to the director. No, wait. He *did* call it, because he *was* the director.

So, only if you're going to direct your own work, can you call the music. Otherwise, it ain't a great idea.

☐ 78. You didn't run your spellcheck, you moron!

This is a hot-button issue for a lot of people. I'm one.

```
She tucks the flower into Raymundo's breats pocket.

A CLUMBSY KID runs across the street, ice cream cone in hand.
```

I used to circle misspelled words in students' homework and write "run your spellcheck." I got tired of writing "run your spellcheck" on the same people's homework week after week, so I changed my policy. If a word is spelled wrong, I just give the homework an F. Spellcheck!! How hard can it be? If you think this is harsh, consider that, if they find a typo, producers will throw your script in the trash!

Remember, they are looking for ANY reason to quit reading so they can go hang out with lifeguards or movie stars or, perhaps not, their mothers.

> *"How come things that happen to stupid people keep happening to me?"*
> Homer Simpson

A good screenplay is the blueprint for a movie. Would you buy a house if the electrical system were messed up? Correct spelling is a basic. No one will buy a script if the basics aren't there. Plus, *a typo takes the reader out of the read* and diverts their attention from the quality of the writing.

So, run your spellcheck. It really, really matters. Maybe not to you, but to the people who might give your script to their boss.

DISSOLVE TO:

FLASHBACK - 20 YEARS AGO

My first screenplay, which, after nine drafts, got made, was written on this typewriter. An IBM Correcting Selectric II, the gold standard of word processing. I still use it sometimes to write dialogue. In 1980, it cost $1,000 and all it did was type. Beautifully. It still has the best keyboard ever conceived by man. Typing with that thing was a breeze. Sometimes, though, I'd make mistakes.

On an IBM Correcting Selectric II, if you made a mistake, you backed up one space and hit the "correction" button. A white piece of film ribbon came up and you typed the wrong letter again. The wrong letter got covered by a white letter. Then you typed the correct letter, covering up the covered-up wrong letter with the right letter. Sound complicated? It was nirvana compared to what had come before. You don't want to know about Liquid Paper.

The correcting feature of the IBM typewriter worked like a charm — as long as the paper was *in* the typewriter, held tightly by a medieval system of rollers and springs. If you typed your way to the bottom of the page, looked back and found a typographic error at the top of the page, you rolled back up to the top, lined up the letter in exaaaaactly the right spot, pressed the "correction" button, covered up the bad letter, typed the good one, and you were back in business.

But, only *as long as the paper was in the typewriter.*

Once you yanked the page out, it was a whole new ballgame. If you found a typo once the paper was lying malevolently on your desk, screaming "You clod, you didn't see this mistake!" there was no way to get the paper back in the typewriter in exaaactly the right place — so this meant, *you had to retype the entire page.*

I repeat. "Retype the entire page."

That means putting in another piece of paper (and a second sheet behind it to protect the platen [roller thing] from being dented because the element [the ball] hit it so hard!) and looking at the page you had recently typed (and proofread poorly) and then retyping the whole damn thing. This maddening operation would take from two to ten minutes, depending how good a typist you were.

And it was doubly horrible, because, all the while you're wasting your time retyping an entire page of your screenplay (wishing you'd written in the Walter Hill style!), you were stewing because you hadn't noticed the damn typo.

DISSOLVE TO:

PRESENT DAY

Almost no one uses a typewriter anymore. Which is why Royal and Smith Corona are pushing up daisies. Almost everyone uses a computer. And, if you find a typo on a computer, *all you have to do* is tap BACKSPACE, correct the little beast, press PRINT, and lo and behold, a shiny new page comes spewing out of your printer, nice and neat as a glass of bourbon.

And it ONLY TOOK YOU ABOUT TEN SECONDS TO DO IT!

So please explain, dear reader, why, when I started writing it took me three minutes to correct a single typo, but people won't take fifteen seconds to do it now? Is it processed food? The insidious effect of television? A worldwide Communist conspiracy to sap and impurify our precious bodily... fluids?

Hard to believe, I know, but producers and agents, some of whom are actually as old as I am, don't *like* typos. And, while this may come as a shock to you in your ivory tower, they don't like people who leave them in their scripts.

The most common reason people get hired in the movie business is not talent or charm or who they know — it's because people like them and want to work with them. If you have typos, people won't like you and won't want to work with you.

"Because?" you ask, with that corn-fed naive smile I've grown accustomed to seeing.

Because they think that if you're too sloppy to proofread a script, or God forbid, a *cover letter,* you're not going to be someone they can rely on. And, in a business where millions of dollars go flying out the door every day, reliability is a key component to hire-ability.

Once upon a time, I did seminars on screenwriting at Borders Books. I brought Hollywood writers and producers to different cities, and they answered questions about writing. I'll never forget when a producer said that if she got a cover letter with a typo in it, she threw it away. A woman in the crowd reacted in horror, "How can you *do* that?! What if the script is fantastic?!" The producer looked at her and said, "I don't care. If you can't write a grammatically correct letter, why should I think you can write a good screenplay?" The woman in the crowd felt that because she'd spent a year writing a script that Someone Out There owed her a read.

Wrong.

They owe you nothing. Nothing. *Nothing*!

So, if you know that, if there's a typo in your letter, they'll just throw it away, perhaps you'll do a really, really, really good job of spellchecking and proofreading your query letter and script. Or not. Your call.

Remember. They don't want to work with people who are stupid. Why would you want them to think you're stupid?

The WGA registers thousands and thousands of new screenplays per year, so rest assured, agents and producers are getting plenty of query letters and scripts with no typos in them. They can afford to throw away a few. Including yours.

☐ 79. You *trust* your spellcheck! Ah haa ha haaa ha ha!

Treat spellcheck like an evil mother-in-law! Use her when you can, but trust her as far as you can throw the Chrysler building. Never, ever forget, just because some computer tells you something's right, doesn't mean it's really right. *Woe unto you if you do not proofread*. Repeatedly, with great vigor.

```
Sally and Jessica both smile and bear their teeth like two
lionesses.
```

If you can't find the problem in the above sentence, you need to find a friend to proofread for you. While I've got your attention, cut "both" and "two." More proofreading mistakes. Don't make 'em.

```
The boy returns to the alter with only the crucifix.
Carmen peaks through the window.
Tommy stops to admire at Colleen.
Rob looks at the books adjacent Elizabeth's bed.
With lightening speed the Priest disarms Kate.
```

Failing to proofread makes you look sooooo stupid.

☐ 80. You think longer is better!

Bigger ain't better. The iron clad rule used to be 120 pages, tops, the theory being, "One page per minute of screen time, a 120-page script = a two-hour movie." Longer than 120 pages, they thought, "Well this Bozo doesn't know what he's doing, so I don't even need to read it."

It's a cinch that every person who picks up your screenplay will do the exact same thing: they will flip to the last page to see how long it is. Everyone used to feel that if you were under 120 pages, you were safe. This is no longer the case.

Because movies are so expensive to make, now it's 110–115.

And don't say, "But some movies are three hours long. Those scripts are way over 120 pages, so I can break that rule if I have to." Yeah, but those movies weren't written by unknown writers trying to get their first agent. They were written by writers paid hundreds and hundreds of thousands of dollars, and if a writer is raking in a quarter of a million bucks *a week* on a production rewrite, she can scoot around a rule or two.

Not you. Not me. If you're trying to break into the industry, get it down between 115 and 110. Closer to 110. Plus, because the executives have all read the screenwriting books, they believe the 115-page rule, so you have to adhere to it.

Remember, *The English Patient* is a three-hour movie they squeezed out of a 104-page script!

☐ 81. You didn't read your script out loud!

John McPhee (my favorite non-fiction author) reads his writing out loud. So should you. Why? Because when you read it in your head, to yourself, it sounds good. Smooth. Like patting baby powder on a baby's bottom. So perfect, what's to fix? If you read something out loud, you have a prayer of hearing the mistakes.

By reading aloud, you find glitches in scene description. You also find story problems. Finally, you hear the dialogue. Actors will be saying it, so how can you NOT read dialogue out loud?

I had a rule when I first started writing. It was a super-duper rule. When I had a draft I was rewriting, I would sit on the sofa with the script in a three-ring binder. I'd read it out loud. If I read a page out loud *three times* and made *no* changes, I'd turn to the next page. If I found something to change, I'd make the edit and start over at read #1. If, on the third read, I was at the bottom of a page and changed a comma, I'd read that page three more times. This was a numbing exercise and required maniacal discipline. It took forever to churn through the script but was a marvelous way to improve the material.

If you want to *really* hear your mistakes, have someone read it aloud to you. What seemed perfect will now stink like garbage in the summer sun. In science, this is called the Observer Effect. "The act of observing will change the phenomenon being observed." It's why we sing top-notch in the car, but tragically at the audition. If the person reading to you stumbles over something or can't make sense of dialogue, or whatever, scribble a note to yourself and beg them to press on. When your friend is done helping you, buy her lunch!

☐ 82. You used a crummy printer!

Is the script printed on a good printer, with good ink? Are pages smeared? Blurry? A little messed up? Quality control is your job. You won't be there to apologize for your cheap ass printer. No one in Los Angeles can see your sharecropper's cabin with the leaky roof. They can't feel sorry for you because you have no shoes and your children haven't eaten in weeks. While you know and I know that you're lucky just to have been able to print out one single copy without your house burning to the ground, no one in Hollywood cares.

They see only your screenplay. It had better look good. Your script makes the impression. Not you. And you only get one chance.

Before you mail it out, have you gone through your entire script to make sure every page is there, in the right order, and right side up? You'd be amazed how copy machines don't have your best interest at heart.

And finally:

Run your spellcheck, I beg you.

FADE OUT.

ACT III:

What Now?

Writing the screenplay was the easy part.

"The universe is like a safe to which there is a combination.
But the combination is locked up in the safe."
Peter De Vries

"The primitive tribe honors the storyteller, but if he doesn't
tell a great story, they kill him and eat him for dinner."
William Froug

"I know. You're like me. You don't want to do any work.
You just want to cash checks."
Producer to Major Actor, setting up a television deal

"I can't believe how much my confidence had been blown by
the brutality of the film business and how much the lack of
money had hurt my sense of self-worth."
former screenwriter

"The pessimist complains about the wind; the optimist
expects it to change; the realist adjusts the sails."
William Arthur Ward

FADE IN:

Screenwriting is 50% writing and 50% selling.

Quit worrying about "are you going to write a great script." If this is your first one, it'll most likely stink. Don't worry about failing. Get some screenplays under your belt, and then sweat about "are you doing it right?" For now, leap into the void and don't worry there's no net. Enjoy the process and damn the consequences. Try to have fun. If this weren't fun, why would so many people want to do it?

If you're worried about failure, Hollywood will eat you alive.

This is a tough business. Lots of people want to get into it. For some reason, it has the reputation of glamour. Beats me why. If you've ever been on a movie set, you'll know there's nothing sexy about it. It's work.

> *"Screenwriting isn't as hard as coal mining. It's just darker."*
> Dub Cornett, writer/producer

People treat writers well when the writer is at the tippy tip top of the pyramid. That's about fifteen men and women. They get treated like the dictator's brother. Other than that, and I can't figure out why, people in Hollywood aren't very nice to writers. Maybe it's because everyone can write a sentence or two, and they resent you because you are better at something they can already do. Maybe it's because no one gets paid until the writer finishes what she's doing. Maybe it's because when the movie goes south, only the writer got paid.

> *"It is a strange thing. A composer studies harmony and theory of musical forms; a painter doesn't paint a picture without knowing something about colors and design; architecture requires basic schooling. Only when somebody makes a decision to start writing, he believes that he doesn't need to learn anything and that anybody who has learned to put words on paper can be a writer."*
> Turgenev

Maybe everybody thinks he can write. I dunno. Whatever the reason, west of Las Vegas they're often unkind to writers. Knowing this, it's best if you don't let get under your skin. Be pleasant. Enjoy the nice meals. Enjoy doing your work. Be glad you have a talent. If it makes you angry, tell your therapist. But getting pissed off at someone who is in the business is not a good way for you to get into the business.

A good way for you to get into the business is to write a crackerjack screenplay. But that's only the first hurdle.

Now you have to sell it.

Don't Be a Jackass, Be Professional

☐ 83. You want to be famous more than you want to write!

Lots of writers don't want to write a screenplay, they just want to be rich.

If this is anywhere close to true for you, spend some quiet time staring at your belly button, and if you decide it *is* true, throw this book away and bail out of the writing game. Writing is tough and you're most likely going to fail. If all you want is money and fame, I can't help.

> *"It ain't all coke and pussy."*
> Older lighting guy to P.A. after P.A.
> dropped a 10K on his foot

You need to be writing for the right reasons, and they are, well, actually, there's only one reason. You need to write because you have to write. Not because you want to have movies made. Not because it will pay your mortgage.

Really, really good writers will write even if they're not paid for it. It's a compulsion for them. And it feeds something in them that goes beyond the financial. You must be writing because if you don't write, you'll die.

If there is any other reason, like having your photograph in *People* magazine, then you are headed for astounding misery. The happy (or semi-happy) writers are the ones who like writing and don't worry so much about success.

Believe me.

Don't be looking for a quickie route to success. You have to spend the time on your screenplay to make it fit together like a Swiss watch. Do not send your script out until you know it's great. And I mean really, really incredible.

The last script I wrote, I cried when I got to the last page. The first two people who read it, cried. The script is amazing. When I hand it to someone, I don't know if they're going to buy it, but they *are* going to think it's an incredible piece of work.

Because I put in the time.

And you have to, too. Do not think that if you write the all-time greatest query letter, that someone will buy your not-really-ready script. Your script has to be fucking *bulletproof* before you send it out. Do the draft. Put it away a while. Write another script. Then pull the first one out and look at it. Go back in, roll up your sleeves, and do the heavy lifting required to make the script sing.

Check to see if there's anything you've seen in another movie. If there is, change it. Make it better. Improve it. Don't copy another movie, because the people reading your screenplay will have seen that movie. I guarantee it. One of my best students' prose and dialogue were smokin' inventive. I asked him about it. He said, "I read it and if it sounds like something I've heard before, I change it."

All artistic pursuits are about discipline. Margot Fonteyn. Julian Schnabel. Mick Jagger. Saul Bass. Ron Bass. Picasso. Donatella Versace. Milton Caniff. Worker bees every one. It's about waking up earlier than the other guy and working harder than the other guy and caring enough to be professional about this craft you say you love.

The people you are trying to sell to are professionals. To be in a position to buy your work, they put in the time. Why would you do any less?

☐ 84. You think _your_ script is special and rules don't apply!

Sadly, despite what your mother tells you, you're not all that special. Well, maybe you are, but your script isn't. It's best you learn this now, instead of later.

Scripts have looked the way they look for going on a hundred years. It's not up to your most wonderful screenplay to change the way Hollywood does things. Readers want to read your script and nothing but your script. They want it to look like every other script. Title page. The script. In regular screenplay format, please.

Do any of these mistakes apply to your script? Hope not.

Don't use three brads. Chucklehead. They put three holes in the paper to lure you into their nefarious trap. Use two brads. During the research for this book, I talked to a producer who smirked when I asked him about three brads. "Yeah, I laugh when I tell beginning writers to only use two brads, because it's such a stupid rule, but then, when I see a script that has three brads, I throw it away." And then he laughed again. Sort of like this: "Mwuu uu ha ha haaaa!"

The reason for this "two brads" nonsense? The assistants, who have to photocopy your screenplay, don't want to take time undoing three brads when two will hold your script together. So, when they see a script with three brads, they know you're not hip to their needs. And they begin to loathe you. Just by _picking up_ your screenplay!

Do you have the _right_ brads? Buy them at _www.writersstore.com_.

They're 1¼" #5 solid brass fasteners. You can't buy them in your hometown. The ones you can buy are thinner metal and won't hold. Nothing shouts "amateur!" like the word "amateur" written on your cover page, but crappy Office Depot brads run a close second.

Don't widen the margins in an effort to make your over-long screenplay look like it's come in at the cherished 110 pages. Do you think these people just fell off the turnip truck? If you widen the margins, they'll just think, "wannabe," and toss your baby out the window. Go ahead, do the work, make it shorter.

Don't include artwork, photos, or maps to help "explain things better." Just the script, ma'am. You have to tell the story with words. Only words. Few things shriek "loser" more than, partway through: "Open the map now...."

No CD of soundtrack music, no list of characters. No photographs of actors who might someday want to play the roles. Nothing but the script. You want to stand out, sure, but you want to stand out because of your writing, not because you look like a goof-ball next to the 1,500 scripts in their office.

Don't extend the dialogue margins.
Don't have it bound at Kinko's.
Don't send it in a three-ring binder.
Only use card stock covers!
Don't photocopy it at 95% size so it will look like there's more white space. Cute idea. Don't do it.

Don't use a dazzling new format, thinking Hollywood has been waiting for the vivid style of genius you're bringing to their lucky table. I'm sorry to report, Hollywood is not waiting for you. If you do something really outlandish, thinking it's new and improved, they'll just think you're nuts.

And they won't return your calls.

☐ 85. You put the wrong stuff on your title page!

No © symbol on the title page.
No reg. WGAw on the title page.
Or WGAe, for that matter.
No WGA registration number 349683 on the title page.
No "All Rights Reserved" on the title page.

MY FANTASTIC SCREENPLAY

written by

William M. Akers

myname@domain.com
The Street Where I Live
My Hometown, State 12345
212/555-1212

Nothing but the title, your name, and contact information. Why, you ask?

At this stage of the game, when you've sweated blood over your screenplay for who knows how long, and you've got a great script — you can *still* blow it at the very last minute. You want to appear, dare I say, cool. What you do not want to appear is *paranoid*.

If you put all that "If you steal my idea, I'll sue you to kingdom come" malarkey on the title page and in your cover letter, you're hosed. If you give the slightest impression you're worried they may steal your precious work, you will earn yourself an INSTANT trip to the round file, my friend.

But wait, there's more! If you and your writing partner put this on the title page:

written by

William M. Akers and William Goldman

It instantly tells them you don't know what you're doing! Don't want that, now, do we? The "and" is a recognized term that means the first writer got fired and the second writer came along and replaced him. An ampersand — "&" — means you are a writing team.

written by

William M. Akers & William Goldman

This means we sat down in a room and wrote it together. As if.

Knowing this, you can now sit in the movie theater and cackle, "Hey, that woman got fired, and they hired those two guys to replace her, fired *them*, and this last guy batted cleanup." Of course, the screen credits tell you nothing about the nineteen other writers who died like flies along the way and didn't get any credit.

Your screenplay sucks because you put a date on the title page! Never, ever, ever!!

Understand that, in Hollywood, youth is prized above all else. A new script is worth more than an old script, even if the old one is better. Stupid, but that's the way it goes.

Once you let it out of your hands, you never know what peregrinations your script will take. If you put a date on that script, someone might pick it up two years hence, think it's a tired old piece of garbage that nobody made, *ergo* it must be junk.

I wrote a screenplay once. Naturally, no date on the title page. My agent sent it out and nobody bought it. Somebody read it and it almost got made into a movie. Then it didn't. Time passed. A different agent sent it out to a development executive, who liked it. Unfortunately, her bosses didn't like it, so she had to keep it in her drawer until she had new bosses, and they did like it. More time passed, and they found an executive producer and a director.

I went to Los Angeles to have lunch with the producers, the exec, and the director. At some point during lunch, the conversation went like this:

> "So, when did you write the script?"
> I had my response well prepared.
> "Gosh, a while ago. I don't even remember."
> The E.P. said, "Yeah, sometimes the old scripts are the best."
> A general chorus of "Yes" and "Absolutely" rumbled around the table.
> The E.P. then said, "I was reading an old script the other day. No one had made it, but it was incredible. And it was written *five* years ago!"

Again, a tangible sensation shot around the table — a script *that* old was written before there were internal combustion engines. I, naturally, kept my mouth shut. *My* screenplay, the object of all this conversation and free lunch, had been written 20 years earlier. Had they known how old it was, they would have dropped it like a hot potato, because everyone knows that if something in Hollywood is old, it is by its very existence, bad — because, if it were any good, someone smarter than they are would have made it into a movie by now!

None of them knew, because, twenty years earlier, I had not put a date on my title page.

☐ 86. You haven't done a table read!

Dialogue is meant to be heard.

Writing it in your head, then putting it on a piece of paper, and then reading it again in your head, doesn't really work. In order to find problems in your dialogue, you have to hear it.

A table read is a great idea, especially if you know some actors. If it's just your friends, it may be less useful, but it's still incredibly helpful. Get people together, give them dinner, sit them around the table, and then take an hour and a half or two hours and read the script. You shouldn't read, not a character or scene description. You need to sit there, listen, and take notes — perhaps on a laptop, or scribbling on a copy of the script in front of you.

Be sure to:

> Give the actors time to familiarize themselves with the material.
> Have plenty of coffee and water.
> Bring your sense of humor.
> Bring chocolate to share.
> Leave your expectations at the door.
> Answer all questions succinctly and directly.
> Be prepared to improvise.
> Be prepared to be disappointed. There are no guarantees.
>
> Breathe.

Allow me to give you a slight *caveat*. If you or the actors aren't prepared for them, table reads can be monumentally depressing. If the actors phone it in (which means you're not feeding or paying them and they are just doing it because they feel they have to), when it's over, you're going to be suicidal.

I was in London for a table read for a producer and financing entities. A fancy hotel private dining room was jammed full of actors, the producer, and myself. They did a read-through before the finance guy arrived. The actors were bland, insipid, uninspired, and uninteresting. It was the lowest point of my entire creative life. I walked out of that room feeling I was talentless, that every movie I've had made was a joke, and that I did not deserve to be in this business. Little did I know that the actors weren't up to "performance level" and were only familiarizing themselves with the material. When the financing guy showed up, they turned in a blistering performance. The dialogue lifted off the page and flew around the room. Based on the table read, the guy decided to finance the movie.

☐ 87. You're dying to send the script out before you're really, really ready!

If you can find someone "real" who wants to read your script, you're a lucky writer. By real, I mean a director or producer or development person or actor who is in a position to help you get your movie made. Someone *in* the movie business.

Treat this opportunity like gold. If you give your script to someone real and they read it and it wasn't FANTASTIC, they'll a) never read anything you write in the future, or b) if they do read your next screenplay, they'll remember the first one wasn't so hot and it will color their perception of your new work. Ghastly, but true.

They can say how excited they are to read your work, but don't you believe it. Don't fall into the trap of, "This guy wants to read it, so I better hurry up and get it to him." They don't care if you *ever* send it, so you may as well take an extra six months to make it dazzling. Do drop them a line every couple of months to say you're not dead, so they won't forget they promised to read it.

The first script I wrote, *The Wolves Of Willoughby Chase*, a book adaptation, took me three or four months of non-stop work.

Maybe six months. One fine day, I finished it. I was ecstatic. I wanted it to go into production the next week. Oh happy day, a friend of my sister's was dating a well-known actress. She volunteered to read my screenplay, and, amazingly, to help me. I was doubly ecstatic. I drove up to the Chateau Marmont and dropped it at the desk. I left on a cloud. My script was finished and the road to wealth and happiness lay shining before me.

I stopped off at my friend Steve Bloom's house. Later on, he would co-write *The Sure Thing* and *Tall Tale*, and *James and the Giant Peach*. He volunteered to read my hot-off-the-presses screenplay. Right then! I trundled off to his living room and read a book. It was dark by the time he finished, and I went back into his office.

I still remember him in his chair, rocked back, my script on his lap. He started flipping through it, but instead of singing my praises, he tore it to pieces. Like he'd shot it with a sixteen inch shell, it exploded in front of my eyes. As soon as he began gently disemboweling it, I was instantly able to see it clearly. I saw tons of mistakes, ones he hadn't even pointed out. It was depressing, of course, because I had thought my work was done, but it was exhilarating because, armed with his stellar criticism, I was going to be able to make the script even better!

Then I remembered the famous actress. She had my script! She was going to read this monumental piece of garbage and not only *not* help me, but probably have me hunted down and killed for wasting her time.

I felt terrible and stupid and a thousand other sweat-inducing emotions. Mortified, I called her back in New York to tell her I had to rewrite the script and, um, er, ah, please not read it. But, before I could say a word, she apologized because the hotel had lost it! Yee ha! Good news!

Dodged a bullet there.

I dove back into my script and spent three more months rewriting it. Total writing time: nine months. But, when I was done, it was good. It got optioned and eventually was produced. I was launched as a writer. All because my friend blasted my half-baked script, that I had thought was perfect, clean out of the water.

Keep in mind these deathless quotations:

> *"Just because you're sick of your script doesn't mean it's finished."*
> William M. Akers

and

> *"How do you know when your script is ready? When the only choice is do another draft or blow your brains out."*
> Max Wong, producer

The Industry

☐ 88. You haven't the first clue how the business works!

Do not show a lack of understanding of how a movie gets made. Do your homework. Be professional.

"He's not just a dentist. He's writing a screenplay!"
Susan Sarandon in *Anywhere But Here*

Now that your script is finished, you have to sell it. That means getting someone to *read* it. Someone other than your boyfriend, unless he runs a studio. If that's the case, call me.

Mine your address book. Then, those of your friends: Do you know a guy who has a cousin who's a gaffer? Is your old boyfriend's mom a friend of Clint Eastwood's script supervisor? Does your teacher have any contacts in Los Angeles? Have you ever met *anyone* who ever *lived* in Los Angeles? Whom might they know?

If you don't know *anybody* with a connection to Hollywood, a way to find someone to read your screenplay is the Hollywood Creative Directory (*www.hcdonline.com*). It lists every production company and the contact information for the people who work there. Never send your script to a studio. Find a company who makes movies like your screenplay and write the Director of Development and try to convince her, sweetly, to read your work. Because people change jobs every 18 months, nearly half the Creative Directory will be inaccurate, so always buy the new one.

Your query letter best be fantastic. Take a looooong time to write it. Like weeks.

Meanwhile, while you're waiting for a reader to agree to read your work: Form a writer's group. Get feedback and take some of it or all of it and work on your material. Remember, anyone who reads your script is doing you a favor.

Meanwhile, give yourself another skill in the business. You can be a performer, you can be a playwright, you can write a novel, etc., but don't be just a screenwriter.

Meanwhile, make short films. The *South Park* trailer was hilarious. It got those guys work. People are getting deals now because they submitted a short to *www.YouTube.com* or *www.funnyordie.com*.

If you can get someone at a company to agree to read your script, they'll send you a release form, which is what they have to combat nuisance lawsuits. You're better off getting an entertainment attorney to submit your screenplay, because you won't have to sign a release form.

When they receive your script, the company will give it to a reader. If it is a small company, the reader will be a receptionist, an assistant, or an unpaid college intern. While a reader at an agency will read your entire screenplay, the production company reader doesn't have to. Therefore, you have to win or lose your reader in ten pages.

When the reader finishes reading, he will write coverage, which is a synopsis of your script and a recommendation for someone else to read it, or not. That coverage will stick around a lot longer than your entire career, and you only get one chance at it. If they don't like your script they will never read your stuff again. Therefore, don't send in your first script, send your first *great* script.

If the reader recommends your work, the Development Executive will read it. If they like it, they'll give it to the Producer. If the Producer likes it, you'll get a phone call.

It's always a good idea to have Script #2 ready to go because the Producer may say, "Hey, this is good writing, but we're not really interested in this story. Have you got anything else?" If you do, they may ask you to come to town and tell them your next idea.

You hear a lot about pitching. It's storytelling.

If you do get a meeting, plan on taking 20 minutes for the whole shebang. As soon as the chit-chat is over, take ten minutes to do your pitch and leave. Rehearse beforehand, to a person — not the mirror.

> I like to set up the world of the story, quickly. A little atmosphere, then move on.
> A bit about the main character, her personality, her problem, and what she wants.
> A bit about the bad guy and what he wants.
> First Act break: how do things change?
> A few of the major bumps in the road leading to and including the Second Act break.
> The hero's low point, where she thinks all is lost.
> What does she do to solve her problem?
> And, when the whole thing is over, how has she been transformed by the experience?

Boom. That's it.
Take your free water and skedaddle.

If they are interested in that idea or your script, then you can get an agent, easy-peasey, because there is automatically money for the agent to make with no effort! The company will option your script and ask you for rewrites. Or, they will option your script and *not* ask for rewrites (woo hoo!) and start trying to attach talent. These days, you will do those rewrites for free. You will whine to your new agent about it, but producers are used to getting stuff for free, so you'll do a raft of rewrites in hopes they can sell the thing. Who else is showing interest in your screenplay? Nobody, right?

Maybe they'll sell it. Maybe they won't. Maybe they'll waste a year or two of your life on useless rewrites. Perhaps not. This is one of the most frustrating areas of the business, and there's no way around it. Development. If you're lucky, the Producer is good with story and your script will improve. If you were born under a bad sign, the Producer has little story-sense and will force you to destroy your screenplay, for free, and then will throw it away because it's no good any more. Tough beans.

If they get a director or an actor attached, they'll go after money.

If they get financing, they'll make your movie and you'll get a big check on the First Day of Principal Photography.

And then, it will be a tiny bit easier to get someone to read your next screenplay.

Never forget, the competition is mind boggling. When he was fresh out of school, future Academy Award winner Tom Schulman was visiting a friend who was house-sitting for Richard Dreyfuss. After dinner, a messenger showed up with a script for Mr. Dreyfuss. If a messenger delivers a screenplay to an actor's home, that means that script has already fought its way darn high up the food chain.

Schulman's friend said, "So you wanna be a writer?" She walked down the hall, opened a door, and tossed the script in. With trepidation, Schulman followed and looked in. He saw a small empty bedroom and in the center of the floor was a four foot pile of screenplays.

He nearly threw up.

Know what to expect. Your life will be easier.

☐ 89. You don't know what time they eat lunch in Hollywood!

Otherwise, you wouldn't call at 1:15 Pacific. Nimrod.

Everyone in the entertainment business eats lunch at 1:00. All over town. So, don't call someone at 12:45 Los Angeles time, just as they are shouting at their assistant about the last phone calls, just as they are cramming into their high heels, and just as they are screeching for the valet to have their car ready downstairs, and — right then! — *you* call from Podunk. Why on Earth would they want to talk to you, someone who obviously doesn't know their ass from third base?

Don't look like a putz. Call during business hours. Call before 12:30 and after 2:30.

Unless — and there's always an "unless."

Don't call at lunchtime *unless* you only want credit for having returned *their* call and don't actually want to talk with them at all. Then, avoiding people is what lunchtime phone calls are all about! If this is why *you* call during lunch, permission granted to move two steps up the Sammy Glick Ladder To Success.

Speaking of phone calls: Hollywood is an ever-changing morass of bad manners, exquisite politeness, and savage cruelty. What used to be considered anti-social, immoral, inexcusable behavior has become the norm. When major league, A-list directors, agents, and producers send material out to actors' agents and are never told that they liked it, didn't like it, or even that they read it, then you and I have got no business expecting anyone to give us an answer to a question about anything.

Silence means no.

It doesn't mean they didn't like it. It doesn't mean they liked it, and aren't back to you yet. It means you're never going to hear from them, and it is your job never to ask why. The law allows you one noodge email or one noodge phone call, and after that give up, lick your wounds, and retire to your cave to plan a better strategy or write a better screenplay.

☐ 90. Your sense of entitlement is in overdrive! a.k.a. "Don't fight the notes!"

No one owes you a read.

> *"If I read a bad script, which takes me forty-five minutes, I can't ask for my money back or my time back and I am filled with incalculable amounts of rage."*
> Los Angeles producer

No one owes you anything. Just because you took the time to write your *fabulous* screenplay doesn't mean anybody Out There is honor bound to read it. It may be the greatest screenplay on earth, but there are plenty of scripts floating around and if they miss out on reading yours, they won't lose sleep over it.

Get into the mind of the person you are asking to read your material. Remember the massive amount of stress and time involved to be in the movie and television business. When you approach someone "real," be aware of their schedule and what you are asking them to do. If you ask someone to read your script, you are begging for a couple of hours out of their life, that you can't give back. You can give them a nice present, a cool book, or a Starbucks gift card, but listening to their advice, and taking their suggestions, is not a bad idea either.

You must be endlessly gracious, not overly pushy, and very understanding. If someone agrees to read your screenplay, you must treat them like a precious jewel and never assume they'll get to it this weekend, despite what they say.

Don't call them Monday to see what they thought. You have to constantly keep in mind how many people are pulling them in how many different, and painful, directions. Don't call for a couple of weeks. Then send them a gentle email noodge. A month later, maybe another one. After that, forget them.

Be sweet. Be patient. Be tolerant. And don't act like an idiot.

The last thing you want to do is come at somebody, guns blazing, put out that they haven't gotten to your phenomenal screenplay quickly enough to suit you. You're lucky they'll take your calls, so act accordingly.

And, if perchance, they are thoughtful enough to give you notes, take them!

> *"No one is as arrogant as a beginner."*
> Elizabeth Ashley

If somebody reads your script and doesn't want to canonize you as quickly as you'd like, but they have notes, then dutifully *write them down* and act interested. I get this a lot with writers who have never had anything produced. Newbies are often less open to criticism. Maybe they figure the advice is worth what they paid.

Do not fight the guy giving notes. Do not say, "but the act break is there, you just can't see it." Do not claw for every yard like it's Omaha Beach. Copy down what they say, murmur gracious acceptance, and say "thank you" at the end. Don't act like you know more about screenplays than they do. Don't act like they're idiots because they don't understand what you've so generously taken the time to have written!

When I was in film school, we showed our pathetic little first projects and one guy's was terrible. It happens. So, we were going around the room and giving our most afraid-of-being-hurtful comments, and he said, really put out, "It's a *personal* film! You're not supposed to understand it!" He vanished soon thereafter.

If you find someone real to read your script, the door to Hollywood opens. Slightly.

If someone reads your script and is kind enough to give you notes, but because of some insane sense of entitlement, you fight them on the notes, that great golden door will begin to close. You won't *see* it close either, because these guys are *smooth*, like the Flusher in college fraternities — the pleasant guy during rush who leads the loser to the back door, all charm and grace and understanding. He gently explains to the dweeb that perhaps he might try his luck at a frat house down the road, and the guy leaves all smiles, unaware he's a dead man walking. That's how it is when the Hollywood door closes. You never feel the needle enter your brain.

These people read 20 or 30 scripts a week. They have no time or tolerance for arrogance. Remember, it only crosses the reader's mind how long it took to read, not how long you took to write it.

If you refute the notes, he or she is absolutely going to think, "Dude, I took an hour of my weekend to read your fucking script. You're a guy who has never done *anything*, and there's a shot I could know what I'm talking about — at least listen!"

And the great, golden door will *lock*. The producer will go off to her production meetings and casting sessions and free lunches and massages and first days of principal photography, and you will be left alone on a raw, windy sidewalk, clutching your screenplay, looking at the high wall and the closed steel door, wondering why it's got no handle.

☐ 91. You don't know what a decent query letter is!

The question the person opening your query letter asks is, "Why should I pay attention to you?" Even the tiniest boutique agency, marked on the WGA agent list as "does not accept unsolicited material" gets five query letters a day.

Creative is good, "creative" is not. Don't be elaborate and appear desperate. Don't send a message in a bottle to fifty agents. Don't send a fake severed finger to a bunch of executives with your horror script. A huge office building got evacuated over *that* one. Guess which writer's name is forever mud?

In your query letter, get to the point. Tell the log line. Give whatever writing credit you have: reporter, playwright, novelist, that says that writing is your life. Perhaps have your letter mailed by a friend in Los Angeles, as non-L.A.-based-writers make the agent's life more difficult. If you don't live in Los Angeles, she will likely pitch your letter. Make your letter and script look normal. If the script is not exactly the right format, or has the wrong weight brads, they just trash it, and it could be worth a million dollars.

> *"I'd look at it and see if this person has a clue. If the log line looks interesting, or the synopsis, I'd go on. Rarely was it. In three years, I only discovered two writers that way, who turned out to be really good, who had come to Hollywood knowing nothing and knowing no one, and tried it via a query letter."*
> Former creative executive

You have to remember, the producer is busy and doesn't care. You have to have something spectacular, and it has to be ready for her to sell — with no effort. Something like this would get a call back, I should think: "I control the life rights of my grandfather, Winston Churchill."

Here are a development executive's thoughts about query letters.

> "These days they mostly come by email. We get some by letter and fax too. Since we get so many, and since we don't technically accept unsolicited submissions, most get ignored. The best strategy would probably be for someone to call me, then I'd ask them to email me information, and because we've had a conversation I would actually read the email versus trashing it."

A thought: If most come via email, why don't *you* send a snail mail letter? Then again, perhaps not.

> "Even if you're sending them by email, still format them as a formal letter. I get lots of emails that start with 'Irene, thought you'd like to take a look at' from people I don't know, which pisses me off since it makes me think they're trying to trick me into thinking I know them."

Don't be a jerk. They know if you're lying.

> "One misspelled word or grammatical error is enough to stop me from reading on. If the writing of the letter isn't perfect, I can only imagine the writing in the actual script."

Remember what I said about spellcheck!? I'm not such a doofus, huh?

> "Avoid the '*Die Hard* meets *Beaches*' comparisons. It's okay to say a movie is in the vein of something (e.g., a high school comedy in the vein of AMERICAN PIE) but the blah meets blah comparison always feels clichéd."

> "Avoid dramatic phrases like, 'or will he?' "

> "It's great when people reference other films we've produced and say how their project would fit in with our general slate (e.g. 'Much like your film, *Silent Swim*, which I loved, this script also combines a personal story with a larger political issue')."

> "If you enter a contest and you are a finalist, put that in the first sentence of your query letter. 'I was a finalist in the _____,' top line."

> "If you've written a comedy, make your query letter funny."

Here are a few query letters, that, um, didn't quite... make it.

Besides appalling grammar, no real sense of the story, listing his WGA#, and using "very" too much, the worst mistake this writer made was continuing to Email the development exec as if she had requested the script by putting *Re*: in the subject line and starting his Emails "Thank you for your reply" even though she had not replied. The ultimate no-no.

From: Young Writer (youngwriter@domainname.com)
To: developmentexec@productioncompanyproductions.com
Subject: Submission

Carolyn, I attached below the Logline and the Short Synopsis for the script. I hope you like them and please let me know if you have any questions.

Feature Script: "Buddy, buddy, buddy", Comedy
WGA Registration # 1234567

I believe that "Buddy, buddy, buddy" could be a good pick for Production Company Productions. The main stars, the two male and female leads, are supposed to be in their early 30's, good looking, smart, intelligent, and also vulnerable people. Right from the opening credits, the movie has many surprises and the laughs begin to come full force. The movie's first Act which takes place in a bar sets the pace and comical environment of the film, and from then on, things get funnier and much more entertaining. This is a very smart story, a very nice lighthearted and adorable romantic comedy dominated by intelligent humor, love and funny surprises.

I hope you enjoy it!

Logline

She was superficial and mean in high school and dumped him on prom night because of his looks "specially his big nose". So when he sees her 13 years later, with a nose job and his three funny friends, it's revenge time.

Thank you,
Have a great day.

Young Writer
(212) 555-1212

The development executive didn't make it past the second paragraph on this beauty. Notice how special the writer has made her feel because of the Email list at the top. "We're sending this to *every*body!" And, a lot of them are blind Email addresses, not even a person's name! Nice research.

From: Young Filmmaker
To: reader@bigfilms.com; edwinag@bigmovies.com; contact@literaryhat.com; mail@fabulousfilms.com; contact@giantmovies.net; timsmith@immensemovies.com; info@bigmoviesentertainment.com; madisonpewitt@bigmovies.org.uk; films@bigmovies.ca; josephine@bigmovies.tv; ipfreeley@hugeproductions.com; prq@thebigmoviecompany.com

Subject: Seeking producer for our film project titled RETROACTIVE

Dear Fellow Producers and Film Makers,

We here at In the Groove Productions are looking for other producers to come on board, to help get our film project titled RETROACTIVE, (with huge international appeal) made and onto the big screen. Below is a synopsis of this true and compelling story. If interested please contact us.

Retroactive is a story of drama, adventure, courage, love and loss. It will take you on a emotional roller coaster ride, because this true story, will touch you deeply, at the core of human emotion.

The story follows the extraordinary adventure of these two young men, their struggle for survival, and the life and love Michael finds in Norway, the land of the free. But freedom always comes at a cost.

Retroactive shows us the lengths one will go, to search for freedom, (something that is still happening today) and the simultaneous desire to find our own place in the world, and the guilt we feel about separating ourselves from our families.

Best Regards,
Young Filmmaker

Here's one from someone the producer never met who Emailed as if they were buddies. He did spell "definitely" correctly, but check out the poor subject line proofreading. Notice the run on sentence in the logline and the clichéd dramatic line at the end.

From: Young Director
To: Mr. Producer
Subject: thought to see project

Hi there David, hope all's been well with you.

There's something I definitely thought you might want a chance to see. It's an available full-length drama script by a produced screenwriter and award-winning playwright who's also been a Nicholl Fellowship finalist.

I can have it sent over to you if you'd like...just say the word.

"ROBBING THE BLUE SEA (full length drama)...

A father whose marriage is in trouble, whose friends think him boring, risks losing his own teenage son who is drifting away from him and there's no hope of preventing it, unless he finally confronts a similar estrangement from his own father...but that man's been M.I.A. in Vietnam for thirty-eight years.

He undertakes a journey that leads him to the comical veteran who fought alongside his father, and then the mysterious bricklayer who was a cook in the war. When he eventually learns the awful secret of what happened to his father, it changes him forever. He goes home to attempt reconciliation with his family, but is it too late?"

Best regards,
Young Director

I heard about a *great* query letter. Never was able to track it down, sadly. The writer was one half of conjoined twins, and had written a screenplay about life as Siamese twins. It was a standard, stupid letter with bad jokes that didn't work, but on the *back* of the letter, written by hand: "My brother is a freak and a total hack. If you want to read *my* screenplay, call me, but if you call and he answers, tell him you're calling from the dry cleaners."

The whole thing was a hoax, and the guy now has a career in comedy writing.

☐ 92. You made boneheaded demands in your query letter!

I re-quote Ms. Ashley. "No one is as arrogant as a beginner."

How to get your letter thrown in the trash in one easy step: "I'm attached to direct, and I've never done anything but I've got the vision for this."

You've got to understand. It's very hard to get a script produced with Will Ferrell attached. It's incredibly hard to get a script produced with no attachments. It's *unbelievably* hard to get a script produced with meaningless attachments. And you, as director, are meaningless.

I hate to be harsh about it, but what have you done? Seen a lot of movies? Remember, they are looking for reasons *not* to read your script. Being an arrogant bonehead is a great one.

They don't let beginners make movies. So, if memory serves, actress Madeline Stowe (who has a higher profile than you) recently wrote a western. The script, apparently, was fantastic. She wanted to direct. They supposedly offered her *five million dollars* for the screenplay. She still wanted to direct. Ha! End of fairy tale. Look her up in the imdb. She's not listed anywhere as "director." If Madeline Stowe can't pull it off, don't you try. Okay?

> *"Take what's there."*
> Richard Sylbert

A career can only tolerate a small number of gigantic mistakes. If you continue making them, you'll look up, at fifty, wondering where the hell it all went.

My advice, in a gentle, Big Brother, benevolent, soothing, all-comforting voice:

> *Just… let them… make… your movie…*

Let them *pay* you for your screenplay. Let them bring your work to the audience. Let it be made for cable. Let it be made for direct to DVD. What do you care? Don't be an arrogant moron. Arrogant morons work on the loading dock at Safeway. People who let other people buy their material get to cash checks and have hot sex with their terribly contented wives!

☐ 93. You don't want to sign their release!

If your query letter thrills them, they will send you a release to sign so they can read your script without being sued. If you don't let them read your script, they can't make your movie.

Most of these documents are pretty basic: "There are only so many ideas out there and we may be developing something like this. We'll be happy to read it, but you must acknowledge that we may be working on something similar." Like that. Yes, these documents are weighted toward the producers, but they're the buyers and you're not.

> *"What's the difference between being a buyer and a seller? The difference between the first half of* A Clockwork Orange *and the second."*
> Brandon Tartikoff

If you're lucky enough to get someone to want to read your screenplay, don't spoil the opportunity by refusing to sign the release! They have a constant flood of scripts coming at them and one less won't matter. You have to understand that they don't care if your script might be the next *Titanic*. They'd rather throw it away because all they want is to get through the week without someone suing them.

Sign the release and hope for the best. That's what this whole business is built on anyway, hope.

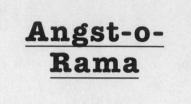

Angst-o-Rama

☐ 94. You think Hollywood will steal your idea!

Be paranoid of paranoia.

> *"Don't worry about people stealing your ideas. If your ideas are any good, you'll have to ram them down people's throats."*
> Howard Aiken

This one I truly do not get. An inordinate proportion of beginning writers are terrified someone is going to steal their idea. People in Hollywood don't have *time* to steal your story! First, it's cheaper to pay you off for your idea and hire someone else to write it. Second, what are you going to do about it? Nothing. Remember, they have *floors* of attorneys. Don't live in the Land of Paranoia. It's not a healthy place to be. Third, if they *even for a moment* get the ghost of a whiff of paranoia, a reinforced steel security gate will drop closed and you will never, ever get them on the phone again. They run from paranoia like Lot leaving Sodom.

So they steal your idea? Come up with another one. If you've only got one good idea, why are you in this business?

> If they want to know your other ideas, tell them.
> If they want to read your script, give it to them.
> Make it easy for them to like you.
> Make it easy for them to help you.
> If you are twitchy or weird or secretive, he will say he needs a refill on his wine, politely turn away, and, like Kaiser Soze, he is gone.
> Do not mention your attorney.
> Do not say you've registered it at the Writers Guild.

> Do not ask them to sign a release before you'll grant them the right to read your script. They'll smile, say no, jet off to Aspen, and never think of you again.
>
> Do not photocopy your screenplay onto dark yellow paper to make it impossible for them to Xerox.
>
> Don't tell them a studio stole your last spec and you're suing.

Who wants to work with a paranoiac who's in a lawsuit with a studio? Nobody.

Instead of wasting time trying to figure out a way to keep them from stealing your screenplay, invest that time in a rewrite.

Do not act paranoid. It's okay to *be* paranoid, just don't let anybody know! Do register your script with the Guild (*www.wga.org* or, if you live east of the Mississippi, *www.wgaeast.org*). I highly recommend copywriting your screenplay (*www.copyright.gov*). You'll be out about $50 if you do both.

You may think someone stole your idea, but it's quite unlikely. I wrote a spec TV pilot about Sherlock Holmes' grandson and Dr. Watson's granddaughter teaming up as detectives in Washington, D.C. A year later, I saw that story on the air. Did I think someone had stolen my idea? I did not. Because, one, I am not paranoid, and two, I had never shown anyone my script.

The business works in cycles. A development executive once told me: "I haven't seen a circus movie in five or ten years. Not one. All of a sudden, last week, three circus screenplays landed on my desk."

From time to time, ideas do get stolen. Google "Art Buchwald" and "*Coming To America.*" But it doesn't happen often enough for you to get your knickers in a twist! The chance that the person who wants to read your screenplay is going to steal it is FAR more remote than the chance the person who wants to read your screenplay is going to run like hell if you act like they might steal it.

Don't believe me? Next time you get in conversation with a producer or studio executive who wants to read your screenplay (and how many of those conversations have you been in up to now?), go all Travis Bickle on them, whip out a release form and demand they sign it. See what happens.

□ 95. You don't understand Hanlon's Razor!

Why should you? You've never heard it.

> *"Never attribute to malice that which can be adequately explained by stupidity."*
> Hanlon's Razor

Does this matter in the entertainment industry? It matters if you're trying to get *into* the entertainment industry.

You're going to be emailing and writing and calling people who do not know you, hoping they will return your call or read your script and get back to you. It's going to take longer than you thought it would. Eons longer. You'll suspect they don't like you, or have decided never to call you, or any of a hundred wicked gremlins that your low self esteem visits upon you. You will assume malice and you will fear they are mad at you or hate your script or are busy stealing your idea.

And 99 and 44/100ths percent of the time, you will be wrong.

If you don't consider the possibility that they may have lost their mind (happened to a friend's agent) or mislaid your phone number or their plane crashed and the script burned up in it (happened to me!) or, again, any of an unlimited number of reasons that incompetence ruled the day — if you write or call them up angry, and say, "Why haven't you read my script, you jerk?!" then they're going to scratch you off their list *forever*.

You will become one of the undead and you will *never* find your way back in their good graces. So be patient with the overworked people you wish to hear from — there can always be a perfectly good reason, stupidity, generally, why someone isn't getting back to you.

Be nice. Be patient. *Never burn a bridge.*

They may not have gotten your email. Chill.

☐ 96. You don't know the difference between Natalie Merchant and Patti Smith!

Go wherever you download or buy music and get "Because the Night" by both 10,000 Maniacs and Patti Smith. 10,000 Maniacs — MTV Unplugged. Patti Smith Group — Easter.

Listen to the 10,000 Maniacs version first. It's fantastic. A great song, incredible music, and a hugely powerful performance by Ms. Merchant. Imagine her rendition of the song to be your screenplay. In the top 5% of all scripts written last year! Maybe the top 2%! Great dialogue, story, characterization. Everything is top drawer all the way.

Now, put in the Patti Smith CD. Turn it up loud. Press "Play," hang on, and pray for mercy. Once she gets that sucker rolling, her performance is so raw, so painfully steel-edged, that, in comparison, Natalie Merchant is a distant also-ran. The scary part is how small the difference is. Both records sound almost precisely the same, but the difference is stunning. Compared to Patti Smith's voice's shearing intensity, Natalie Merchant's seems like lukewarm tap water.

Going back to screenplays: the slight but gigantic difference between the two versions of "Because the Night" is like the difference between a screenplay that gets written, and is *really* good, and one that gets *made.*

> *"When nothing seems to help, I go and look at a stone-cutter hammering away at his rock perhaps a hundred times without as much as a crack showing in it. Yet at the hundred and first blow it would split in two, and I know it was not that blow that did it, but all that had gone before together."*
> Jacob A. Riis

Before you send it out, your script *has* to be at the Patti Smith level. Sad to say, if you're only at Natalie Merchant, you won't get to first base.

☐ 97. You don't know you can write your way out of a hole!

No matter how un-Zaillian-esque your screenplay may be, you *can* save it!

"If I have a good trait, it's probably relentlessness."
Bruce Springsteen

For the beginning writer, when you get into trouble with a screenplay it's difficult to know that you can fix it. It's like being dumped by your very first boyfriend. Your heart was broken, your mind was shattered and you thought the future held only blackness, death, depression and endless agony. Eventually you learned you could get over that cretin, and, similarly, as a writer, you will come to understand you can rewrite a script until you solve its problems.

The first pitch I ever sold is a great example. This was back when a schmo like me could sell something based on three pages. Hollywood would give you enough money to live on *for a year* if you gave them three really good pages! Sadly, those days are long gone.

Anyway, I wrote three killer pages. My agent sent them out. A big-time Hollywood producer loved them, and I came to town to work with him on a pitch to take to the studio. The plane landed on Saturday morning and I took a cab to his office. He and his assistant and I worked and worked all weekend long. Basically, he beat me up about the story. Pounding, pounding, pounding. Unfortunately for me, he did not understand the mindset of a beginning, terrified writer, and starting five minutes after I walked into the room, he made me feel like I was the wrong guy for the job.

Working on the outline was agony because I felt like he thought I was never going to be able to deliver. When we went to the studio on Monday to pitch, he started to tell the story we had worked out over the weekend, and much to my amazed surprise, he couldn't tell a story *to save his life*. He was Godawful! After he said about five sentences, I realized that this thing was going in the toilet unless someone stepped up to the plate. So, *I* took over the pitch. I'm a pretty good storyteller, partially because I'm from the South, and mostly because I've been telling stories my entire life. I sailed through the pitch, the studio bought my idea, and I started to write the screenplay.

The development process was not easy, and the script turned into a sticky, gooey mess. Man, was I depressed. I ended up getting writer's block. I would write a sentence, look at it, and think, "He wouldn't like this." And I would erase the sentence. It was ghastly — the lowest point I have ever been in my writing career. I pushed away from the computer, didn't work for two days, and then I came back, sat down, gritted my teeth and decided, "Screw him, I don't care what he thinks," and I pressed on.

Once I decided I didn't care any more, it got better. I loosened up. If I messed something up, I worked on it until I solved the problem.

What I did not know then that I do know now is that, no matter how deep a hole you put yourself in as a writer, if you keep pushing and prodding and poking, eventually you'll write your way out of the hole, and solve the problem.

What's important is that you don't abandon ship. Don't quit writing something just because it's difficult. Don't bail out just because you run into turbulence in the middle of Act II. Don't stop just because you've made a mess of your genius idea. If you're getting paid, you do get to keep the money, no matter what a hash you make of it, but keep on going. It is helpful to know that every screenwriter has problems, that every script becomes a quagmire at some point, but *you have to finish it*. If this is your first script and you don't finish it, you're going to end up with a bunch of half-written screenplays lying around.

Keep turning the problem over in your head. Talk to friends. Read books about screenwriting. See movies that are like your movie. Do anything you can to solve your problem and, after investing enough time and pencil lead, you *will* solve your problem. If you abandon it, the problem will never be solved, and you'll have an abandoned screenplay sitting there on the shelf looking at you, making faces, and giving you the finger.

There are few things worse than a pile of unfinished screenplays. Especially if they are giving you the finger.

☐ 98. You don't know how to get an agent!

Neither does anybody else.

At seminars about writing, when they get to the "how can I get an agent?" question, the people on the podium just throw up their hands and moan.

It's a bit like the grim "how do I get a girlfriend?" conundrum. If you don't have a girlfriend, you're blue as Picasso and slouching around like you expect to be struck in the face. You're miserable. You need a girlfriend, badly. So what happens when you meet the Right One? She smells desperation and runs for the horizon. True? When you've got a girlfriend, and she digs your chili, you're walking on air. Of course, you're the *same* guy you were the week before, only now, women are coming up to you, shoving phone numbers in your pocket and writing "I love you" on their eyelids. Also true.

Getting a movie made seems like cake compared to getting an agent. Which is why I advocate making your OWN movie and saying, "Pah!" to the agent machine. Once you've made your own film, Hollywood will march on you like Napoleon went after Russia.

But for now, a bit about getting an agent.

First, write a couple of FANTASTIC scripts. I don't mean good ones, either. I mean scripts where people say, "Holy cow, this is amazing! Can I give it to my friend who knows someone who sweeps the floor of the body shop across the street from UTA? Please, please, please?"

There's not a body shop across from UTA, but you get my drift.

I hate to say, the query letter thing has never worked for me. Not once. And I've had more agents than I care to admit. Every one came from some friend or buddy of a friend holding a gun to an agent's head and saying, "Read this guy's stuff. You'll thank me. He walks on water." Once, after I'd had two films produced, I was looking for a new agent. I'd sold pitches, sold spec material, and right then was supervising producer on a national cable television series. I had killer writing samples. Not that it mattered, because, by that time, I'd exhausted every avenue to get someone to hand an agent a script. Translation: my friends were sick of me.

So I tried the query letter approach. Spent a week writing one and sent out forty of the little suckers. *One* assistant called me back. He said, "Your letter is one of three she's considering to be the one she calls back this month." That agent answers twelve query letters *a year*! I never heard from her again.

I waited until I had some new friends who weren't sick of me. Then I got a new agent.

> Make friends with people who know agents. Not easy to do.
> Never pay to have your material read (critiqued is another matter).
> Even in large agencies, new agents are the ones who will read new material. Read the trades. See who has just gotten promoted to agent.
> Before you send the letter, get a name to send it to.
> Your letter must introduce you, and introduce the material. It has to tell about who you are and what you're trying to sell. Tell a little bit about the script.
> Don't do a standard letter. Catch their eye. Be creative.
> Send it out to large and small. Boutique and big. Of course, big agencies can package. Of course, at a big agency, writers get lost.

Enter contests. Win or come close.

Call every college filmmaking professor in the country and ask if they have any students who are agents' assistants. Send your stuff to them.

Move to Los Angeles and meet people through your hobbies.

Here is advice worth the price of this book. If you ever *are* fortunate enough to meet agents or producers or someone "real," DO NOT TELL THEM ABOUT YOUR STUFF.

That sounds counterintuitive, but bear with me.

Be different from the last fifty or three hundred people they met! Talk about model railroading or your interest in speaking French. Tell them a killingly funny joke. Ask about their problems raising their children. Talk about the last good book you read. Ask them why John Hughes doesn't make movies any more. Talk about *anything* OTHER than your illustrious career and your dazzling ideas and your damn screenplay.

I have a friend in Los Angeles, a manager. Long ago, before I knew the little bit I know now, I was having dinner with him. I said, "Hey, last night, I met Steve Martin's attorney." He stared at me with despair laced with horror. "You didn't ask him to read your script, did you?" I thought, "Isn't that what I'm supposed to do?" I nodded and my friend sagged, slowly put his face in his hands, and sighed.

I never spoke to the lawyer again. If, instead of trying to shove a script at him, I'd told the guy a filthy joke, maybe he'd have taken me to lunch.

They don't want to read your stuff. So, if you meet someone at a seminar, ask, since you've got a car, if they need to run an errand. Take them to the drugstore. Or an antique mall. Or offer to get them coffee. Swear you won't pitch them and you'll probably get a laugh. Make them like YOU and then let them ask to read your stuff.

It may take a year.

But, if they ask *you*, they'll read it.

☐ 99. You get excited when they say they like it!

Hollywood is where you go to die from encouragement. Nobody, but nobody, wants to make you angry in case you turn out to be the Next Big Thing. Consequently, no one is going to tell you your script sucks. Except, maybe, me. But probably not.

There are two ways to know someone likes your work. Two and only two. Anything else, they're shining you on.

> 1) A check. Duuh.
> 2) If they give your script to someone else.

They can *say* they liked it:

> "I loved your screenplay. I kid you not. It's fantastic!"
> "Best script I've read this year."
> "You are a real *writer*."
> "This is amazing."
> "We've got something like this in development, but I'd love to see your next one."
> "Wonderful plotting. Great action scenes. You write killer dialogue."
> "My girlfriend loved it."

...but these lovely sentiments mean precisely nothing. They may have loved it. They may have hated it. You'll never, ever know.

It's not because they're liars. Well, not necessarily. They don't want to hurt your feelings. They want to get out of the conversation conflict-free. Who can blame them? They are not there to give you notes. You gave them a script to read. They didn't like it. Maybe they did like it, but they don't want to buy it. End of story.

This is a long and deeply rutted road. It doesn't do to get too excited over what will likely turn out to be nothing. When you get good news, enjoy it. There are few highs in this business, and you should take the ones that come your way. However, don't start telling everyone your good news, unless it's really solid.

Just because "Mr. Big Star is reading it" doesn't mean you're going to get a check. You can wait months on someone, and then realize they passed without ever reading it.

It's not a good idea to let your imagination run away with you. Keep your day job. Keep thinking about your family and what's important. If something good is going to happen, it's going to happen, but no time soon. The more you bounce off four walls, all revved up because of a tiny piece of good news, the more disappointment you and yours will have to endure when that bit of joy turns out to be dross. And, like as not, all joy will end as dross. Welcome to Disappointmentville.

> Producer (excited): We're one "yes" away from a movie!
> Me (to myself): Yeah, and I'm one "yes" away from a blow job from Princess Caroline of Monaco.

It's a disappointing business. That's the nature of the game. Embrace that and be aware of it and don't let yourself get too wrapped up in it. If something swell happens, be ready to capitalize on it, but please don't spend all day every day all thrilled because something great *may* be about to happen. Only when it REALLY DOES HAPPEN are you allowed to go nutso.

Until you get a big green light, or a first day of principal photography, or an Emmy nomination, keep your excitement on simmer. It's a bit pessimistic, but in the long run, it's better for your soul and for the sanity of those around you.

Be cool. Sometimes, it's not easy.

☐ 100. You're confusing hope with denial!

At some point, you must ask yourself if you should quit.

Finally, after you've been rejected and rejected and rejected, you're going to have to realize you can't write a screenplay. A lot of people can't; there is no shame in it. If someone is a good writer, they get it quickly. The entertainment business is a cruel dragon and will burn you to a crisp if you allow it to. The line of people trying to get in is endless; the doorway, tiny. If you can't figure out a way to shrink yourself down to fit in that door, you'll never get through. Unfortunately, there is no tour guide. It's like *Alice in Wonderland* without the cookie asking you to eat it. Waking up earlier in the morning, more days a week, will not get you what you want. Finally, you have to decide this is not going to work, ever.

How you figure that out is something I can't answer. When do you draw the line, when do you realize that encouragement from people in Los Angeles is a waste of your precious and irreplaceable time?

It is a craft; you can get better at it, but someday you must ask yourself, "Is this working or not? Are the people I am giving my material to helping me do something with it, or are they just patting me on the head saying, 'Very nice, I'd love to see your next effort'?"

While it may be unimaginable to consider not writing screenplays or not being a success in Hollywood, failure after failure after failure, or encouragement after encouragement after encouragement, finally means you're not going to get anywhere. You owe it to yourself to sit down and take a long hard look at what people are telling you about your material — or, what they are not telling you.

At some point, you may have to let it go.

Fading Out

Well, that was depressing, wasn't it?

Pay all this money for a book, and right at the end the guy tells you to give up.

If I can convince you to quit, and only for the price of this book, you should name your next son after me.

You don't want to quit? Then don't. But keep your head when all about you are losing theirs.

> *"There are millions to be grabbed out here and your only competition is idiots. Don't let this get around."*
> screenwriter Herman J. Mankiewicz, in a 1926 cable
> from Hollywood to Ben Hecht in New York

Just because you read in the trades about some guy selling his first script for $500,000 doesn't mean you're going to sell your first, or your second, or your ninth. That may have been his ninth screenplay, but the first he ever tried to sell and he's *telling* everybody it's the first script. Maybe it actually is his first script. My first script got made. Big deal, because what about the next one, and the next five? Your main job will be to write a script, and then write another script. And another after that. And then more. And then even more after that; and somewhere in there, you're going to learn what you're doing.

After you put in thousands of hours at your typewriter, pad and paper, computer, or perhaps dictating to a comely secretary, you're going to begin to know how to write a screenplay. Some people get it right off the bat. They're lucky. With some people it takes time. You may be one of those people. But the important thing is to not think your first script is genius and that Hollywood is idiotic because they're not buying it. Write one, and then write another one. It's a learning process. I am a better writer now than I was when I started. I remind you:

"The competition is grotesque."
Richard Sylbert

Recently, Hollywood has gotten a lot more difficult.

The studios don't buy scripts like they used to. They want movies that come from franchises. Used to be, they'd buy a script and build a movie around it. No more. The game is too risky. The studio business is all driven by brand recognition and marketing.

Screenplays used to be mini-movie stars, but big spec sales happen rarely now. It *can* happen, but not every weekend like before. Plus, the studios found out development was a bad economic model, as writers will write even if they're not paid. Now, the studios let the producers and writers do the work and bring it to them, without spending a dime.

What's good for writers is that there is an independent market outside the studio system, where you can make movies and sell them in lots of places.

What's bad for writers is that producers can get away with asking you to work for free. If someone's interested in your idea and tells you that they *may* want to make it, if you write it, what will you do?

It's an impossible situation.

But, then again, it's always been impossible, and is even more impossible than whatever previous level of impossibility it had managed to achieve five years ago. "It's worse than it's been in 20 years!" "I'm sure glad I'm not trying to break in now!" "Whooee, thank God my wife is swimming in money!" are lines you hear whenever enough alcohol has flowed.

Because the process is so savage, it will help a lot if you know *why* you are pursuing this writing foolishness. As you finish the *Your Screenplay Sucks!* checklist and send your script off, ask yourself "Why am I doing this?" Are you doing it because you are compelled to write? Do you have stories in you bursting to get out and you can't stop yourself from writing them down? Or are you trying to get rich and be a big success in Hollywood? If it's the latter, you will have a more difficult road, because, even if you have talent and good ideas, it's difficult to get rich and it's difficult to be a success in Hollywood, because you have to get lucky. You have to be in that right parking lot and bump into the right person at just the right time:

> *"So you just have to ask yourself just one question. Do you feel lucky? Punk."*
> Dirty Harry

In the Army they say: "Keep to the high ground even if it kills you." In writing, keep your reader in mind, even if it kills you. You've got to remember who's reading your script and keep their point of view right in front of you, no matter what. That said, because this is a semi-artistic endeavor, you still have to write for yourself. You have to please yourself. This business is so difficult, the chances of what you're writing getting made are so small, that you have to enjoy yourself in the writing.

> *"It's very weird to succeed at 39 years old and realize that in the midst of your failure, you were slowly building the life that you wanted."*
> Alice Sebold

As odd as it may seem, if it's fun when you're broke, it'll be fun when you're cashing checks. If you don't enjoy it when no one likes your stuff, you won't feel any better when A-List Talent is committing to be in your movie.

However; if you are writing because you *have* to write, if you are writing because you're a *writer*, then the act of creating your screenplay may be enough. Chances are you're going to have to write four or five of them before you know what you're doing. Maybe as many as ten. But if you enjoy the process and don't sweat the end result: riches, fame, or marrying Charlize Theron, then this could be a good thing for you.

Consider this for the last time:

> *"Write a screenplay that will change your life. If you don't sell it, at least you will have changed your life."*
> John Truby

All the stuff all your writing teachers and all the books say about "it's the journey that matters" is totally true. Disregard that *bon mot* at your peril. Writing is so painful and so heartbreaking and takes so long, that if you aren't having a wonderful time while you're a failure, you won't have any fun when you're a success.

You need to enjoy writing. Every aspect of it. Complaining about how tough it is does you no good and only puts off people who might be in a position to help you. No one wants to be around a whiner. Assume everybody's got it tough and press on.

There is an invisible line out there. On one side is everyone NOT in the movie business. This probably includes you. From time to time, I'm there too. On the other side of the line, are all the people who are getting paid to write, having meetings with directors, getting material optioned, having actors attach to their screenplays — and some of those people are actually making money.

But, never you fear, they are just as unhappy and miserable and suicidal as you are. Being on the side of the line with the people who are IN the business does *not* make you happier. Getting a paycheck for your work is satisfying, make no mistake about it, but it has less effect than you'd think on your psyche.

Stepping across the line INTO the movie business does not change the fundamental relationship you have with your work. Getting paid does not make you a better writer. It will not make you happier. Having a famous director attach himself to your screenplay does not make the script any better than it was a week before he read it. It makes other people *think* it's better, but what has that got to do with your soul?

> *"How do you know when a script is good? When Tom Cruise hands it to you and says, 'This is a really good script.' "*
> Anonymous

If Tom Cruise never says those magic words about your script, you still have to figure out a way to be content.

> *"Endeavor to persevere."*
> Chief Dan George in *The Outlaw Josey Wales*

You have to be happy at your desk, at that laptop in the coffee shop, or in the front seat of your car, doing your writing, whether you ever get paid or not. Otherwise, it is no fun. Getting paid should not affect what you want to do.

Because, if it's not what you want to do, why are you doing it?

FADE OUT.

THE END

Visit *www.yourscreenplaysucks.com*. Lots of useful stuff I couldn't find room for in the book!

Send suggestions and I'll put them online or in the book's second edition. Assuming there is one.

Again, I hope the book proves helpful.

About the Author

A Lifetime Member of the Writers Guild of America, William M. Akers has had three feature films produced from his screenplays. Akers has written for MGM, Disney, and Universal Studios as well as Fox, NBC, and ABC networks. Currently, his script about the fall of Saigon is under option to Overture Studios with director Jon Amiel. He teaches screenwriting and filmmaking at Vanderbilt University.

Akers speaks reasonably decent French, has two well-behaved dogs, and was a *Jeopardy!* contestant. He didn't win.

www.yourscreenplaysucks.com

THE WRITER'S JOURNEY
3RD EDITION

MYTHIC STRUCTURE FOR WRITERS

CHRISTOPHER VOGLER

BEST SELLER
OVER 170,000 COPIES SOLD!

See why this book has become an international best seller and a true classic. *The Writer's Journey* explores the powerful relationship between mythology and storytelling in a clear, concise style that's made it required reading for movie executives, screenwriters, playwrights, scholars, and fans of pop culture all over the world.

Both fiction and nonfiction writers will discover a set of useful myth-inspired storytelling paradigms (i.e., "The Hero's Journey") and step-by-step guidelines to plot and character development. Based on the work of Joseph Campbell, *The Writer's Journey* is a must for all writers interested in further developing their craft.

The updated and revised third edition provides new insights and observations from Vogler's ongoing work on mythology's influence on stories, movies, and man himself.

"This book is like having the smartest person in the story meeting come home with you and whisper what to do in your ear as you write a screenplay. Insight for insight, step for step, Chris Vogler takes us through the process of connecting theme to story and making a script come alive."
> – Lynda Obst, Producer, *Sleepless in Seattle, How to Lose a Guy in 10 Days;* Author, *Hello, He Lied*

"This is a book about the stories we write, and perhaps more importantly, the stories we live. It is the most influential work I have yet encountered on the art, nature, and the very purpose of storytelling."
> – Bruce Joel Rubin, Screenwriter, *Stuart Little 2, Deep Impact, Ghost, Jacob's Ladder*

CHRISTOPHER VOGLER is a veteran story consultant for major Hollywood film companies and a respected teacher of filmmakers and writers around the globe. He has influenced the stories of movies from *The Lion King* to *Fight Club* to *The Thin Red Line* and most recently wrote the first installment of *Ravenskull*, a Japanese-style manga or graphic novel. He is the executive producer of the feature film *P.S. Your Cat is Dead* and writer of the animated feature *Jester Till*.

$26.95 · 300 PAGES · ORDER NUMBER 76RLS · ISBN: 193290736x

SAVE THE CAT! GOES TO THE MOVIES

THE SCREENWRITER'S GUIDE TO EVERY STORY EVER TOLD

BLAKE SNYDER

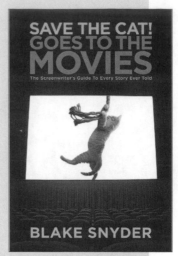

In the long-awaited sequel to his surprise bestseller, *Save the Cat!*, author and screenwriter Blake Snyder returns to form in a fast-paced follow-up that proves why his is the most talked-about approach to screenwriting in years. In the perfect companion piece to his first book, Snyder delivers even more insider's information gleaned from a 20-year track record as "one of Hollywood's most successful spec screenwriters," giving you the clues to write *your* movie.

Designed for screenwriters, novelists, and movie fans, this book gives readers the key breakdowns of the 50 most instructional movies from the past 30 years. From *M*A*S*H* to *Crash*, from *Alien* to *Saw*, from *10* to *Eternal Sunshine of the Spotless Mind*, Snyder reveals how screenwriters who came before you tackled the same challenges you are facing with the film you want to write — or the one you are currently working on.

Writing a "rom-com"? Check out the "Buddy Love" chapter for a "beat for beat" dissection of *When Harry Met Sally...* plus references to 10 other great romantic comedies that will make your story sing.

Want to execute a great mystery? Go to the "Whydunit" section and learn about the "dark turn" that's essential to the heroes of *All the President's Men*, *Blade Runner*, *Fargo* and hip noir *Brick* — and see why ALL good stories, whether a Hollywood blockbuster or a Sundance award winner, follow the same rules of structure outlined in Snyder's breakthrough method.

If you want to sell your script and create a movie that pleases most audiences most of the time, the odds increase if you reference Snyder's checklists and see what makes 50 films tick. After all, both executives and audiences respond to the same elements good writers seek to master. They want to know the type of story they signed on for, and whether it's structured in a way that satisfies everyone. It's what they're looking for. And now, it's what you can deliver.

BLAKE SNYDER, besides selling million-dollar scripts to both Disney and Spielberg, is still "one of Hollywood's most successful spec screenwriters," having made another spec sale in 2006. An in-demand scriptcoach and seminar and workshop leader, Snyder provides information for writers through his website, *www.blakesnyder.com*.

$22.95 · 270 PAGES · ORDER NUMBER 75RLS · ISBN: 1932907351

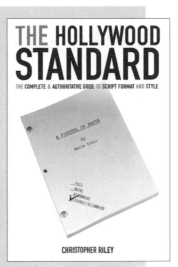

CINEMATIC STORYTELLING

THE 100 MOST POWERFUL FILM CONVENTIONS EVERY FILMMAKER MUST KNOW

JENNIFER VAN SIJLL

BEST SELLER

How do directors use screen direction to suggest conflict? How do screenwriters exploit film space to show change? How does editing style determine emotional response?

Many first-time writers and directors do not ask these questions. They forego the huge creative resource of the film medium, defaulting to dialog to tell their screen story. Yet most movies are carried by sound and picture. The industry's most successful writers and directors have mastered the cinematic conventions specific to the medium. They have harnessed non-dialog techniques to create some of the most cinematic moments in movie history.

This book is intended to help writers and directors more fully exploit the medium's inherent storytelling devices. It contains 100 non-dialog techniques that have been used by the industry's top writers and directors. From *Metropolis* and *Citizen Kane* to *Dead Man* and *Kill Bill*, the book illustrates — through 500 frame grabs and 75 script excerpts — how the inherent storytelling devices specific to film were exploited.

You will learn:
- How non-dialog film techniques can advance story.
- How master screenwriters exploit cinematic conventions to create powerful scenarios.

"Cinematic Storytelling scores a direct hit in terms of concise information and perfectly chosen visuals, and it also searches out... and finds... an emotional core that many books of this nature either miss or are afraid of."
— Kirsten Sheridan, Director, *Disco Pigs*; Co-writer, *In America*

"Here is a uniquely fresh, accessible, and truly original contribution to the field. Jennifer van Sijll takes her readers in a wholly new direction, integrating aspects of screenwriting with all the film crafts in a way I've never before seen. It is essential reading not only for screenwriters but also for filmmakers of every stripe."
— Prof. Richard Walter, UCLA Screenwriting Chairman

JENNIFER VAN SIJLL has taught film production, film history, and screenwriting. She is currently on the faculty at San Francisco State's Department of Cinema.

$24.95 · 230 PAGES · ORDER # 35RLS · ISBN: 193290705X

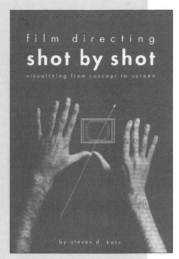

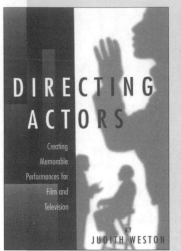

{ THE MYTH OF MWP }

In a dark time, a light bringer came along, leading the curious and the frustrated to clarity and empowerment. It took the well-guarded secrets out of the hands of the few and made them available to all. It spread a spirit of openness and creative freedom, and built a storehouse of knowledge dedicated to the betterment of the arts.

The essence of the Michael Wiese Productions (MWP) is empowering people who have the burning desire to express themselves creatively. We help them realize their dreams by putting the tools in their hands. We demystify the sometimes secretive worlds of screenwriting, directing, acting, producing, film financing, and other media crafts.

By doing so, we hope to bring forth a realization of 'conscious media' which we define as being positively charged, emphasizing hope and affirming positive values like trust, cooperation, self-empowerment, freedom, and love. Grounded in the deep roots of myth, it aims to be healing both for those who make the art and those who encounter it. It hopes to be transformative for people, opening doors to new possibilities and pulling back veils to reveal hidden worlds.

MWP has built a storehouse of knowledge unequaled in the world, for no other publisher has so many titles on the media arts. Please visit www.mwp.com where you will find many free resources and a 25% discount on our books. Sign up and become part of the wider creative community!

Onward and upward,

Michael Wiese
Publisher/Filmmaker